TOUCHING HOME

TOUCHING HOME

Baseball and the Liberal-Republican Tradition in America

Mary Craig

University of Missouri Press, Columbia, Missouri 65211
Printed and bound in the United States of America
 First printing, 2025.

ISBN 9780826223401 (hardcover : alk. paper)

Library of Congress Control Number: 2025022643

∞™ This paper meets the requirements of the
American National Standard for Permanence of Paper
for Printed Library Materials, Z39.48, 1984.

Typeface: Bernina Sans and Minion Pro

Sports and American Culture

Adam Criblez, Series Editor

This series explores the cultural dynamic between competitive athletics and society, the many ways in which sports shape the lives of Americans, in the United States and Latin America, from a historical and contemporary perspective. While international in scope, the series includes titles of regional interest to Missouri and the Midwest. Topics in the series range from studies of a single game, event, or season to histories of teams and programs, as well as biographical narratives of athletes, coaches, owners, journalists, and broadcasters.

For my parents

Contents

Preface

As is the case with most baseball fans, I inherited my fandom from my parents, and so much of my life was oriented around the sport before I was even cognizant of it. It was not a choice of whether I would be a fan, but of how much of my life I would allow baseball to occupy. And as I came to know the game, I gave to it a greater and greater percentage of my time. I watched as many games as I could and talked to as many of my family members and friends as I could about it. There was no doubt that it was my favorite hobby, but I did not expect to welcome it into my career, as well.

What drew me so completely to baseball were the ideals it proposed to uphold: teamwork, sacrifice, equality. Unlike many other sports, winning in baseball is a full team effort in which having one or two dominant players is not enough on its own. Its grueling daily schedule requires constant dedication from its players and its fans—it's not easy to watch your team get obliterated in August games day after day, but there is merit in sticking by your team. And on its surface, baseball is a game that can be played by anyone so long as they have a bat and a ball. In these ways, baseball is a deeply beautiful game. But it is also clear to me that baseball as it exists in America often fails to live up to these ideals. Teamwork and sacrifice often give way to greed and the sport's history with racial and gender equality is troubling at best.

This book is an effort to understand the root of these failures so that we—fans, players, and communities—can work toward creating a version of baseball worthy of the dedication it demands from us. The project led me to examine the principles on which America was founded, because if baseball is representative of America in some way, understanding the sport requires understanding the country. What I discovered is that at the heart of America is a contradiction: a desire to reduce politics to the level of the individual while also maintaining a great concern for community. Every aspect of American political life is an effort to normalize this contradiction, enshrining it in our political institutions, governing documents, and social life. Doing so has required the creation of a mythic American society in which the contradiction is the key to prosperity on both the individual and communal levels.

The argument about baseball and American politics presented in this book is not meant to be comprehensive; it would be a fool's errand to attempt to analyze the entirety of baseball and American history in a single book. Rather, it is my intention to provide a framework for readers to think about their relationship with baseball and America in a different way. I have therefore focused on a handful of examples from baseball's storied history that best represent the complicated relationship I present in my argument. Proceeding in this way should help readers understand the sport's entanglement with issues of class, race, gender, and more, both in the present day and in the future.

Finally, while the book is at times deeply critical of both organized baseball and American politics, I do not intend for it to be a work of despair. The bonds I have formed from interacting with baseball as both a fan and a scholar have left me hopeful about the future of the sport. Baseball cannot exist without us, and therefore the power to shape it lies with us. The future of the sport is what we make of it.

Acknowledgments

First, I would like to thank David Nichols, who responded to me when I presented him with a much more conventional dissertation topic by asking, "Why aren't you writing on baseball?," thus paving the first steps of this journey that has at times seemed more laborious than a Red Sox–Yankees Sunday Night Baseball game. Without his constant support (and gentle mockery), this project would not exist. Next, I would like to thank Mary Nichols for her encouragement and wisdom, which she freely offered even in retirement. I also owe my other dissertation committee members, Benjamin Kleinerman, Dave Bridge, and Barry Hankins, a great deal of thanks for their helpful comments as I refined my argument. And I would, of course, have been lost a million times over at Baylor without Jenice Langston's and Melanie Pirelo's constant willingness to solve every single problem I brought to them.

I extend my thanks to my Furman colleagues, Akan, Brent, Buket, Cleve, Danielle, David, Glen, Jim, Kate, Liz, Lucy, Mike, Rob, Tammy, and Teresa. Since my arrival at Furman, they have daily provided a welcoming and supportive environment. I could not have asked for a better first job out of grad school than to work alongside a group of people so dedicated to helping our students and one another.

I have a great many friends to thank for providing insightful comments on my project and, at other times, absurd distractions from it. Most notably, I want to thank Catherine Craig, Brigid Flaherty, Matthew Reising, Christopher Ruiz, Hannah Norman-Krause, Jacob Boros, and Ben Slomski, all of whom provided me with many hours of laughter and support.

I am also grateful to many people outside of academia. Kelsey Pye, Cole Altmann, and Shakeia Taylor graciously allowed me to spend hours explaining to them the intricacies of both this project and academic life in general, providing just enough excitement, insight, and confusion to assure me that I was on the right track. Furthermore, the book may not have existed at all if not for Patrick Dubuque, Paul Swydan, Meg Rowley, and many others who first provided me the opportunity to write about baseball and politics with both whimsy and sincerity, demonstrating time and again to me that seriousness does not mean joylessness.

Speaking of joy, next to watching baseball, my greatest joy is teaching. I would like to thank my students at Baylor and Furman for the enthusiasm and earnestness with which they approach political theory. My scholarship would be far inferior were it not for the lessons my students have taught me about politics, life, and crafting an argument.

And I would especially like to thank Andrew Davidson, Adam Criblez, and everyone else at University of Missouri Press for the enthusiasm, care, and efficiency with which they have treated me and this book.

I am most of all grateful to my parents for instilling in me a passion for baseball and inquisitiveness about the world around me. They have shown me copious amounts of support through all stages of my life and have miraculously seemed happy to do so. It is from them that I have truly learned what it means to belong to a community, and it is to them that I dedicate this book.

TOUCHING HOME

Introduction

> There are a lot of people who know me who can't understand for the life of them why I would go to work on something as unserious as baseball. If they only knew.
>
> —A. Bartlett Giamatti

It is a common refrain among both baseball fans and political scientists that baseball and politics do not mix, and that combining them would do a grave disservice to both. It would be taking baseball too seriously and politics not seriously enough.[1] However, I believe that it is essential for us to take seriously the things that bring us joy, and—as a Red Sox fan in the twenty-first century—baseball has brought a great deal of joy to my life. This book is an attempt to take baseball seriously by examining the extent of its political nature.

Since at least the 1840s, writers and public figures have connected baseball to America's political life, arguing that the game captures the essence of the country. In 1889 Walt Whitman declared that baseball "is just as important in the sum total of our historic life" as our political institutions and laws.[2] Writing a century and a half later, Major League Baseball Commissioner A. Bartlett Giamatti clarified Whitman's statement, arguing that "baseball fulfills the promise America made to itself to cherish the individual while recognizing the overarching claims of the group."[3] In this book, I evaluate these two statements, uncovering precisely what promises America made to itself about the individual and the community and how baseball embodies these promises.

Any exploration of baseball and America must begin with a discussion of the centrality of myth to the existence of both the sport and the nation.[4] While myths have been integral to the life of every political community, I am inclined to agree with Richard Slotkin's argument that "no modern nation is more indebted to, or dependent on, its myths than the United State of America."[5] Slotkin further states that the importance of myth is to "give us the power to control the present and future" by producing public acceptance of political actions that conform to these founding myths.[6] Founding myths, then, perhaps particularly for America, limit the political imagination; all solutions to new political problems must adhere to the accepted mythology of America's founding. The challenge of this country's founding myths has been to reconcile its supposed commitment to natural rights with its dependency on chattel slavery and genocide. What emerged from this seemingly impossible project was a new conception of the relationship between the individual and the political community in the form of a peculiar synthesis between the theories of liberalism and republicanism.

My project therefore differs from the handful of other works connecting political theory to baseball, although there are two works in particular that seem on the surface to argue in a similar vein. First, in *The Protestant Ethic and the Spirit of Sport: How Calvinism and Capitalism Shaped America's Games*, Steven J. Overman argues, as I do, that the development of professional sports and the development of corporate capitalism are closely linked. However, he attributes this relationship to the Protestant work ethic rather than liberalism and republicanism, and, while he analyzes baseball, his work extends to sports as a whole in America.[7] Secondly, Thomas David Bunting's *Democracy at the Ballpark* applies democratic theory to baseball, attributing the sport's significance to its ability to direct America toward a more democratic society concerned with equality, liberty, and civic virtue.[8] While Bunting (as I do) analyzes baseball's relationship to issues of class, race, and gender, among other things, he does so primarily in relation to the democratic power fans have as spectators of the game, and he connects this theory to theories of sports beginning in ancient Greece.

During the founding era, from the 1770s through the 1790s, debates concerning the theoretical foundations of the new American regime and its governing document relied heavily on liberalism and republicanism. Emerging from the writings of seventeenth-century English philosopher John Locke, the theory of liberalism emphasizes the individual as the origin of political life and thus the protection of individual rights as the goal of political society. More specifically, liberalism privileges a self-interested pursuit of property rights within a capitalist economic system and thereby a justification for unequal distribution of property in society. Republicanism, on the other hand, dating back to ancient philosophers like Aristotle and Cicero, characterizes liberty as a product of the cultivation of civic virtue through a concern for the whole of a political community. In other words, liberalism individualizes notions of freedom through promoting self-interested conceptions of property rights, while republicanism aims at a collective sense of freedom as something greater than pure self-interest.

These theories generated several enduring myths about America, namely its agrarianism, its dedication to equality, and its reliance on manliness as a civic virtue. These myths in turn united to create the idea of the self-made man—one whose success is solely the product of his own hard work and ingenuity. In America, it is proclaimed, there is enough land and opportunity for one to rise from poverty to unimaginable wealth so long as one is industrious, and through this individual pursuit of success America as a whole will achieve success. Paul Heike writes of this myth that it "creates a usable past and a hopeful future by bypassing the manifold discrepancies between mythic text and lived reality."[9] Essentially, it rhetorically eliminates the challenges inherent in America's political life by presenting a fictitious account of past, present, and future.

Baseball embodies these theories of citizenship and myths in a number of ways. The foundation of the sport is a battle between individuals, the pitcher on one side and the hitter on the other, and the strikeout and the home run are frequently the two most sought-after outcomes of this battle. Yet, no single pitcher or hitter is capable of leading their team to victory, either in the course of a single game or over an entire season. It is the team that comes together to win, or lose. Moreover, through its professionalization, baseball has spread the American founding era's conception of liberalism and republicanism throughout the country, providing opportunities for individual owners to expand their liberal property rights while also creating a sense of belonging for a diverse number of communities.

Furthermore, baseball promotes the myths associated with the "self-made man" narrative through its conception as a game that embodies American pastoralism and develops physical and moral health in its players and spectators. It is a game played predominately outdoors on patches of grass, offering respite from the dreary insides of the factory or office building. It teaches children and adults alike the values of fair play and teamwork. It presents the perfect blend of strength and intellect necessary for the creation of engaged citizens and provides men a safe outlet for their combativeness and aggression. Echoing Heike, baseball is the American game par excellence because it connects future generations of American citizens with previous ones. The combination of liberalism and republicanism at the heart of these myths, however, has often resulted in baseball's insufficient efforts to address fundamental problems of citizenship and the security of individual and communal rights and liberties.

This book discusses these insufficiencies by detailing baseball's involvement with the class, race, and gender conflicts of twentieth-century America. In each case, I trace the development of liberal-republican debates on class, race, and gender from the founding era through baseball's evolution from hobby to multi-billion-dollar industry. Ultimately, I argue that baseball has been instrumental in creating a new blend of liberalism and republicanism that equates civic virtue with corporate consumerism, pushing individuals to think of supporting large corporations as a public good.

Chapter Outlines

The book is divided into four chapters. The first chapter examines the role of myth in establishing baseball as America's national game. I focus on the efforts of player, manager, and sporting goods magnate A. G. Spalding, who dedicated much of his life to making baseball synonymous with America. I analyze Spalding's arguments for baseball's superiority to other sports, particularly cricket, namely that baseball is democratic, fast-paced, and the perfect American blend of brains and brawn. While Spalding did not use the terms "liberal" and "republican," I argue that the sentiments he espoused echo founding-era debates about liberalism and republicanism. In particular, I emphasize liberalism's and republicanism's connection to baseball's mythic pastoralism, using the myth of Abner Doubleday's invention of baseball to demonstrate the sport's reliance on this simplified, fictitious image of America.

In chapter 2, I link baseball's class and labor issues to those of the broader community. In particular, I examine how America's political principles of liberalism and republicanism play out in debates concerning the reserve clause throughout the history of baseball. After providing an overview of the liberal and republican debates concerning property rights during the founding era, I demonstrate how the sport's practitioners applied these theories to class and labor issues surrounding the reserve clause and the resulting antitrust exemption, beginning with baseball's professionalization in the 1870s. I analyze the arguments within the three Supreme Court cases concerning baseball: *Federal Baseball Club v. National League* (1922), *Toolson v. New York Yankees* (1953), and *Flood v. Kuhn* (1972). Through an investigation of these Supreme Court opinions and the 1994–1995 player strike, I argue that the reserve clause's extension into an antitrust exemption for MLB helped produce a new conception of civic virtue as consumerism.

Chapter 3 takes up the topic of race, focusing on Black participation in baseball. I argue that professional baseball's handling of anti-Black racism might initially be an example of the powerful way in which the sport can provide a moral guide for American society, but it ultimately illustrates the problem of individual ambition overtaking the public good. I begin this chapter with an overview of liberalism's and republicanism's relationship to the constitutional classification of enslaved people as being both persons and property. I argue that founding-era debates on slavery reduced emancipation to the individual Black person's "free" participation in the emerging capitalist economic system—a system that relied on slave labor. I then discuss how the rise and fall of the Negro Leagues and the context surrounding Jackie Robinson's MLB career and civil rights activism further cemented this liberal-republican synthesis as the framework within which the integration of Black people into American society has proceeded. Ultimately, I argue that baseball's relationship to Black Americans demonstrates the problem with reducing civic virtue to individual economic gain.

Chapter 4 examines baseball's role in shaping women's place in American society. I begin by outlining founding-era arguments about the role of women, namely liberalism's linking of freedom to property ownership and republicanism's emphasis on domestic life as civic virtue. I then discuss how men have used baseball as a means of boxing women into strict gender roles and women have used it as a means of aiding them in their pursuit of the rights guaranteed to men in the Declaration of Independence and the Constitution. At its best, baseball has been a force through which women can demonstrate that they are entitled to protection of their equal rights by creating public spaces in which to demonstrate their virtue. Ultimately, however, I argue that baseball's role as a feminist tool has been limited by its role as a means for wealthy men to achieve their personal ambition, which is at odds with the liberation of women.

My conclusion examines the "Baseball As America" touring exhibit and the way the sport was used as a response to 9/11 to further illustrate how each of these threads—class, race, and gender—have helped create this new consumerist liberal-republican theory. In both instances, baseball was used to celebrate American values like freedom and equality while burying the reality of the sport's role in upholding class, race, and gender divisions in American society. I argue that the ideals of baseball and thus America cannot be achieved unless we deconstruct the myths surrounding these ideals and address the realities of contemporary American life. Once we begin this project, baseball in its simplest form might provide a guide for the correct combination of liberalism and republicanism, one in which the good of the individual does not come at the cost of the good of the community.

CHAPTER ONE

Myth and Money

A. G. Spalding Makes a National Pastime

> Baseball has realized—through individual brilliance or teamwork or racial harmony—the highest of our country's ideals. But the game's greatest gift to America has been to provide a haven from it—a Providential antidote to our raging, tearing, relentless progress, an evergreen field that provides rest and recreation, myths and memories, heroes and history.
>
> —MLB historian John Thorn

Speaking before an audience comprising Mark Twain, Theodore Roosevelt, and future US Senator Chauncey Depew, Abraham G. Mills declared at a celebration for A. G. Spalding's 1889 baseball world tour that baseball was "in its present perfected state, an evolution of American genius." The audience, in response to Mill's hyperbole, began chanting "no rounders!," affirming that regardless of the extent to which the American game evolved from the English one, they viewed baseball as their own.[1] This dinner and the tour that it honored were part of sports magnate A. G. Spalding's efforts to solidify baseball as America's national game. These exertions were recognized by the 1905 Mills Commission Report, which declared that baseball was invented in 1839 by Abner Doubleday in Cooperstown, New York. Whatever the factual truth about Abner Doubleday, the commission's report about the American origin of the game confirmed baseball's popularity and promoted Spalding's larger vision for its role in American society. That vision, as we will see, portrays baseball as the perfect blend of liberal and republican components, and thereby an appropriate response to America's identity crisis in the final decades of the nineteenth century.

While baseball's popularity in America cannot be solely attributed to Spalding, his desire to turn the game into an organized political project laid the groundwork for its corporatization throughout the twentieth century. He was the impetus for Chicago White Stockings owner William Hulbert's founding of the National League in 1876, which led to territorial rights and the creation of the minor league farm system.[2] His prominence as a player and executive allowed him to forge connections with politicians, further turning the growth of baseball into a political project to inculcate a specific notion of Americanness in the country's citizenry.[3] Any attempt to reckon with the realities of baseball's place in America must include an analysis of Spalding's work in making baseball America's national game, in a way that emphasized the sport's role as civic educator and purveyor of pastoral innocence.

This chapter does just that, investigating what Spalding says about the differences between cricket and baseball and why baseball is particularly suited to the American people. I then discuss Spalding's claim that baseball unifies and strengthens the mind and the body, focusing on the sport's relation to the American judicial system and to liberal and republican conceptions of pastoralism producing individual freedom and fostering communal bonds. Finally, I analyze the enduring Doubleday myth as the embodiment of these elements of Spalding's project.

A. G. Spalding's Baseball Project

Albert Goodwill Spalding, born September 2, 1849, in Byron, Illinois, served as a player, manager, and executive in baseball before becoming a sporting goods magnate. His relationship with baseball began when he took it up as a child to combat the loneliness he felt after the sudden death of his father. His skill as a pitcher was almost immediately evident, and after he led the amateur Chicago Excelsiors to a defeat of the Cincinnati Red Stockings (the first professional baseball team) in 1870, he was offered a spot on the Boston Red Stockings of the National Association (NA). During his five seasons with Boston, he excelled on the mound and in the batter's box, propelling the team to four consecutive championships. Then, after becoming disillusioned with the rampant drinking and gambling among the players in the NA, he switched his red stockings for white ones, joining the Chicago White Stockings in the newly formed National League (NL). He won forty-seven games in 1876 for Chicago and his .796 career winning percentage remains the highest ever for a pitcher.[4] He was inducted into the inaugural Baseball Hall of Fame in 1939 as the "organizational genius of baseball's pioneer days."[5]

As innovative as he was as a player—he pioneered the padded glove—most of Spalding's contribution to baseball came after he retired in 1878 to become the White Stockings' president. While in this position, he began his quest to cement baseball as America's game, making it synonymous with all aspects of American life. In so doing, Spalding hoped to enrich his personal fortune by turning his sporting goods store into a chain of stores across the country. Indeed, when speaking to an Australian reporter during his 1889 Baseball World Tour, Spalding admitted that he had created the tour "for the purpose of extending my sporting-goods business to that quarter of the globe and to create a market for goods there."[6] Central to Spalding's plans to embed baseball within American society, then, was the liberal individualist desire for property in the form of money.

In 1911, four years before his death, Spalding provided great insight into his efforts to make baseball synonymous with America in his book *America's National Game: Historic Facts Concerning the Beginning, Evolution, Development and Popularity of Base Ball.*[7] Early in the book, he declares that "to enter upon a deliberate argument to prove that Base Ball is our National Game; that it has all the attributes of American origin, American character and unbounded public favor in America . . . is to undertake the elucidation of a patent fact; the sober demonstration of an axiom; it is like a solemn declaration that two plus two equal four."[8] Yet, *America's National Game*, functioning as part autobiography, part history of baseball, attempts to do just that.

Furthering the American break from England established during the founding era, Spalding's project begins with differentiating baseball from English cricket. He declares that "cricket would never do for Americans" because while English people can wait days for the conclusion of a match, Americans can only wait mere hours.[9] Furthermore, cricket is too aristocratic and genteel a game to suit Americans, who are a democratic, "cosmopolitan people, knowing no arbitrary class distinctions."[10] When it comes time to play baseball, Americans, unlike the English, are unconcerned with dirtying their clothes and instead eagerly acquiesce to the sport's demands. In essence, "it would be as impossible for a Briton who had not breathed the air of this free land as a naturalized American citizen; for one who had no part or heritage in the hopes and achievements of our country, to play Base Ball, as it would for an American, free from the trammels of English traditions, customs, conventionalities, to play the national game of Great Britain."[11]

Spalding does not provide much of the history of cricket in America to support his claims, but the historical record does produce multiple accounts in line with the above version. Despite cricket being used by Britain as a means of "transferring the appropriate British moral code from the messengers of empire to the local populations" in the empire's other colonies, it did not truly emerge in America until the mid-1700s.[12] Prior to cricket, colonists passed the time with horse racing and tavern-based games like billiards and cards, but once the population expanded as a result of the slave trade and new commercial centers were created, colonists began to play the game of their motherland.[13] In 1754, three years after the first recorded cricket match in the American colonies was played, Benjamin Franklin brought with him to Philadelphia from London a copy of the 1754 Cricket Laws, referred to as the "London Method," providing the colonies with the first uniform cricket rules.[14]

Having codified rules made it easier for members of the upper class to form cricket clubs, which they did in each of the colonies, although New York and Philadelphia remained the two epicenters of the sport in America. These rules also made it easier for children of aristocrats to learn the game, ensuring its survival for at least another generation. Games were commonly played in politically significant green areas of towns, such as Lexington Green in Massachusetts and outside the House of Burgesses in Virginia, further cementing cricket as a symbol of wealth and power in these societies and maintaining a connection between the local colonial governments and the Crown.[15]

Although cricket remained a way for the English upper class to maintain their ties to their aristocratic cousins in England, by the end of the eighteenth century it had spread to select middle-class colonists who enjoyed being able to take on the English at their own game. However, for many Americans, the formality and pageantry of these games was far too English, and so they created their own version of the sport, which they called "wicket." This version of the English classic used a narrow-handled bat with a round, spoon shaped bottom, not the traditional rectangular bat, and allowed each team to field up to thirty players instead of the usual nine. By making outs far easier to obtain, these changes sped up the game from the usual two to five days to a single afternoon. Additionally, they allowed more people to take part in the contests, contributing to a livelier atmosphere and increasing the popularity of the sport.[16] This version of cricket proved more popular than its original, particularly in Connecticut and parts of the Midwest, and even managed to entice George Washington to play it during the American Revolution.[17]

This American desire to distinguish themselves from the English, particularly in the years leading to the revolution, prompted further distancing from cricket, which was banned in many of the colonies. Despite these bans, however, both cricket and wicket managed to survive the war for independence, due in part to a push to recognize them as democratic rather than aristocratic games. The bulk of this conception of cricket as democratic rested on the fact that it was much cheaper to participate in than yachting and horse racing, and as working-class English people continued to immigrate to America, they began to teach their communities all over the country to play the sport.[18] But by the 1840s, cricket was largely played by older working-class people who had learned it from post–Revolutionary War English immigrants, while younger working-class people played baseball.[19] Due to its English aristocratic trappings, cricket's popularity continued to dwindle, and it was rapidly replaced by baseball as the premier stick-and-ball sport in America.

Beginning in the 1780s, references to the playing of "base-ball" emerged throughout Massachusetts, Pennsylvania, and New York, although there remain no detailed accounts of the rules of any given game of "base-ball."[20] By the 1840s two distinct prototypes of the sport existed in America: the Massachusetts and Philadelphia–style game called "town ball" and the New York "base ball." The major difference between these types was that town ball featured six bases and no foul territory, meaning players could run wherever they wanted to avoid getting tagged out, while baseball utilized either three or four bases and included foul territory. In 1837 the New York Gothams became the first baseball club, mainly playing intra-team games until the formation of the Knickerbocker Base Ball Club in 1845. This new club became the first team to issue a written list of rules, which allowed anywhere from seven to eleven players per side and specified no number of innings per game, with victory awarded to the first team to score twenty-one runs.

Despite the Knickerbockers' attempt to restrict baseball to the upper class, its more widespread grassroots development prevented these elite clubs from dominating the game.[21] Indeed, as Spalding pointed out, baseball remedied many of the inherent problems within cricket that left the English game unsuited to the American people. Practically speaking, baseball was far more accessible than cricket because baseball fields required much less maintenance than cricket pitches, which needed smooth grass to control the bounce of the ball between the bowler (pitcher) and the batsman. This change, in addition to baseball's faster pace of play, made baseball a more egalitarian game that could be played virtually anywhere, such that an 1856 *Porter's Spirit of the Times* article estimated that every empty plot of land within a ten-mile radius of New York City had become a baseball field.[22] Concerning the pace of play, Knickerbocker member William R. Wheaton stated that he and his teammates "found cricket to[o] slow and lazy a game . . . The difference between cricket and baseball illustrates the difference between our lively people and the phlegmatic English."[23]

The final nail in the coffin for cricket's popularity in America was an 1859 match between England's All-Eleven cricket team and the Manhattan-based St. George's Cricket Club. At the end of the four-day match attended by twenty-five thousand spectators (the largest-attended sporting event in the country to that point), the American team was humiliated, losing by sixty-four runs. In the wake of this loss, many American newspapers promoted baseball as the superior sport. *The New York Daily Herald* published an explanation of cricket's unsuitability to the American people:

> base ball—an American national game—was too like cricket to be superseded by it . . . Even if there were no base ball in existence cricket could never become a national sport in America—it is too slow, intricate and plodding a game for our go ahead people . . . [cricket] is suited to the aristocracy, who have leisure and love ease; base ball is suited to the people . . . both games seem suited to the national temperament and character of the people among whom they respectively prevail.[24]

The account echoed Wheaton's praise of baseball's faster pace, while also attributing its popularity to its comparative simplicity, arguing it was uniquely suited to the American people.[25]

Early accounts of baseball's usurpation of cricket as America's go-to stick-and-ball sport confirm Spalding's argument about the sport's egalitarian and energetic nature, but they do not exhaust his argument. Spalding's likening of baseball to the American temperament extends beyond these two points to produce a more nuanced picture of the sport and therefore American democracy. Although Spalding does not use the vocabulary of "republican" and "liberal," we will soon see that his understanding of the sport and his efforts to cement it as America's national game relied on a combination of republicanism's civic virtue and liberalism's individualism.

Spalding's Conception of Human Nature

In order to understand Spalding's project, one must begin with his conception of human nature, which he provides in *America's National Game*. Taking up the perspective of "Boy," he narrates a child's progression from playing with a ball by himself to finding other children with whom to play and thus moving from a solitary pursuit to playing baseball. He writes:

> It is quite conceivable that the average boy, upon being presented with a Ball, would find immediate and pleasurable entertainment throwing it to the ground and catching it upon the rebound; but such pastime would be of temporary duration. The lad would soon tire of the monotony of the sport. Unselfish, he would want someone to share his fun—moreover, everybody recognizes that thing in human nature, in youth as well as maturity, which delights in the exploitation of ownership, possession . . . human nature is not only social in its demands ; it is also enterprising—and fickle . . . as the pastime became more popular, and more boys wanted to play, it became necessary to devise a new form of the game which would admit a greater number of participants and at the same time introduce the competitive spirit that prevails in teamwork.[26]

This sketch of human nature exhibits both liberal and republican elements. First, his belief that humans are naturally concerned with ownership and are naturally enterprising follows from the Lockean liberal understanding of property rights contained in many founding-era documents.[27] For instance, the Continental Congress declared in 1774 that "by the immutable laws of nature," the people "are entitled to . . . property." The Virginia declaration of rights in 1776 then clarified that the right is "the means of acquiring and possessing property," language found in many other state declarations.[28]

Spalding's description of human nature does not rely on liberalism alone, but also rests on the republican notion originating with Aristotle that human beings are political animals predisposed to form communities.[29] The goal of these communities is the advancement of the common good and therefore the happiness of the people. According to Spalding, children will naturally come together to play ball-based games in which they are united by a common goal—winning—as well as the desire to "share [the] fun," or promote individual and communal happiness. This republicanism is contained in many founding-era documents, such as the Massachusetts Bill of Rights, which declares that "government is instituted for the common good; for the protection, safety, prosperity and happiness of the people; and not for the profit, honor, or private interest of any one man, family, or class of men."[30] Likewise, Adams, Franklin, and Jefferson frequently spoke of happiness in terms of the ability of a regime to orient the public toward virtue.[31] Spalding's characterization of human nature here suggests that he thinks baseball can perform this function.

According to Spalding, then, the combination of these republican and liberal traits produces the innovation necessary to create something like baseball, a game in which one's competitiveness and acquisitiveness will be tempered by the necessity of community—one's teammates.[32] Thus, he declares, "I know of no other medium which, as completely as baseball, joins the physical, mental, emotional, and moral sides of a man's composite being into a complete and homogenous whole."[33] For Spalding, baseball is both a natural interest and one that creates the best version of a human being, and more specifically, an American.

In the introduction to his 1889 *Official Base Ball Guide*, the first of forty such guides and sporting goods catalogs published between 1889 and 1939, Spalding notes the ways in which baseball benefits American society:

> The game has attained its present position of popularity, not only from its adaptability to our peculiar national characteristics . . . but also from its value as a field sport which presents sufficient excitement in itself to draw thousands of spectators, without the extrinsic aid of betting as its chief point of interest . . . base ball first taught us Americans the value of physical exercise as an important aid to perfect work in cultivating the mind up to its highest point. It is to the introduction of base ball as a national pastime, in fact, that the growth of athletic sports in general in popularity is largely due; and the game pointed out to the mercantile community of our large cities that "all work and no play" is the most costly policy they can pursue, both in regard to the advantages to their own health, and in

> the improvement in the work of their employes, the combination of work and play judiciously, yielding results in better work and more satisfactory service than was possible under the old rule.[34]

This description highlights the communal aspect of the sport in its ability to instill in Americans both moral and physical virtues in line with the country's "peculiar" characteristics. The two virtues Spalding highlights, baseball's lack of a gambling infrastructure and its ability to engage industrial workers in physical activity, speak to prevalent moral concerns of the time. Middle- and upper-class Americans during the Gilded Age—the mid-1870s to the mid-1890s—spoke frequently of the supposed rampant immorality of the working class, manifested in increased gambling and physical laziness.[35] More concisely, baseball "is the American game *par excellence* because its playing demands Brain and Brawn, and American manhood supplies these ingredients in quantity sufficient to spread over the entire continent."[36]

Once again stressing the mind-body connection necessary for baseball, Spalding states, "Base Ball, I repeat, is war! And the playing of the game is a battle in which every contestant is a commanding General, who, having a field of occupation, must defend it; who, having gained an advantage, must hold it by the employment of every faculty of his brain and body, by every resource of his mind and muscle."[37] So great is the cultivation of mind and body through playing baseball that "there are men of eminence . . . who have graduated from the ball field to enter upon honorable careers as American citizens of the highest type, each with a sane mind in a sound body."[38] The key to understanding baseball for Spalding, then, is the way it incorporates the mind-body relationship and directs Americans to think about this relationship, particularly with respect to the liberal-republican underpinnings of America and the sport itself.

Baseball's Cultivation of the American Mind

Central to Spalding's considerations of how baseball enhances the mind are its republican elements, specifically that it is open to a great number of people and is governed by laws. Concerning the former, Spalding posits that baseball is the one sport in which spectators have an actual impact on the outcome of the games.[39] Diehard fans, whom he calls "rooters," provide entertainment for fellow fans and players with their "words of encouragement to the home team [and] shouts of derision to the opposing players."[40] These types of fans endear themselves to their home teams, in some sense becoming extensions of the team. Like those who participate in town halls and elections, fans make their voices heard in this manner, ensuring they have a relationship with their chosen "representatives" on the field.

Furthermore, Spalding argues that baseball is a contemplative game rather than a purely adversarial one, allowing diehard fans to become philosophers. In making this argument, he draws upon the form-based republican element of the game:

> The true fan is not only a spectator, enthusiast, and historian, but also must be a student of the ethics, aesthetics, and ontology of the game. The thoughtful fan investigates more than simply the obvious lore; he pursues the essence of baseball, its shape and meaning, its resonant possibilities. One of the most fundamental and significant truths of the game derives from the peculiar shape of its playing area. With the exception of cricket (which you have to be English to understand) baseball is the only team sport played with a ball that does not use a rectangular field. All other ball games are territorial and circumscribed; all play occurs within a box, where a team defends one end and attempts to penetrate the other.[41]

Spalding recognizes that sports that use rectangular fields are naturally more adversarial in nature, with each team adopting a particular "side" such that teams and fans are more directly pitted against each other in a physical back-and-forth contest. Baseball's circular field of play enables it to function as the modern equivalent of the ancient polis, a public space in which individuals can gather to engage in conversation about political and philosophical questions. Consequently, rather than arguing that baseball's appeal lies in its simplicity, Spalding applauds its creation of well-rounded, thoroughly knowledgeable fans.

As the game has developed, Spalding notes, ballparks have progressively come to play a republican role in society, offering a place for every American:

> Time was, and not long ago, when comparatively few understood the playing rules; but the day has come when nearly every man and boy in the land is versed in all intricacies of the pastime; thousands of young women have learned it well enough to keep score, and the

> number of matrons who know the difference between the short-stop and the back-stop is daily increasing.[42]

As more of the population learns the game, they "are able to become participators in the game itself," meaning that knowledge leads to participation.[43] Spalding links this knowledge of baseball to knowledge of America, claiming that "each generation will produce a little higher type of citizenship than that which went before it, and Base Ball and the principles which underlie it will help to bring this about."[44] In other words, baseball can guide American politics and dictate the future of the country, a future that increasingly recognizes the distinct American struggle for liberty and equality of all.

Central to Spalding's conception of baseball as civic educator is the sport's basis in the rule of law. Baseball possesses the most detailed rulebook of any North American professional sport, the development of which began in 1857 with the inaugural convention of the National Association of Base Ball Players. This convention adopted the nine-inning format, replacing the commonly used "first team to 21 runs" format, and the following year, adopted the called strike.[45] On this subject, Spalding writes, "Base Ball is governed by inflexible rules, and it is the function of the umpire to enforce the laws to the letter. Just insofar as he can do this to the satisfaction of magnates, managers, players and spectators he is efficient."[46] He further links umpires to judges, arguing that "a crooked umpire at a ball game is as offensive as a scoundrelly jurist on the bench," in part because "he must hand down his decision instanter before an audience composed of hundreds who know Base Ball law as well as he."[47] Umpires, then, both guard the rule of law against the passions of the players, managers, and fans, and encourage them all to engage with it.

This comparison of umpires to judges has become something of a staple in thinking of both the sport and the American judicial system. Multiple Supreme Court justices have turned to baseball as a way of explaining their role in American government. For instance, in the Senate Judiciary Committee's hearings on the nomination of Samuel Alito to the Supreme Court, Chief Justice Roberts stated, "Judges are like umpires. Umpires don't make the rules, they apply them. The role of an umpire and a judge is critical. They make sure everybody plays by the rules."[48] Umpires, of course, do more than simply apply the rules, and judges do more than merely apply existing law to cases, so Roberts's simile does not hold up to scrutiny. However, it does reveal a great deal about the way baseball fans understand laws. One of the biggest complaints many fans have about baseball is the fact that, though the rulebook describes the parameters of the strike zone, the zone is in reality the discretion of each individual umpire, leading to drastically different interpretations.[49] In this sense, the sport, according to historian Paul Finkelman, "prepares Americans for [the] legal and social reality" that the rule of law necessarily incorporates judicial discretion.[50]

Moreover, Finkelman argues that almost the entirety of the application of rules during a baseball game mirrors the American judicial system:

> Just as umpires are much like judges, and occasionally like police officers, managers and players often resemble litigants and lawyers. Where else but in a baseball game do we see a coach charge on to the field waving a rule book in his hand. The argument is often not only about how two observers, the umpire and the manager, saw the play but also how the "rule" should be applied to the play. Every manager is a rule-bound formalist, while most umpires are common law judges. In baseball, as in the American court system, there is even the possibility of appeal. Often enough a first base or third base umpire will reverse the judge at the plate on whether the batter swung at the ball. But, like our court system, the "higher court" judge only says something if an appeal has been made.[51]

Baseball theoretically teaches its players and fans to learn the rules and argue their case when they think a rule has been unfairly applied, but it also teaches them to respect the final outcome of the case. Indeed, without this ultimate deference to umpires, the game would potentially descend into chaos. Therefore, baseball has the capacity to cultivate and moderate public spiritedness, creating sharp minds capable of understanding the scope of the rule of law that provides the foundation for the sport and the country.

Baseball, the Body, and Pastoral America

The second aspect of baseball that makes it particularly American, Spalding argues, is the specific physicality it instills in men and boys. He states that the professional ballplayer "is doing more for his native country than any one engaged in any form of sport has ever done for any country in the past."[52] This is because baseball naturally develops "the American boy's inborn love of manly, skillful, outdoor sport," and it therefore "has done a lot to keep the Yankee lad from being brutal."[53] Rather than sports like football that rely on "brute force," the physicality of baseball directs boys toward patience, self-reliance, and skill.[54] In this explanation of strength, Spalding relies on the Gilded Age's linking of manliness to both liberal and republican theories of American pastoralism.

The late 1800s in America ushered in the Gilded Age and the "New Woman," both of which eroded the Victorian Era's conception of manliness as gentlemanliness. In its place, a new conception of manliness as physical strength and athletic prowess was formed, with baseball acting as the purveyor of this conception. Indeed, Theodore Roosevelt stated that baseball was one of the few "true sports for a manly race."[55] Simultaneously, the rise of the factory worker created a longing for a reclamation of the innocence found in nature. Baseball offered the intersection of these twin cultural shifts, providing images of manliness for boys to study and upholding both liberal and republican-based myths of the pastoral in the face of rapid urbanization.

First, focusing on farming, French American writer J. Hector St. John de Crèvecœur exemplifies the liberal veneration of pastoralism. In *Letters from an American Farmer*, first published in 1782, de Crèvecœur argues that in America, man's "labor is founded on the basis of nature, self-interest," producing "a new man, who acts upon new principles." Freed from the "involuntary idleness, servile dependence, penury, and useless labor" that characterized England's aristocratic land ownership, the American man "must therefore entertain new ideas and form new opinions" because "he has passed to toils of a very different nature, rewarded by ample subsistence. This is an American."[56] This characterization of agrarian individualism differs from the common conception of individualism as linked to commercialism, with de Crèvecoeur commenting on a supposedly novel relationship with the land that produces a new kind of continuously innovative man born out of self-interest.

Conversely, Jefferson's championing of America as a country of small farmer-landowners emphasized the system's ability to inculcate civic virtue, in contrast to the viciousness of urban life. Echoing the tendency to refer to America as a Garden of Eden, Jefferson declares, "Those who labour in the earth are the chosen people of God, if ever he had a chosen people, whose breasts he has made his peculiar deposit for substantial and genuine virtue . . . Corruption of morals in the mass of cultivators is a phaenomenon [*sic*] of which no age nor nation has furnished an example."[57] He restates this position in a letter to John Jay in 1785: "Cultivators of the earth are the most valuable citizens. They are the most vigorous, the most independent, the most virtuous, & they are tied to their country & wedded to its liberty & interests by the most lasting bonds."[58] In contrast to manufacturing-based economies, which have "distorted relationships among men, bred dependence and servility, and spawned greed and corruption which became a canker on the society," a farming-based nation "would assure the preservation of those qualities on which the strength of a republic depended."[59] As Christopher Michael Curtis puts it, Jefferson assumed that linking citizenship to the ownership of land would "reconcile the indulgent characteristics of economic individualism with a vested social attachment to a particular local community and, accordingly, foster civic virtue through self-interest."[60] This creation of civic virtue, according to Jefferson, would also emerge because agrarian societies supposedly are more predisposed to classical education and the production of learned citizens who would eschew the vices prevalent in cities.[61]

During the postrevolutionary westward expansion of the first half of the 1800s, Americans latched onto this romanticization of the individual's relationship with nature, expanding it beyond farmland to incorporate the wilderness. Coined "The Frontier Thesis" by Frederick Jackson Turner in his 1893 seminal work, *The Significance of the Frontier in American History*, this ideal posits that "the frontier promoted the formation of a composite nationality for the American people."[62] As "the meeting point between savagery and civilization," the frontier offered the noble goal of furthering the project of civilization by capturing Indigenous land.[63] Thus, westward expansion gave European laborers "an exit into a free life and a greater wellbeing among the bounties of nature" characterized by "manly exertion" and "the chance for indefinite ascent in the scale of social advance."[64] This depiction of pastoralism focuses on a figure that is "at once more primitive and more dynamic than the farmer, unfettered in his individualism, superior to mere labor, and free of any vestigial deference towards traditional social superiors."[65] This mythical frontiersman, inhibited solely by his physical limitations and responsible to none of his fellow men, is the apex of America's romanticization of individualism and the mythic self-made man.

Many of the most revered American writers of the 1800s—Whitman, Thoreau, Emerson, for instance—championed some combination of these interpretations of pastoralism, calling forth "a purer American vision of a society founded on the order of nature" rather than on industrialization.[66] J.G.A. Pocock describes this Gilded Age attachment to pastoralism as the American "in search of . . . his own nature as a man, which is civic, military, commercial, and in a word active."[67] Additionally, Richard Hofstadter argues that agrarianism "represents a kind of homage that Americans have paid to the fancied innocence of their origins . . . Its hero was the yeoman farmer, its central conception the notion that he is the ideal man and the ideal citizen."[68] These pastoralism myths provided select Americans with an unwavering image of the self as innocent, industrious, civic-minded, and manly at a time when the changing economic and civic relationships continuously undercut the notion of a unified national whole.

Building on the liberal individualist and republican virtuous conceptions of the country's mythic pastoralism, baseball offered itself as the means through which a singular national identity could be achieved. In 1888 baseball historian Henry Chadwick observed of the South that "manly games and athletic skill have taken the place of the bloody contests on the field of battle," providing a far better outlet for the "inherent attributes of manliness" than warfare.[69] Baseball combined this novel conception of manliness with a sense of innocence, offering the chance for both Northern and Southern soldiers to regain their innocence by playing a childlike game that associated manliness with morality.[70] As the nineteenth century neared its end, concerns of morality moved from the Civil War to the corrupting influences of rapidly growing urban centers, and baseball became a "sign of how rural virtues could redeem the excesses of the city," according to historian Christopher H. Evans.[71] The game, via its connections between pastoralism and urbanism and childhood and manliness, enabled men to acclimate themselves to the new industrial capitalist order of American society.[72]

Baseball possesses many characteristics that naturally lend it to promoting a nostalgia for pastoral innocence. As an outdoor game lacking a clock, it is reliant on the cycle of nature; games draw to an end as the sun sets, and the baseball season emerges with the spring and withers away in the fall. Relatedly, it can be played anywhere there is a patch of grass, and the earliest ballparks were rough patches of grass encompassed by quickly erected wooden stands, creating an intimate environment among the players, onlookers, and the greenery of the field. In many cities, these ballparks were among the few green spaces open to the public, creating a natural association of the game with the pastoral. Indeed, historian Frederick Paxson argued in his seminal 1917 article "The Rise of Sport" that baseball had come to be "a partial substitute for pioneer life," an argument adopted by many early historians of the game.[73] Even as ballparks became concrete structures designed to squeeze every last dollar from spectators, their form remained tied to pastoral sentiments. As opposed to the regulated dimensions of a basketball court or a football field, each ballpark has its own outfield dimensions, offering a reprieve from the cookie cutter approach inherent in industrial society.[74]

When linked with home plate, these outfield dimensions evoke another component of pastoralism: the Turner frontier thesis. Beginning at home plate, the baseball field opens outward into the large green area of the outfield, mimicking to some degree the "open" borders of the frontier and allowing the outfielders to exercise their individualism in interacting with this space.[75] This limitless individualism, however, is constrained by the symbol of "home" as beginning and end (rendered in the way a child is taught to draw it), as representation of America's constant effort to return to some past innocence. On this notion, Canadian poet and baseball enthusiast David McGimpsey surmises that "the baseball pastoral has less to do with the intrinsic qualities of what makes baseball beautiful than it does with American fascination with innocence and corruption."[76]

The new Gilded Age manliness Spalding links to baseball, then, relies on the game's ability to evoke America's longing for the pastoral. The inherently pastoral elements of baseball enabled it to respond to the crisis of identity caused by the post–Civil War rise of industrialism. Specifically, baseball allowed players to pursue individualism while disseminating the importance of morality and civic virtue. Spalding further blended these iterations of liberalism and republicanism in his creation of the Doubleday myth, which remains integral to understanding baseball's political presence in America.

The Myth of Abner Doubleday

The greatest indicator of baseball's obsession with the pastoral is the myth that Abner Doubleday invented the game. This story was created in 1907 by the Mills Commission, established by A. G. Spalding for the purpose of countering historian Henry Chadwick's more truthful claim that baseball evolved from the English game "rounders." Although this origin story is now commonly understood to be a myth, its effects on baseball's image as a uniquely American, pastoral game remain to this day.

The Mills Commission was composed of its namesake, Abraham G. Mills, fourth president of the National League; Morgan G. Bulkeley, US Senator and first president of the NL; Nicholas E. Young, first secretary and fifth president of the NL; Arthur P. Gorman, US Senator and former player and ex-president of the Washington Base Ball Club; James E. Sullivan, president of the Amateur Athletic Union; and Alfred J. Reach and George Wright, sporting goods owners and former players. It was crucial for Spalding that this commission consist of both statesmen and ballplayers, thereby placing congressional politics and baseball on the same level of national importance. Indeed, *The New York Sun* declared of the committee, "If the sessions are begun early in the fall, it is believed that the work will be over in time to let Senators Bulkeley and Gorman take their seats in the Senate at the opening of Congress. Otherwise, Congress must suffer."[77] The senators did make it to the opening of Congress, but it took the committee far longer than those few months to reach a verdict on the origins of baseball.

Unsurprisingly, after nearly three years of "investigation," the handpicked commission concluded:

> *First*—that baseball had its origin in the United States;
>
> *Second*—that the first scheme for playing it, according to the best evidence obtainable to date, was devised by Abner Doubleday, at Cooperstown, New York, in 1839.[78]

The evidence consisted almost entirely of testimony from Doubleday's supposed schoolmate, Abner Graves, a mining engineer from Denver who responded to the commission's advertisements in local papers asking for written testimonials from anyone with knowledge of baseball's origins. In his testimony, Graves fancifully recalled Doubleday—who was at West Point, not Cooperstown, in 1839—overtaking a game of marbles one day to draw a large diamond in the dirt, thus establishing the four-base shape used for the game of baseball.

Graves's testimony was not the first time the commission had heard of Doubleday, however, as both Mills and Spalding were already aware of his existence. Mills had been a longtime friend of Doubleday, having met him during the Civil War, in which they both served as generals.

Spalding, meanwhile, had first become aware of Doubleday via an 1893 obituary of him printed in the journal of the Theosophical Society, to which Spalding belonged. In 1905 the obituary was reprinted with a final line crediting him with naming baseball and "in large degree its development from a simpler sport; or indeed . . . its very invention."[79]

Spalding and the commission were eager to name Doubleday the inventor of baseball because of his ability to link pastoralism and the Civil War and thus speak to a conception of a unified America, albeit a mythic one. After making note of the origins of baseball, Spalding offers a biography of Doubleday that recounts his military accomplishments in the Civil War. He quickly rose up the ranks, becoming a general before he was "sent to Gettysburg . . . and took command of the field till the arrival of General Howard . . . and on the third day aided in the repulse of Pickett's charge."[80] Spalding boasted, "The founder of our National Game became a Major General in the United States Army!"[81] Doubleday, then, confirms Spalding's belief that "the best ball players were born fighters," thereby equating baseball with manliness.[82]

Spalding further uses this Doubleday–Civil War connection to cement the sport's ability to cultivate civic virtue and craft a facade of innocence in American identity. Referring to the spread of baseball during the Civil War, Spalding declared that the sport

> had its early evolution when soldiers, North and South, were striving to forget their foes by cultivating, through this grand game, fraternal friendships with comrades in arms . . . It was a panacea for the pangs of humiliation to the vanquished on the one side, and a sedative against the natural exuberance of victors on the other. It healed the wounds of war, and was balm to stinging memories of sword thrust and saber stroke. It served to fill the enforced leisure hours of countless thousands of men suddenly thrown out of employment. It calmed the restless spirits of men who, after four years of bitter strife, found themselves all at once in the midst of a monotonous era, with nothing at all to do. And then, when true patriots of all sections were striving to forget that there had been a time of black and dismal war, it was a beacon, lighting their paths to a future of perpetual peace. And, later still, it was a medium through which the men who had worn the blue, found welcome to the cities of those who had worn the gray, and before the decade of the sixties had died the game of Base Ball helped all of us to "know

> no North, no South," only remembering a reunited Nation, whose game it was henceforth to be forever.[83]

Although this account of early baseball contains a great deal of exaggeration concerning the ease with which society could move past the Civil War, there is also truth in it. After the war, baseball spread throughout the South, and it was not uncommon for southern and northern teams to play one another, resulting often in warm receptions from each host city, both North and South.[84] While baseball on its own, of course, could not solve the problems caused by racism, particularly at the start of the Jim Crow era, in which southern states rapidly legalized segregation, the sport did offer an example of what America could become should it embrace republicanism's foundation of civic friendship.

The Doubleday myth spread quickly around the country and was immediately championed by writers and fans alike. *The Chicago Inter Ocean* declared, "Let the joyous tidings that baseball was founded in America . . . be spread abroad, and let every fan rejoice."[85] *The Wichita Daily Eagle* echoed that sentiment and added that the origin "was, in a way, connected with politics," randomly placing Doubleday's invention of the game at a William Henry Harrison presidential campaign event.[86] All publications stressed Doubleday's connection to the Civil War, declaring his most honorable qualities his invention of baseball and his dedication to America. In this way, he helped shape the country twice over.

So taken with this myth was Major League Baseball that it built its Hall of Fame and Museum in Cooperstown in the 1930s, where Doubleday had lived several years prior to his supposed invention of baseball. In his speech at the opening of the Hall of Fame, MLB Commissioner Kenesaw Mountain Landis emphasized the relationship between baseball and America, dedicating the museum "to all America: to lovers of good sportsmanship, healthy body, team mind. For those are the principles of baseball."[87] Here, again, we see the association of baseball with the cultivation of mind and body, not only for the few players who were inducted into the Hall of Fame but for the nation as a whole.

The opening of the Hall of Fame and Museum cemented baseball's reliance on myth over fact, in part because there is ample evidence that baseball existed prior to 1839 and was even played in Cooperstown, though never by Doubleday. For instance, James Fenimore Cooper's semi-autobiographical 1838 novel, *Home as Found*, includes a passage in which a group of boys plays a baseball game in a field adjacent to the place where the Hall of Fame would be built a century later.[88] Nonetheless, baseball's mythological origins proved here to stay.

In 1923 the Village of Cooperstown created a ballfield with stands seating roughly ten thousand fans on the site at which Doubleday supposedly invented the game. In 1940 the famous "Sandlot Kid" statue was erected next to Doubleday Field. The statue depicts a barefoot young boy sporting the typical farmer outfit of overalls and a straw hat and holding a bat over his shoulder. This statue demonstrates the desire to link baseball to pastoral innocence, prompting spectators to conjure memories of playing baseball in their childhoods, when life was much simpler and their time was less in demand. To this day, over three hundred games per year are played on this field, demonstrating the centrality of this myth to baseball fans and players of all ages.[89]

The persistence of this myth despite it being recognized as such speaks to the desire in American society for simplicity over uncertainty and for individual figures to immortalize. Bud Selig, the MLB commissioner who oversaw the 1994 strike and the steroid era, clung to the Doubleday myth, writing in a letter in 2010, "I really believe that Abner Doubleday is the 'Father of Baseball.'"[90] Essentially, the myth has endured because it is easier to believe the perfect relationship between the individual and the common good within the story than to confront the realities of the sport and the country. Thus, even in its falseness—or maybe *because* of its falseness—it captures something true about baseball and America itself. It is crucial for us to confront this truth about America if we are to understand how we ought to live in community with one another.

CHAPTER TWO

Courts and Communities

The Development of MLB's Antitrust Exemption

> Baseball is most of all an enormous and cold-blooded corporate enterprise, and as such is probably a more revelatory and disturbing part of our national psyche than we had supposed.
>
> —Roger Angell

From the late nineteenth century through the end of the twentieth, professional baseball transitioned from a disparate group of teams that each rarely lasted more than a couple of seasons to a multi-billion-dollar corporate enterprise that monopolized the sport. Central to this transformation was a group of owners who insisted that professional baseball would not reach its true potential unless it became a stable enterprise guided by their business acumen. In essence, they argued that the players themselves could not be trusted with upholding the good of America's emergent national pastime. The legitimacy of this argument stemmed from a general distrust among the middle and upper class in America toward professional athletes, who they thought would introduce "gambling and fraud" and therefore "weakness and wickedness" into both sports and American society.[1]

In their quest to make money from the professionalization of baseball, these businessmen had to present themselves as more virtuous than the players, who were infinitely corruptible due to the greed that supposedly did not extend to these new team owners. Thus, as they came to extract greater and greater profits from the game, the owners increasingly needed to maintain the myths within the sport. The more economically interconnected professional baseball became, the greater the need to understand it as a fundamentally local sport; the more corporatized it became, the more it relied on notions of the pastoral; the more exclusionary it became of different races and genders, the more it hid behind false notions of equality. Indeed, the primary tool these owners used to control players and therefore profit was the reserve clause, which bound players to teams indefinitely and granted select teams exclusive territorial rights in many cities, demanding loyalty from players and fans which has not been reciprocated. The more control these owners assumed of the game, the farther away professional baseball has drifted from genuine civic virtue.

This chapter contextualizes the reserve clause in liberal and republican arguments concerning the nature and scope of property rights in society and the efforts of the federal government to regulate monopolies. It questions whether an emphasis on individual property rights can foster civic virtue. Ultimately, this chapter argues that organized baseball's antitrust exemption reveals how republican civic virtue has been directed toward supporting liberal property rights, with the result being the monopolization of baseball at the cost of both individual rights and the common good.

To anchor this account of baseball's class and labor issues in the political thought that has shaped America, this chapter begins with a discussion of the liberal and republican conceptions of property prevalent during the American founding. It then provides a brief overview of baseball's professionalization in the late 1800s, which culminated in the implementation of the reserve clause. Next, it discusses the players' reaction to the reserve clause, namely John Montgomery Ward's arguments against it and the creation and demise of the Players' League. The chapter then moves on to the extension of the reserve clause in the twentieth century, focusing on a trio of Supreme Court cases that granted Major League Baseball an antitrust exemption. The chapter concludes with an examination of the 1994–1995 player strike, after which the reserve clause was officially abolished while the territorial elements of the antitrust exemption remained in place.

Property Rights During the Founding Era

The American Revolution coincided with a shift in Western society from feudalism to commercial capitalism, generating many debates concerning property rights and the nature of property itself. So central was property to this new American government that historian Gordon S. Wood claims "the entire Revolution could be summed up by the radical transformation Americans made in their understanding of property."[2]

Much scholarship of the founding era has attempted to illuminate the precise nature of this transformation, focusing primarily on the interplay between the different ways republicanism and liberalism understand property's relationship to citizenship and liberty. Several scholars argue that liberalism's emphasis on individual property rights formed the basis of political thought in this era, but even more maintain that the founding era combined liberalism and republicanism in some way.[3]

The liberalism of the American founding began with English philosopher John Locke's conception of property. In short, Locke argues that private property is derived from the idea of self-ownership—a person's labor is an extension of themselves and so once a person mixes their labor with something, it becomes their property.[4] Government, then, exists for the protection of individual rights, primarily this property right. Locke's argument about individual ownership of labor leads to a prioritization of the individual over society, wherein the individual believes "he owes no debt to civil society" since he is the source of his own labor.[5] In this account of property, Locke gives special consideration to America, which he saw as a vast amount of land ripe for appropriation through individual industriousness. It is no surprise, then, that his theory was appealing to many of America's founders.

Emerging from this Lockean liberalism was a theory of property that emphasized individual property rights and the individual accumulation of capital as a public good. This theory, embodied by Alexander Hamilton, argued in favor of commercialism and the granting of public powers to charter corporations. Hamilton, like Locke, argued that the purpose of government was the protection of private property and personal liberty, which would necessarily produce inequality of property.[6] In essence, government protected the self-interested *pursuit* of property, which Hamilton thought would naturally create "commerce and industry."[7] Thus, Hamilton declared that compared to agriculture, manufacturing is "more *constant*, more uniform and more ingenious . . . and] at the same time more productive."[8] He ultimately believed that the success of America rested on the national government's investment in manufacturing and its ability to tie the good of the national government to the good of the few wealthy manufacturers at the head of this emerging industrial economy.[9]

Contrary to Hamilton, both John Adams and Thomas Jefferson championed an agrarian attachment to property that cultivated republican civic virtue. Like Locke, Adams related governmental power to ownership of property, but his emphasis on the preservation of both "equal liberty and public virtue" led him to argue for making "the acquisition of land easy to every member of society" to minimize the concentration of power in a wealthy elite.[10] Jefferson shared much of Adams's thought on property rights and civic virtue, but to it he added a greater disdain for commercialism and a greater appreciation for natural aristocracy.[11] In defense of agrarianism, he argued that "cultivators of the earth are the most virtuous and independent citizens."[12] It was thus imperative to abolish feudal laws restricting the ownership of land so that more equal property ownership could be "an opening for the aristocracy of virtue and talent" and the "laying [of] a foundation . . . for a government truly republican."[13] He thought that individual ownership of land would both protect against tyranny and result in a desire to take greater care of the land.

Finally, there existed a strand of republican thought that centered the laborers absent from the Hamiltonian and Jeffersonian theories of property. Proponents of this theory, such as Thomas Paine and William Manning, argued for a community-based approach to property rights that promised to create true economic equality. Refuting Locke and Hamilton, Paine argued that individuals could not acquire property without the aid of society, and therefore one "owes on every principle of justice, of gratitude, and of civilization, a part of that accumulation back again to society whence the whole came."[14] Thus, Paine's solution to wealth inequality was to organize society "upon such principles as to act like a system of pullies, that the whole weight of misery can be removed," rather than rely on "the choice of detached individuals" to provide charity to the poor.[15] Paine's republicanism argued that rather than being individual and natural, property rights are collective and granted by the state.

Manning offered an even more radical departure from the Jeffersonian agrarian republicanism, adapting the republican principles of civic virtue and self-government to the plight of wage laborers. In his 1792 book *The Key of Liberty*, he analyzed the relationship between the Many (wage laborers) and the Few (landed gentry, merchants, and lawyers), arguing that the Few, who do not labor themselves, create monetary scarcity in order to "compel [the many] into a state of dependance on the few for favours & assistance in a thousand ways."[16] Contrary to other accounts of republicanism that have a virtuous few guiding the many away from self-interest and toward the common good, Manning conflated the many's self-interest with the exercise of virtue and the common good: it is in their self-interest to establish republican government. In order to establish true republican government, Manning called for the creation of a "Sociaty of Labourers" [*sic*] to facilitate the publication of their own newspapers and establish free public schools for teaching civic education, with the expectation that this education would free laborers from "individuals who may be interested to deceive" them.[17] Manning's account of republicanism, then, extends beyond agrarian and aristocratic conceptions, positioning the political theory in dialogue with the growing industrial capitalist landscape in America.[18]

Emerging from these liberal and republican debates is the fundamental question concerning the degree to which individual property rights can be understood as separate from one's community. This question encompasses the relationship between self-interest and the public good, as well as the government's role in regulating property rights and labor. Professional baseball, in its transition from amateur game to multi-billion-dollar industry, provides unique insight into the development of property rights through America's industrialization and corporatization. An analysis of baseball's role in this transition will help illuminate the degree to which it is possible to combine liberal and republican notions of property.

Baseball's Professionalization and the Development of the Reserve Clause

The late nineteenth century, known as the Gilded Age, was a period of rapid industrialization bolstered by increased immigration largely from Ireland, Germany, and Italy. For the first time, manufacturing industries outpaced farming, giving rise to great economic disparities between business magnates and their millions of new wage laborers.[19] These economic relationships were characterized by the liberal idea of property ownership and freedom of contract as the foundation of individual liberty. This era also produced more radical republican calls for worker solidarity across ethnic and class lines in service of the common good. Baseball, with its unique blend of liberal and republican elements and its entrenchment in American society, offered a different conception of labor and the class conflicts of this time.

In the immediate post–Civil War years, baseball was a local, amateur game played by all members of society for the purposes of recreation and civic pride, but people soon realized there was money to be made in the sport.[20] Between 1865 and 1869, baseball players earned money by agreeing to sham jobs as storekeepers, clerks, and other middle-class positions to disguise their being paid to play baseball. Fielding a competitive team was such a source of community pride and power for business owners that players were paid more than other workers in their industries.[21] In 1869 the Cincinnati Red Stockings became the first professional team—all players were openly paid to play baseball as their primary job.

In 1871 ten professional teams formed the National Association of Professional Base Ball Players (NAPBBL), each represented by a wealthy business owner who had purchased stakes in these teams.[22] Then, in 1876, William Hulbert, member of the Chicago Board of Trade, created the National League of Professional Baseball Clubs to replace the fragmented and weak NAPBBL. This league sought to stabilize professional baseball through creating the "League Alliance," which gave each team territorial rights over its city, forcing players to play for their hometown teams. It also blacklisted any player who tried to "jump" to another team and any team who signed such a player, further granting teams monopolies in each city.[23] Hulbert's three goals for the league—eliminating players from positions of power concerning league financial matters, outlawing gambling, and curbing player drinking—embodied the paternalistic notion that workers needed owners to control their welfare.[24] This consolidation of ownership power was therefore explained as putting the game on a "sound financial and moral basis" through assuring players "lucrative employment as long as they are honest and work hard."[25] This combination of liberal individualism with republican morality set the tone for future discussions of professional baseball.

In 1878, after the third season in which no team made a profit, the owners implemented a policy to further bring players under their control: the reserve clause. This clause was a form of indentured servitude that allowed each team to "reserve" five players from their roster for at least a year after their contracts ended, preventing these players from signing with another team. With players denied the ability to receive contract offers from multiple teams, salaries almost immediately declined, some by almost half.[26] Owners justified these moves by claiming it was a travesty to pay players $2000 annually when the general working population received far below that—for instance, the average "unskilled" laborer in New York at the time made roughly $550 annually, a fraction of what ballplayers were making.[27]

The reserve clause proved instrumental to the longevity of the National League in these early years as it helped the NL fend off challenge first from the American Association (AA) and then from the Union Association (UA). In 1881, the Cincinnati Red Stockings, who had been banned from the NL for selling alcohol and playing Sunday games, formed the AA. This new league marketed itself to the working class by selling alcohol, playing Sunday games, and setting ticket prices at 25 cents, half the cost of an NL ticket.[28] The absence of the reserve clause initially prompted NL players to sign with AA teams. However, when multiple challenges in court of the reserve clause and whether players were "club property" threatened the stability of both the NL and the AA, the two leagues in 1883 agreed to respect each league's territorial rights and blacklists, increase the reserve list to eleven players per team, and set minimum player salaries at $1000. In 1957 MLB Commissioner Ford Frick called the first two elements of this agreement the "keystones of organized baseball."[29] Thanks to this agreement, nearly every team made a profit in the 1883 season. The UA, which also marketed itself as reserve clause–free, lasted only one season before folding, and the league's president, St. Louis millionaire Henry Lucas, who had previously called the reserve clause the most "arbitrary and unjust rule ever suggested," gladly joined the NL, reserve clause and all, once his league went bankrupt.[30] Following this collapse, the NL and AA signed a new agreement in October of 1885 to cap salaries at $2000 per season and expand the reserve clause to twelve players per team.[31]

The expansion of the reserve clause drew the ire of the working class, prompting multiple trade unions to speak out against the blacklisting of UA players. The general consensus among these union members was that the players were "workingmen kept out of employment by a body of capitalists."[32] This conclusion urged many of these unions to call for a boycott of professional baseball. Professional baseball thus came to intersect with a period of rapid unionization across America in response to the Gilded Age's widening wealth gap that saw 4000 millionaires own 20 percent of the country's wealth, while 40 percent of industrial laborers lived below the poverty line.[33] By the mid-1880s, the Knights of Labor—the country's largest labor union—had exceeded 700,000 members, including white women and non-white workers.[34] The Knights aimed to "make individual and moral worth, not wealth, the true standard of individual and national greatness," thereby reversing the moral and economic degradation produced by industrial capitalism's monopolistic paternalism. They argued this could be done through securing "to the worker the full enjoyment of the wealth they create, sufficient leisure in which to develop their intellectual, moral and social faculties . . . in a word, to enable them to share in the gains and honors of advancing civilization."[35] The solution to wage labor, in their view, was a "co-operative industrial system" in which workers would own their businesses and share the fruits of their labor with one another.

This approach to property rights and issues of labor set the tone for all other unions during this time. Professional baseball's continued use of the reserve clause prompted multiple trade unions to speak out against it and professional baseball as whole. The consensus among these union members was that the players were "workingmen kept out of employment by a body of capitalists."[36] This conclusion urged many unions to call for a boycott of professional baseball until the NL reinstated blacklisted players. In response to this potential boycott, the heads of the NL declared their willingness to reinstate four players who had recently violated the reserve clause and allow them to choose their own team, provided they pay a $500 fine.[37] The owners' pseudo-capitulation prompted players to recognize the amount of power owners had accumulated via the reserve clause and planted the seeds of the coming battle and the players' own unionization efforts.

John Montgomery Ward's Critique of the Reserve Clause

Frustrated by this updated NL and AA agreement and the inability of new leagues to establish themselves, in 1885 nine players formed the National Brotherhood of Professional Base Ball Players, the first player union. The Brotherhood was headed by New York Gothams multiposition player John Montgomery Ward, who had just graduated from Columbia Law School. Known for his manliness and cleverness, like his supposed invention of the curveball, as well as his authorship of the popular guide, *Base-Ball: How to Become a Player, with Origin, History, and Explanation of the Game*, Ward was the perfect player to lead this union. As union leader, he voiced to the public the Brotherhood's concerns with the reserve clause, presenting the union as a collective response to the infringement of individual property rights.

Laid out in its constitution, the aims of the Brotherhood were to "protect and benefit ourselves collectively and individually; to promote a high standard of professional conduct; [and] to foster and encourage the interests of the game of Base Ball," linking individual property rights to the collective good.[38] By the end of the 1886 season, the Brotherhood encompassed 90 percent of NL players and had established a chapter in each of the league's eight cities (Chicago, Detroit, New York, Philadelphia, Boston, St. Louis, Washington, and Kansas City). While the union grew its membership, it largely remained private, primarily collecting dues to be distributed to sick or injured players who were not being paid by their clubs. However, when Chicago sold pitchers Michael "King" Kelly and Jim McCormick in 1887 after they beat up a Pinkerton Spalding hired to follow them to bars, Ward became incensed that they had no say in the matter.[39]

After NL president Nick Young refused to meet with Ward over his concerns with the reserve clause, Ward published an article in *Lippincott's Magazine*, titled "Is the Base Ball Player a Chattel?" This article more exhaustively and passionately voiced the critiques of the reserve clause, which had existed since its implementation.[40] After a brief introduction to the reserve clause, Ward outlined the players' gripes with it:

> As new leagues have sprung up, they have been either frozen out or forced into this agreement for their own protection, and the all-embracing nature of the reserve-rule has been maintained. There is now no escape for the player . . . Like a fugitive-slave law, the reserve-rule denies him a harbor of a livelihood, and carries him back, bound and shackled, to the club from which he attempted to escape. We have, then, the curious result of a contract which on its face is for seven months being binding for life, and when the player's name is once attached thereto his professional liberty is gone forever. . . . [the Constitution of the National League] inaugurated a species of serfdom which gave one set of men a life-estate in the labor of another, and withheld from the latter any corresponding claim. No attempt has ever been made to defend it on the grounds of abstract right. Its justification, if any, lay only in its expediency.[41]

Ward's emphasis here is on the restriction of individual liberty, leading him to compare the reserve clause to the fugitive slave clause as something that hangs over a player for life, reminding him that he is property, not a person. Furthermore, Ward defined freedom as the ability to enter into a fair contract with one's employer, thereby asserting ownership as an integral component of professional baseball. Moreover, he suggested that liberal individualism led to the sacrifice of natural rights when capitalists deemed them contrary to their economic goals, although, as we will see, Ward does not pursue the full implications of this final argument.

In accordance with this liberal definition of freedom, Ward refrained from engaging in discussions of baseball's civic role with respect to players, instead focusing on the abuse of individual rights. Using the example of pitcher Charlie Foley, whom Buffalo refused to sign or release during and after an illness, Ward pointed out that the reserve clause's enactment extended beyond the length of player contracts. Moreover, the clause enabled teams to buy, sell, and loan players at will, to the point that even those players who played for disbanded teams were auctioned to the highest bidding team in the NL and AA.[42] Thus, the teams were infringing on the players' freedom of contract, an argument that was sure to win over the millions of Americans in similar relationships with their employers.

Contrary to the popular republican solutions to labor disputes, Ward's more liberal solution to the owners having "seized absolute control over the labor of another" was to eliminate the reserve clause and allow the free market to regulate itself. Professional baseball needed to cut away the "tangled web of legislation which now hampers the game" and allow the sport to "rest on the ordinary business bases" of "supply and demand." He posited that, with the reserve clause gone, multiyear contracts would increase parity, eliminate contract-breaking, and cause players to view baseball as "more of a business and less of a pastime," presumably making them savvier negotiators.[43]

This account of property rights underscores two things: the individualism inherent in baseball and a desire to combat the owners' narrative of immorality. First, individualism appears in baseball in several ways. Fans are attracted by the individual skills of players; they come to the ballpark to watch Buck Ewing throw out runners, marvel at Mike Kelly's innovativeness, and to debate player merits among themselves. Second, the labor force is much smaller than in other industries and the careers of ballplayers are much shorter, pushing them to maximize their earnings through competition. It is difficult to understand things in terms of the collective when a player is only part of the collective for two or three years. Compounding this draw toward individualism was the owners' strategy of using individual player behavior to represent all players. Ward noted this problem, stating, "The public reasons from the individual to the class" even though "ball-players are selected not so much with reference to their social habits or intellectual attainments as to their ability to play ball."[44] His argument, then, is that individual rights should not be dependent on moral qualifications.

The Rise and Fall of the Players' League

In November 1887 the National Brotherhood of Professional Base Ball Players sent Nick Young an ultimatum: He could either formally recognize the Brotherhood and begin reserve clause negotiations, or the union members would "consider themselves absolved from all allegiance to the league."[45] Young partially capitulated, agreeing to write the reserve clause into contracts and giving Ward and other stars a raise for the 1888 season. In the offseason, however, while Ward and other high-ranking Brotherhood members were on Spalding's World Tour, the owners announced a classification system that capped salaries at $2500, punishing the union's many veterans by ensuring they would never reach top classification. This system also attempted to weaponize the players' individualism and acquisitiveness by pitting veterans and youngsters against each other, with the hope that veterans would become resentful of the younger players who were outearning them.[46]

Members of the Brotherhood gathered on July 14, 1889, the centennial of Bastille Day, to finally solidify plans to create a player-run league. On November 4, after the NL claimed a profit of nearly $750,000 (roughly $24 million today) over the 1886–1889 seasons, the players announced their new league.[47] They distributed a manifesto among themselves and to fans in New York explaining this decision:

> We believe that it is possible to conduct our National game upon lines which will not infringe upon individual and natural rights. We ask to be judged solely by our own work, and, believing that the game can be played more fairly and its business conducted more intelligently under a plan which excludes everything arbitrary and un-American, we look forward with confidence to the support of the public and the future of the National game.[48]

The Brotherhood upheld the liberal theory of natural, individual property rights as the foundation of American society and therefore the legitimate foundation of professional baseball as representative of America. The owners, who "have come into the business for no other motive than to exploit it for every dollar in sight," had thereby corrupted the natural labor relationship in baseball.[49] Rather than understanding monopolies as inherent in capitalism, the Brotherhood understood them as a distortion of the free market.

In accord with this understanding of liberalism, the union's "cooperative" league was funded by player contributions and the selling of $100 stock shares to local businessmen in each team's city. Rather than the players themselves, the primary backers of the Players' League were these businessmen, who were said to be men "of good judgment, wealthy, and to a man deeply interested in the welfare of the new organization."[50] Unlike with his fellow players, Ward emphasized these men's civic mindedness, claiming that "many of them were even willing to put in the capital without any return whatsoever, but of love for the sport and a desire to see it placed on a plane above that upon which it was being operated."[51] Publicly, these investors, like Cleveland-based trolley car mogul Albert Johnson, spoke of their desire to "liberate [the players] from the tyrannical rule of the League."[52] Privately, though, they admitted that they "owned businesses . . . or land, which would directly benefit from the presence of a major league baseball team."[53] This league, then, would test the ability of private interests to promote the common good.

The Players' League contract was an amalgamation of player and "backer" interests. The players received a roughly even share of the profits, three-year contracts with guaranteed salaries and free agency thereafter, and a prohibition of in-season trades and sales at any point. While the players received freedom from the reserve clause, the backers received a 50-cent ticket price and bans on Sunday games and the sale of alcohol, thus allowing them to advertise the league to the middle class as a moral, gentlemanly enterprise. These decisions brought the league into conflict with the working class, who could largely only attend Sunday games.[54]

More than Ward and the Brotherhood, NL owners and labor unions understood the stakes of this league. Very simply, the owners viewed the issue as the "irrepressible conflict between Labor and Capital" in which the players must be crushed.[55] Spalding, the owners' leader, knew that if the players were to succeed, it would demonstrate the illegitimacy of owners extracting profits from a game they do not play, a principle that could be applied to other industries. The owners therefore preyed on the middle- and upper-class desire to control the working class.

Spalding again relied on their preoccupation with gentlemanliness, accusing "certain overpaid players" of again trying to "control [baseball] for their own aggrandizement, but to [baseball's] ultimate dishonor and disintegration."[56] Spalding further called the players "hot-headed anarchists" and "terrorists" who had been tricked by "capitalists, whose only possible interests in the matter . . . is the amount of money they hope to realize" from supporting the Players' League.[57] Spalding reaffirmed the fundamental conflict between labor and capital and linked the Players' League to the likes of the labor radicals who had been falsely charged with firebombing Chicago's Haymarket Square in 1886.[58]

In conjunction with these statements, the NL and AA further distanced themselves from the working class. Several teams built new stadiums with more rigid class-based seating divisions, confining the working class to cheaper uncovered, backless bleachers while providing more comfortable and expensive grandstand seating to the middle and upper classes.[59] Furthermore, the AA, originally the working class league, doubled ticket prices from 25 cents to 50 cents in 1888, matching NL prices, and stopped playing Sunday games.[60] The leagues upheld their wealthy patrons as the "gentlemanly" opposition to the rowdy, vulgar "bleachers," despite the fact that wealthy fans instigated most fights at games.[61] This appeal to gentlemanliness extended to "Ladies Day" promotions, where upper-class men could bring women with them in order to "smile upon the horrid men" in the bleachers.[62] The working class was more than ever being priced out of the ballparks its labor had built.

The labor movement, then, was also invested in the success of the Players' League. For many years, labor unions had used amateur ballparks as communal meeting grounds to build camaraderie and class solidarity.[63] It was natural to extend the same principles to professional baseball. American Federation of Labor (AFL) leader Samuel Gompers stated that "laboring men all over the country are in sympathy with the players in this fight," and the Brotherhood would have the AFL's "moral and financial support."[64] This financial support largely took the shape of calls for the working class to patronize Players' League games over NL and AA ones, with both the AFL and the Central Labor Union encouraging their members to do so.[65] Moreover, Samuel Leffingwell, head of the International Typographical Union, summarized precisely what was at stake in the conflict: "It will be seen whether mere capital is to rule with despotic sway over the masses of the people in baseball as it would like to do in many other leading industries in the country."[66] For labor organizers, the player-owner conflict extended far beyond the confines of the ballpark.

The Brotherhood's determination to unite labor and capital, however, prevented it from comprehending the scope of its project. Ward marketed the league to the public as one consisting of workingmen who had "the sympathy of the labor organizations," and whose success would demonstrate the viability of having "the men who do the work participate in the profits of the pastime," but the Brotherhood rejected Gompers's invitation to join the AFL.[67] Moreover, the players' decision to have only "backers" as league officers brought the league into conflict with the working class. Needing quickly constructed ballparks to begin the season on time, John Addison, league vice president and Chicago contractor, authorized the use of non-union carpenters in Boston and Chicago to circumvent the national carpenters' strike for the eight-hour workday and a forty-cent-per-hour wage. The Chicago ballpark, the only site in the city to continue construction post-strike, instigated multiple confrontations between striking carpenters and strikebreakers, one of which ended in a police confrontation.[68] Despite these setbacks, the Chicago team continued to find small groups of laborers willing to cross the picket line, and the ballpark was constructed on time. Somewhat ironically, the ballpark featured "covered stands, with comfortable opera chairs, in place of the old bleachers" such that the "merchant, mechanic, and professional man" could sit side by side.[69]

By the end of the 1890 season, though, both the NL and the Players' League had lost money, and it was clear that not enough fans could afford to attend both leagues.[70] While Ward remained firm in his commitment to his league, the offseason brought to light backdoor deals between Spalding and the Players' League "backers" that resulted in the NL and AA absorbing six of the eight Players' League teams. Ward, who had been working out a compromise "for the benefit of players and capitalists," was furious at the "capitalists of the Players League clubs conducting negotiations without the aid of the players," who were willing to "play for almost nothing next season to continue the fight."[71] The vast majority of "backers" were eager to recoup their losses through merging their teams with their NL counterparts and quickly agreed to end the Players' League in exchange for majority stakes in these consolidated teams.

As part of this resolution, the owners reinstated all reserve lists from 1889 for the 1891 season. Reflecting on the failure of the Players' League, Spalding—one of the men most responsible for its demise—attributed its failure to the nature of capitalism: "Like every other form of business enterprise, Base Ball depends for results upon two interdependent divisions, the one to have absolute control and direction of the system, and the other to engage—always under the executive branch—in the actual work of production." In attempting to combine the roles of ownership and labor, Spalding argued, the Players' League had violated the fundamental liberal economic principles governing the country. As this conception of labor hung over professional baseball, the carpenters' union won their battles, with over 23,000 carpenters in forty-two cities gaining an eight-hour workday and 32,000 more across 313 cities gaining a nine-hour workday.[72]

The final step in this early monopolization of baseball came in 1903, with the creation of the National Association of Professional Baseball Leagues (NAPBL), an agreement between the NL and the new American League (AL). The AL, originally called the Western League, was declared a major league in 1901 by its president Ban Johnson. Immediately, it drew in many NL stars, like Cy Young, Jack Chesboro, and Nap Lajoie, who wanted higher salaries. In revenge, the NL instituted rule changes, including widening home plate and making the first two fouled pitches strikes, for the purpose of lowering offensive statistics, making players unappealing to AL owners and giving NL owners cause to lower their salaries.[73] When this plan backfired by driving strong hitters to the AL, resulting in massive attendance for the AL, the NL decided instead to negotiate a commission to preside over inter-league disputes and fix contracts for player sales. Under this commission, player salaries dropped to their lowest in over a decade, capped at twenty-four hundred dollars.[74] This agreement also instituted both a minor league classification system that defined salary ranges for minor league players, capping them at fifteen hundred, and a draft that would dictate upward mobility of players, with major league clubs choosing the minor leaguers over which they had territorial ownership.[75] The result of this agreement was an extension of organized baseball's monopoly over professional baseball and the beginnings of the contemporary minor league farm system.

The first three decades of professional baseball tell the story of ownership monopolization at the expense of the freedom of players and the inclusion of the working class. The players' inability to comprehend their exact relationship to both labor and capital allowed the owners to equate their concentration of capital with the common good, prioritizing the liberal conception of property rights over any republican alternative. The resulting extension of the reserve clause over the entirety of professional baseball and the communities in which it resided set the stage for the enduring labor battles of the twentieth century, occurring first through a trio of Supreme Court cases.

The Antitrust Exemption and the Creation of the Farm System

The NL and AL had roughly a decade of peaceful coexistence and salary suppression before the emergence of the Federal League (FL) presented the reserve clause with its most serious challenge to that point in history. The short-lived existence of the FL and the ensuing suit brought to the forefront for the first time organized baseball's status as a monopoly and therefore its potential violation of the Sherman Antitrust Act. While the Supreme Court in this era vigorously enforced the act against a variety of corporations, its failure to do so against organized baseball seemingly reaffirmed baseball's special status in American society and brought about the creation of the formal minor league classification system.

Passed in 1890 at the beginning of the Progressive Era, the Sherman Antitrust Act, invoking Congress's power to regulate interstate commerce, prohibited the construction of monopolies, which had become a problem in many industries, from railroads to oil to salt.[76] In *U.S. v. E.C. Knight Co.* (1895), however, the court narrowed the scope of the act by asserting a difference between manufacturing and commerce and ruling that Congress did not have the power to regulate things only "incidentally and indirectly" affecting interstate commerce.[77] In 1914 Congress passed the Clayton Antitrust Act to supplement and strengthen the Sherman Act. This new act more explicitly outlawed the creation of monopolies through corporate mergers and acquisitions, such as what happened with the NL and AL agreement, and determined that "the labor of a human being is not a commodity," distinguishing unions from monopolies.[78]

Although organized baseball had long been recognized as a monopoly, the first challenge to its existence as such came in 1915 from the new Federal League.[79] The league initially challenged the reserve clause, but after district court judge Clarence Sessions ruled that players were morally bound to the team with whom they had first signed a contract and thus the reserve clause would remain binding so long as NL and AL teams agreed to enforce it, they switched tactics.[80] The initial 1915 suit charged the NL and AL with violating federal antitrust law, state antitrust laws, and "conspir[ing] to injure or destroy the Federal League."[81] As compensation, the FL asked for the reserve clause to be voided, and for $900,000 in damages, roughly $27 million today. The FL filed the case in Illinois because the state's federal judge, Kenesaw Mountain Landis, was a notorious trust buster as well as a massive baseball fan who might be sympathetic to the FL's plight.

The FL and NL and AL presented their arguments in court before Judge Landis and roughly one thousand baseball fans packed into a two-hundred-seat courtroom. The FL's argument echoed Spalding's republican conception of baseball as "an honest, moral, uplifting, healthy entertainment and recreation of a nation, a thing which is as necessary to a people as life or law itself," while also contending that professional baseball is "commerce and intercourse within the meaning of the commerce clause of the Constitution."[82] Meanwhile, organized baseball argued that professional baseball could be considered neither labor nor interstate commerce because baseball was entertainment and did not involve the sale of physical goods, thereby failing to meet the commonly understood standard of interstate commerce at the time.[83]

While waiting for Landis's ruling, the NL and AL reached agreement with the FL for it to cease operation and to have FL owners purchase the Chicago Cubs and St. Louis Browns, two existing major league clubs. Although this agreement satisfied seven of the eight FL owners, Baltimore Terrapins' owner, Ned Hanlon, filed his own antitrust litigation.[84] His complaints were the same as those in the FL suit of 1915, namely that the NL and AL had created a monopoly, prohibiting the success of a rival league. His brief took aim at organized baseball's longstanding argument that it is steward of the national pastime, instead stressing the distinction between the sport of baseball and the business of baseball. It argued that the NL and AL "are voluntary associations and corporations engaged upon a vast scale, involving the investment of millions of dollars" and are therefore "not engaged in a sport"; rather, they are "a moneymaking business enterprise in which all of the features of any large commercial undertaking are to be found."[85] In monopolizing professional baseball, these owners were actually damaging the sport they claimed to protect.

In the case's journey to the Supreme Court, each side scored a victory. The district court sided with Hanlon, awarding him $240,000 in damages and declaring organized baseball to be an illegal monopoly.[86] Court of Appeals Judge Constantine Smyth sided with organized baseball. He did not rule on the validity of the defendants' argument that the FL had caused "destruction of the morale of teams and a deterioration in the quality of the baseball furnished to the public," rather simply agreeing that baseball "is local in its beginning and in its end" and therefore "is not commerce, though some of its incidents may be."[87] Nonetheless, the scope of both Hanlon's and organized baseball's arguments concerning baseball as business and civic institution meant that whatever the Supreme Court's ruling would be, it was sure to affect how players, owners, and fans viewed their relationship to the professionalization of the sport.

In 1922 the court ruled in favor of professional baseball. In the opinion, Chief Justice Oliver Wendell Holmes reiterated organized baseball's argument and the logic of *E.C. Knight Co.*:

> The business is giving exhibitions of baseball, which are purely state affairs. It is true that, in order to attain for these exhibitions the great popularity that they have achieved, competitions must be arranged between clubs from different cities and states. But the fact that, in order to give the exhibitions, the Leagues must induce free persons to cross state lines and must arrange and pay for their doing so is not enough to change the character of the business. . . . the transport is a mere incident, not the essential thing. That to which it is incident, the exhibition, although made for money, would not be called trade or commerce in the commonly accepted use of those words.[88]

Holmes upheld organized baseball's position that it does not qualify as interstate commerce, and that strictly the games themselves constitute organized baseball. Although this opinion has since been ridiculed, it was at the time accepted as in line with the court's narrow definition of interstate commerce.[89] Contrary to future readings, it did not gift organized baseball with a blanket antitrust exemption. Nonetheless, we will see that it is an opinion that has not aged well.[90]

In the wake of the court's decision, professional baseball increasingly became consumed by big business and a desire for the owners to extend their monopoly. One of their main targets was minor league baseball, which had shrunk from 283 teams in 1910 to just 57 by 1918. Many teams were forced to sell players to major league teams in order to avoid bankruptcy.[91] In 1921 a revision of the National Agreement expanded the drafting of minor league players and enabled MLB teams for the first time to own part or all of any minor league team.[92] By 1950 every single MLB team had an extensive minor league ownership system, called the "farm system," expanding the number of minor league teams in the country while classifying all MLB teams as big businesses.

The debate over these changes amalgamated the individual economic rights of the owners with the civic duty of citizens. Minor league owners, whose revenues primarily came from the sale of players to the highest MLB bidder, argued that the draft and MLB ownership infringed on their rights to "buy and sell their players in the marketplace."[93] Landis, now MLB commissioner, touted minor league baseball as a "civic proposition" but ultimately argued for a universal draft on the grounds that MLB teams have a right to the most talented players.[94] *The Sporting News* offered one perspective on the players' rights, stating that "a ball player entering upon his 'profession' and under the system that prevails signing his life away when he puts his name to his first contract" has "the right . . . to advance in [his] calling."[95] This argument asserted that the reserve clause linked the players' professional interests with the owners' economic interests, a position the minor league owners found difficult to counter.

To offset their losses, minor league owners pushed economic support of teams onto their communities. Joseph Cantillon, manager of the AA Minneapolis Millers, stated in 1924 that "the only salvation for smaller cities" was for civic organizations to "guarantee enough money to keep the club going during the entire season," and that such a financial arrangement could expand the minor leagues to every city with at least 5,000 inhabitants.[96] In 1930 New York Yankees general manager Ed Barrow declared that the success of minor league baseball depended on its "patronage by civic leaders."[97] More than at any previous point in its history, baseball would test liberal individualism's ability to foster civic virtue.

Due to this new broadened scope of MLB and its owners, organized baseball came into direct conflict with labor movements throughout the country. In the 1910s and 1920s, new factories predominantly in the South instituted "welfare programs" designed to eliminate labor unrest by bringing workers and owners into closer contact. As part of these programs, factories sponsored their own baseball teams, seeking to eliminate the more grassroots sandlot baseball that had previously existed in these cities and become the primary the link between industrial urbanism and the rural agrarianism from which their workers migrated. In a widely read article, University of Michigan professor Everett P. Partridge argued that "possibly the best means of counteracting radical labor agitation lies not in the riot guns, but in attractive sanitary industrial villages supplied with baseball diamonds."[98] This argument infuriated union organizers, who argued that factories should instead give the money spent on baseball to the workers, who could then be responsible for their own leisure. While factory team games had been well-attended events, the labor unrest and increased poverty during the Great Depression pushed workers to disentangle their lives from their work and instead support independent minor league teams.[99]

MLB owners capitalized on this shift from factory to minor league baseball by partnering with municipal and state government officials to build new ballparks, particularly in the South, for the purpose of luring fans and players from factory teams with the promise of providing a higher level of play. MLB owners then purchased these teams, granting them control of professional baseball in each city and town. This strategy achieved success in places like Durham, Charlotte, and Asheville, all members of the Piedmont League, where minor league baseball almost completely replaced factory baseball as the object of workers' leisure time.[100] This acquisition of the minor leagues enabled MLB owners to more thoroughly define civic virtue as participation in big business and expand organized baseball's sphere of influence over class and labor relations.

Edgar F. Wolfe, a sportswriter for *The Philadelphia Inquirer* and *Sporting News*, characterized the change in baseball in a 1923 piece titled "The Benevolent Brotherhood of Baseball Bugs." He writes, "Only in that country in which baseball is known—America—does democracy achieve a close approach to a real fact . . . Nothing in all history has so gripped an entire people as baseball has gripped the American nation . . . nothing has ever been known to form such a bond of common interest between men of all ranks."[101] He attributes this democracy to magnates' investments in the sport, stating, "the biggest percentage of baseball 'fans' is really found among the leaders in the markets of trade and the social world," and if the sport were left in the hands of the working class, "there wouldn't be any $100,000 ball players or million dollar ball parks." The fact that baseball fans are "the soul of the solid citizenry of the nation" is due to the victory of capital over labor.[102]

Congressional Inaction and MLB Expansion

By the time the antitrust exemption was next challenged in court, organized baseball was even more undeniably a monopoly engaged in interstate commerce. Its role in perpetuating the anti-communist crusade of the 1950s by further affixing itself to American patriotism granted it special status in society.[103] Furthermore, the emergence of television as the dominant broadcast medium expanded MLB's reach and offered new financial opportunities for team owners through franchise relocation. In addition to the continued use of the reserve clause, the 1950s introduced new ways for organized baseball to shape the economic and social relationships among the players, the fans, and their wider communities.

Capitalizing on increased demand for cities to host MLB teams, Commissioner Ford C. Frick, appointed in 1951, pushed for municipal subsidization of new stadiums.[104] Milwaukee, home of the minor league Brewers, was the first of five cities in the decade to take this step.[105] The city, which had wanted a major league team for decades, built a $5 million publicly funded stadium in order to entice a team to relocate there. This new stadium drew the eye of St. Louis Browns owner Bill Veeck, but he was beaten out by Lou Perini, whose ownership of the Boston Braves and their minor league affiliate, the Brewers, gave him territorial rights to the area. He settled with Milwaukee on paying $1,000 in rent each of the first two years and then 5 percent of ticket sales and concessions each subsequent year in exchange for a year-round lease of Milwaukee County Stadium.[106]

The construction of this stadium and the relocation of the Braves coincided with the second Supreme Court challenge of MLB's antitrust exemption. This second challenge began in 1947 when New York Giants outfielder Danny Gardella, who had moved to the Mexican League for a higher salary ($8,000 plus a $5,000 bonus) and secured roster spot, was blacklisted when he attempted to return to the Yankees. Gardella sued the league on the grounds that the reserve clause is "monopolistic and restrains trade," seeking $300,000 in damages. MLB Commissioner Happy Chandler tapped into the rising anti-communist and anti-labor sentiment among the country's elite, calling Gardella's case un-American and arguing that "no major league player receives less than $5,000 a year and some of them get close to $100,000. If that's slavery or servitude, then there's a lot of us who would like to be in the same class."[107] The District Court sided with MLB, citing the *Federal Baseball Club* precedent, but the Court of Appeals voted two to one to reverse the dismissal of Gardella's complaint and send the case back to the District Court for a trial. While awaiting trial, Gardella and Chandler reached a $60,000 settlement in 1949, but Gardella had already inspired other players to issue their own challenges.[108]

Sensing the difficult road ahead for MLB, Chandler in 1950 contemplated asking Congress for an antitrust exemption. Although he eventually decided against the idea, four members of Congress, motivated by the desire to save professional baseball from what they saw as its ruin, independently introduced bills seeking an exemption for baseball. In 1952 Congress's subcommittee on the study of monopoly power issued a report on the matter. It began, of course, with a discussion of the significance of baseball to America: "Professional baseball typifies the basic ideals of the American people . . . it is a melting pot of men of all races, religions, and creeds . . . the success of the individual player rests not on who he is or where he came from or what he believes . . . baseball stands out as a model of honest competition."[109] In light of this conception of baseball, the report concluded that the sport is "intercity, intersectional, interstate," marking a departure from Holmes's conclusion in *Federal Baseball Club*.

Despite this conclusion and the declaration that the commerce clause grants Congress the jurisdiction "to investigate, and pass legislation dealing with professional baseball . . . if that business is, or affects, interstate commerce," the subcommittee ultimately handed jurisdiction back to the courts.[110] While it recognized that "organized baseball has for years occupied a monopoly position," the report found that the evidence contained within it "established baseball's need for some sort of reserve clause." Moreover, it seemed counterproductive to the committee to "enact general legislation for baseball . . . until the reasonableness of the reserve rules has been tested by the courts," and there were pending cases.[111]

With Congress passing the buck to the courts, attention landed on one suit filed by George Toolson, a pitcher in the New York Yankees' farm system who argued that the reserve clause confined him to the minor leagues. As with *Gardella*, the district court judge adhered to the

Federal Baseball Club precedent, arguing the importance of "stability in law" and warning of the dangers in a judge becoming a "pseudo legislator."[112] After the court of appeals also upheld the precedent, the case went before the Supreme Court where it was combined with two similar cases, *Kowalski* and *Corbett*.[113]

Most commentators believed the Supreme Court would overturn baseball's antitrust exemption because the sport took in "more than $1,000,000,000 in annual revenue," much of which came from radio and television contracts, two industries subject to antitrust laws.[114] At stake in this case was not only whether organized baseball was a monopoly, but whether it could be subject to any congressional commerce clause legislation. In *Federal Baseball Club*, it was determined that "Congress could not regulate baseball because it was not a form of interstate commerce," but with *Toolson*, the source of this exemption was now Congress—"Congress *could* regulate baseball, but thus far Congress had chosen not to."[115]

Although several justices, including Earl Warren, admitted that there were "very substantial differences in the game" compared to 1922 and that organized baseball was interstate commerce, the court ruled seven to two to uphold the *Federal Baseball Club* precedent. Justice Hugo Black wrote a one-paragraph per curiam opinion, affirming Congress's findings that the regulation of monopolies falls under the jurisdiction of Congress, not the court:

> In *Federal Baseball Club of Baltimore v. National League of Professional Baseball Clubs* . . . this Court held that the business of providing public baseball games for profit between clubs of professional baseball players was not within the scope of the federal antitrust laws. Congress has had the ruling under consideration but has not seen fit to bring such business under these laws by legislation having prospective effect. The business has thus been left for thirty years to develop, on the understanding that it was not subject to existing antitrust legislation . . . We think that if there are evils in this field which now warrant application to it of the antitrust laws it should be by legislation.[116]

In essence, the court ruled that overturning the antitrust exemption would be too complicated due to professional baseball's reliance on the exemption since the *Federal Baseball Club* ruling thirty years prior.

The Supreme Court almost immediately received the opportunity to reflect on its ruling in *Toolson* when the NFL brought its own antitrust case to the court in 1957. In a six to three ruling, the court found the NFL subject to the Sherman Antitrust Act. In a defense of *Toolson*, Justice Tom C. Clark wrote in the opinion that "more harm would be done in overruling *Federal Baseball* than in upholding a ruling which, at best, was of dubious validity" and that "the Court was careful to restrict *Toolson's* coverage to baseball." Without its own similar precedent, then, it seemed obvious to the court that "the volume of interstate business involved in organized professional football places it within the provisions of the Act." Finally, Clark reaffirmed the jurisdiction of Congress, stating that "the resulting product" of congressional baseball antitrust legislation is "more likely to protect the industry and the public alike" than would a Supreme Court ruling.[117]

The court and Congress's unwillingness to subject Major League Baseball to antitrust laws granted owners the power to alter the landscape of both organized baseball and municipal politics. In 1950 there were 430 minor league teams across the country, but by 1959, only 145 remained, most of which were affiliated with a major league team. Part of this decline was due to the expansion of television broadcasts of major league games. By 1960 the broadcasting of evening and Sunday afternoon games on local and national television brought in over $10 million in rights fees all while competing with minor league games that were played at the same time. As a result, Minor League Baseball (MiLB) attendance dropped from forty-two million in 1949 to twelve million in 1959.[118] When MiLB president George Trautman appealed to both Congress and Frick to protect Minor League Baseball, they cited the antitrust exemption to explain their inaction.[119] In 1962 MLB instituted the Player Development Plan, which officially reorganized the minor leagues as MLB affiliates and instituted the A, AA, and AAA system still in use, while shifting much of the financing of player salaries from independent owners to major league franchises.[120] Because so many minor league teams were now financed by their major league affiliate, they feared retaliation if they attempted to weaken MLB's antitrust exemption.

The desire to monopolize new, lucrative television markets also propelled owners to expand to the west and south, in cities like Los Angeles, San Francisco, and Houston. As a result, between 1952 and 1968, eight teams relocated and seven were created as expansion efforts. Most of these new teams followed the Milwaukee model, requiring the promise of a publicly funded stadium before agreeing to the move. Even more so than with the Braves, these owners hoped to maximize stadium profits by requiring the construction of glassed-in luxury box seats above the regular seats. As teams extracted television revenue from working-class fans, they increasingly catered the ballpark experience to the wealthy.

Moreover, these new stadiums were often built in neighborhoods predominately home to the non-white working class, with the promise of stimulating economic development and providing civic identity and pride. In reality, however, the stadiums displaced the city's poor, used up tax dollars, and failed to provide economic or civic benefits.[121] In Los Angeles in 1957, for instance, Dodgers owner Walter O'Malley purchased part of Chavez Ravine, the largest Mexican American neighborhood in the city, erecting a new ballpark for the Dodgers on what was originally supposed to be land reserved for public housing. In defense of the sale, the city argued that part of the land would be a public recreation area, thus fulfilling the "public" stipulation in the original contract; however, left in the O'Malley's hands, this recreation area was never built.[122] While teams pushed working-class fans out of stadiums and communities, they continued to make money off them through embracing television and radio broadcasts of games, establishing the ground for the third Supreme Court antitrust case.

Curt Flood and the Road to Unionization

As was the case in 1953 after the 1922 ruling, the state of baseball at the time of the third Supreme Court case was markedly different than at the time of the two previous cases. An increase in television revenue made MLB a very lucrative investment, leading to extremely wealthy businesses and individuals purchasing teams that had previously been family-owned, such as CBS purchasing an 80 percent stake in the Yankees in 1965. More than ever, these owners sought to monetize every aspect of professional baseball by using the antitrust exemption and reserve clause to their fullest extent.[123] Thus, even as attendance declined in the late 1960s, MLB's value increased. In response to the owners' unwillingness to share this increase in revenue with them, players formed the first real union since the Brotherhood of Professional Baseball Players. This union proved crucial in the players' fight to finally end the reserve clause.

The Major League Baseball Players Association (MLBPA) was headed by Marvin Miller, a labor lawyer who had been a force with the United

Steel Workers.[124] Miller's first job was to convince players of the importance of union membership. In talking to each team during spring training, he found that many players had bought into the owners' argument that professional baseball would collapse without the reserve clause. Nonetheless, Miller won the players' vote to become head of the MLBPA, a victory he partially attributed to the increasing number of Black and Latino players, who were better able to "think in terms of what was wrong with society, what was wrong with the conditions" than their white teammates.[125] In 1968, after only two years in the position, he successfully negotiated the first collective bargaining agreement (CBA) in professional sports, a two-year contract that increased minimum player salaries to $10,000 from the $6,000 it had been for the past decade, raised pension contributions from owners, and established an arbitration system with an outside mediator.[126]

Rather than wait for owners to modify the reserve clause, the players made the first move. On October 7, 1969, the St. Louis Cardinals traded centerfielder Curt Flood to the Philadelphia Phillies as part of a multiplayer trade. Flood, a Black twelve-year veteran, was furious at being traded despite no longer being under contract with the Cardinals and traded specifically to the notoriously racist Philadelphia, dubbed the "northernmost Southern city."[127] His refusal to play in Philadelphia stemmed in part from his time in the minor leagues, playing in southern cities so segregated he had to eat all of his meals and dress for games on the team bus because he was not allowed in the same clubhouse as white players.[128] Despite Miller's warning that he was unlikely to win a challenge to the reserve clause and that doing so would get him blacklisted from professional baseball, Flood was determined to bring forward a lawsuit. He, quite simply, was tired of being part of a plantation-esque system in which an owner allowed "his players to play for him in the same way a plantation owner allowed the sharecropper to work his land while at the same time keeping him deep in debt and constantly beholden."[129] Miller, impressed by Flood's ability to relate baseball labor to other industries, gave Flood his backing.

With the support of Miller and the MLBPA's executive board, composed of representatives from each team, Flood sent a letter to Commissioner Bowie Kuhn notifying him of his decision to opt out of joining the Phillies. He wrote, "I do not feel I am a piece of property to be bought and sold irrespective of my wishes. I believe that any system which produces that result violates my basic rights as a citizen and is inconsistent with the laws of the United States and of the several States."[130] Kuhn wrote back to Flood, "I certainly agree with you that you, as a human being, are not a piece of property to be bought and sold. That is fundamental in our society and I think obvious. However, I cannot see its applicability to the situation at hand."[131] Kuhn, as commissioner—a position appointed solely through a vote by the owners—was tasked with upholding the reserve clause no matter the cost, which explains his contradictory and tone-deaf reply to Flood. Unfortunately for Kuhn, Flood did not accept his reply, instead filing a $1 million lawsuit against Kuhn and MLB, claiming the reserve clause violated federal antitrust law, state antitrust law, and the Thirteenth Amendment's abolition of indentured servitude.

Flood, alongside Miller, appeared on ABC's *Wide World of Sports* to explain his decision to sue. In response to the common refrain among fans and commentators that he was too well-paid to be a slave, Flood replied, "A well-paid slave is nonetheless a slave."[132] In addition to containing some truth, this slavery framing was deliberate, even more so than it had been for Ward. Flood, as a Black man, knew that baseball did not exist in a vacuum and therefore "the hypocrisies of the baseball industry could not possibly have been sustained unless they were symptoms of a wider affliction." Flood was up against Kuhn's position that, for baseball, "the image is more vital than the legal aspects," which translated into the notion that Flood's case was the MLBPA's attempt to use "judicial semantics" to harm baseball's image.[133] The task for Flood was to demonstrate that "baseball was socially relevant, and so was [his] rebellion against it," and this framing did just that, making central the issues of freedom, labor, and community.[134] The case became colloquially known as the "Curt Flood slavery case."[135]

The overwhelming narrative established by the press was that the slave nature of the reserve clause prevented Flood and other players from exercising their free enterprise rights. Red Smith of *The New York Times* called the 1970–1971 offseason a trading of bodies "as if the slave trade was going out of style, which, indeed, may be the case."[136] *Los Angeles Times* writer Jim Murray concurred, characterizing the trading of Flood as the player being "bartered away to another plantation" and quipping that "the Emancipation Proclamation does not apply to centerfielders."[137] Black newspapers like *The Chicago Defender*, *Pittsburgh Courier*, and *Baltimore Afro-American* compared Flood to plumbers and autoworkers, arguing that all workers, regardless of salary, deserve to be paid what their labor is worth.[138] Nonetheless, no paper called for the full abolition of the reserve clause, merely its modification.

In the spring of 1972, while waiting for the Supreme Court's *Flood v. Kuhn* ruling, the players went on strike. Owners had signed a new $70 million television deal with NBC, a $40 million increase over the previous contract, yet refused to increase pension contributions to keep up with inflation.[139] After a 663–10 vote, the players began their strike on April 1, lasting two weeks before owners agreed to their pension demands for the season, with future pension benefits to be negotiated the following offseason. In retaliation for the strike, sixteen of the twenty-four teams traded or released their player union representatives.

On June 19, the Supreme Court delivered its *Flood v. Kuhn* verdict. Both the District Court and Circuit Court had ruled against Flood, upholding the *Toolson* and *Federal Baseball Club* precedent, despite recognizing that both cases were "inconsistent" and "illogical."[140] Both courts parroted *Toolson*, arguing that while MLB was undoubtedly a monopoly, it was a well-run one that should only be altered by "voters through their elected representatives."[141] The Supreme Court, in a five to three decision, upheld these rulings, refusing to overturn *Toolson*.[142]

Justice Harry Blackmun, the court's biggest baseball fan, wrote the opinion, beginning with an ode to baseball as America's "national pastime" or "the great American tragedy."[143] The rest of his opinion was a more straightforward upholding of the *Toolson* precedent, in which he stated that although "professional baseball is a business," its exemption "is an established one . . . that has survived the Court's expanding concept of interstate commerce." The court passed the ball back to Congress on the basis that Congress's "positive inaction" in legislating against professional baseball made any court decision redundant, and that "if there is any inconsistency or illogic in all this . . . [it] is to be remedied by the Congress and not by this Court."[144]

With the abolition of the reserve clause off the table, Miller set to work negotiating modifications to it that would allow for some level of free agency. After a two-week-long lockout from February 8 to 25, 1973, the owners and players eventually agreed to a three-year CBA that established outside salary arbitration for unsigned players with two-plus years of service and instituted the "ten and five" rule, giving ten-year veterans with five years on the same team a right to veto trades.[145] For the first time in history, players would have some free enterprise rights.

These new provisions, particularly the outside arbitration system, proved crucial in the fight to obtain free agency. In 1975 Miller found the perfect players to utilize the arbitration system in Dodgers All-Star pitcher Andy Messersmith and Expos former All-Star pitcher Dave McNally, both of whom had played the 1975 season without a contract. Messersmith wanted a no-trade clause in his contract extension with the Los Angeles Dodgers, and McNally wanted the two-year, $230,000 contract he was promised instead of the one-year, $110,000 one he received.[146] Unable to reach an agreement with their teams, both players went to arbitration. Kuhn and the owners once again relied on the argument that without the reserve clause, MLB would descend into chaos. The MLBPA simply pointed to the language of the CBA that stated if a team and player could not agree on a contract, the team had the right "to renew this contract for the *period of one year* on the same terms."[147] The head arbitrator, Peter Seitz, ruled in favor of the MLBPA and was promptly fired by the owners.

Reeling from this loss, the owners explored legal routes for revenge, first asking a federal court to grant an injunction on Seitz's decision and then appealing the decision to the Eighth Circuit Court in St. Louis. Both courts, however, sided with the players, each instructing the owners to leave behind nineteenth-century business practices. The owners then locked players out of spring training complexes while negotiating a new CBA. The owners wanted a "six-and-one" clause wherein the clubs would control players for a total of seven years, six outright and one arbitration year. The players countered with "five-and-one," and the sides eventually settled with a "one-and-one" for current players and a "six-and-one" for future players, granting all existing players free agency after the 1976 season while retaining control of prospects for seven years.[148]

In contrast to their major league counterparts, minor league players reaped little reward from Flood's sacrifice. They were excluded from the MLBPA and their salaries remained stagnant at only $500 to $2,500 per month, depending on level, for the following six decades.[149] Their exploitation was rebranded as the antidote for "communities . . . which have lost their original reason for being," and minor league baseball became representative of something "true and simple, an unaffected world where men work hard."[150] When faced with a changing economic system, Americans once again turned to pastoral nostalgia for respite and a reaffirmation that labor produces virtue. Being paid fair compensation for their labor, the argument went, would diminish minor leaguers' virtue, making them both lazy and greedy.

Unsurprisingly, then, it was not a desire to support these players that drove the minor league's resurgence in the 1980s; rather, a host of new owners marketed games as entertainment rather than player development opportunities. By the middle of the decade communities clamored to reap the supposed economic and civic rewards of hosting a team, committing to building or renovating eighty stadiums, with an average cost of $4 million apiece. These stadiums rarely provided economic benefits for their communities, but stadiums continued to be built and fans continued to set record attendance numbers.[151] The lingering question stemming from this further integration of baseball into communities throughout America is not whether the civic benefits of professional baseball outweigh its economic burdens, but whether these burdens are necessary in the first place.

The 1994 Player Strike

The expansion of the minor leagues throughout the 1980s and '90s coincided with heightened major league player hostility toward the reserve clause, resulting in the 1994 player strike. Led by Milwaukee Brewers' owner and acting MLB commissioner Bud Selig, the owners had spent the early '90s pushing for a salary cap tied to a gate receipt and broadcast revenue sharing plan that aimed to lessen the financial difference between so-called large-market and small-market teams.[152] Meanwhile, the players, who were still furious over ownership collusion in the '80s, argued that such a plan would limit their salaries, making them the ones paying for this competitive balance.[153] This labor dispute brought to the forefront questions of liberalism and republicanism as owners and players yet again tried to market baseball to fans as both a public good and a private business that created ownership property rights.

By the early '90s, baseball had become a $2 billion annual industry with record profits of $214 million, thanks to new national broadcasting contracts with CBS and ESPN and record attendance numbers.[154] Despite this economic growth, many "small-market" team owners argued they could not compete against teams like the Yankees and Dodgers, whose roster payrolls were almost double theirs and who received more lucrative local broadcast deals.[155] These concerns joined with all twenty-eight owners' desires to limit player salaries—which averaged $1.2 million with a median of $410,000 by 1993—and thereby reduce the players' 56 percent share of revenue.[156] After three years of debate over how, precisely, to tie a salary cap to revenue sharing, the owners reached a unanimous agreement in June of 1994 on a seven-year contract in which revenue would be split fifty-fifty with players, a salary cap would be phased in over a four-year period, and "small-market" teams would receive $5 to $9 million each season coming from "large market" teams. Moreover, owners needed a supermajority of 75 percent rather than a simple majority to veto contracts from here on in, thereby granting greater power to "small-market" owners like Selig.[157]

The 1994 season, which was played under the expired CBA while negotiations continued, was immediately threatened when the owners sent the players this proposal on June 14. While the owners argued this contract would guarantee players $1 billion in revenue shares, MLBPA executive director Donald Fehr estimated that, through the salary cap, a reduction in revenue sharing percentage from 56 to 50, and the elimination of ownership contribution to pension and health care funds for current and past players, this contract would actually cost players $1.5 billion in profits over its seven-year term.[158] After another month of fraught negotiations, players set an August 12 strike date. In response, owners withheld the $7.8 million pension contribution from the players' All-Star Game revenue share. The players went on strike, and in September, the World Series was cancelled for the first time since 1904.

Media coverage of the strike frequently framed it as a dispute between millionaires and billionaires, in which the greed of overpriced players was destroying the game. This formulation repeatedly emphasized baseball's special place in society while reducing fans' civic participation in it to the level of consumerism; the best way for fans to voice their displeasure was to spend their money elsewhere. While there were groups like Sports Fans United who encouraged fans to petition Congress to lift the antitrust exemption, they received little media coverage in comparison to calls for fans to attend non-MLB games.[159] Both minor league games and the Little League World Series (LLWS) were romanticized as the antidote to major league player selfishness, places where fans could "thumb their noses at the no-show big-leaguers" and "watch what real baseball is."[160] One of the souvenirs at the LLWS was a t-shirt that read "players rarely STRIKEOUT and NEVER STRIKE" on the front and "no to the strike, yes to the cry of PLAY BALL" on the back.[161] In essence, the pervading narrative that players should be grateful to play a game for their livelihood once again erected a barrier between baseball players and other laborers, portraying communal labor issues as ones of individual self-interest.

Players, owners, and politicians, however, correctly understood this dispute as one not purely over money but over MLB's antitrust exemption. Fehr, who said of the owners, "what we have here is a cartel that's acting like a cartel," petitioned Congress in December of 1994 to repeal the league's antitrust exemption.[162] On January 5, 1995, after owners declared an impasse and unilaterally added a salary cap to the CBA, Fehr declared every single MLB player a free agent. This move coincided with the introduction of five congressional bills aimed at ending the strike, all of which were supported by President Bill Clinton, who stated that the labor dispute threatened both to do "substantial economic damage to the cities and communities in which major league franchises are located" and "serious harm to an important national institution."[163] New York Senator Daniel Patrick Moynihan introduced the most significant of these bills. Titled the "National Pastime Preservation Act," the bill aimed to repeal the entirety of the antitrust exemption on the grounds that it gives the owners "substantial power over wages and work rules" that allows them to "act as a cartel."[164]

By the time Moynihan's bill reached the Senate Judiciary Committee in February, however, it had been renamed the "Professional Baseball Antitrust Reform Act" and only covered labor issues between major league players and owners, not franchise relocation or minor league baseball. In support of this bill, Senator Orrin Hatch of Utah stated:

> A limited repeal of this antitrust immunity is now in order. Labor negotiations between owners and players are impeded by the fact that baseball players, unlike all other workers, have no resort under the law if the baseball owners act in a manner that would, in the absence of the immunity, violate the antitrust laws . . . is an aberration that Government has created, and it is an aberration that Government should fix . . . far from involving any governmental intrusion into the pending baseball dispute, the legislation would get Government out of the way.[165]

According to Hatch, rather than an argument for government regulation, the bill was designed to remove arbitrary impediments to the free market. Other members of the Senate Judiciary Committee, however, argued that Congress had no place intervening in "an ongoing labor dispute between millionaires" and that rather than creating a "labor panacea," repealing the exemption would cause "unbridled litigation" of MLB's labor issues.[166] This second argument won out, and Congress once again passed up the opportunity to repeal the antitrust exemption.

This development proved beneficial for owners, who used it to threaten communities with relocation should they refuse to fund new stadiums. This tactic proved quite successful, and by the mid-'90s only five of the twenty-eight MLB teams used privately funded stadiums.[167] For instance, George W. Bush, then–part owner of the Texas Rangers, threatened to relocate the team from Arlington to Dallas in 1990 in order to procure $193 million from the municipal government for a new stadium.[168] In 1992 Selig appeared before Congress's "Hearing on the Validity of Major League Baseball's Exemption From the Antitrust Laws" to testify about Fay Vincent's forced resignation and MLB's relocation policies. As part of his testimony, he characterized franchise relocations as "flagrant breach[es] of that special covenant that Baseball has with its fans" and argued they should only occur "in the most dire of circumstances when the local community has over a sustained period demonstrated that it cannot support the team."[169] In emphasizing the republicanism of baseball, Selig laid the groundwork for his later argument that without revenue sharing, the small-market Brewers would be unable to afford a new stadium and would therefore have to relocate.[170]

Fearing the loss of the team, the Wisconsin state senate eventually agreed to Selig's terms: the new stadium would be built next to the existing one, on the outskirts of the city so that fans were forced to spend more on food and parking, and it would be 77.5 percent publicly funded through a 0.1 percent sales tax.[171] By the time the stadium was completed in 2001, it had cost $424 million, almost double the initial $250 million projection, and Selig's share of the cost had shrunk to 2.3 percent, topping out at $10 million.[172] Conversely, the tax, which will remain in place until 2040, will ultimately cost Wisconsin residents roughly $1 billion.

While he was negotiating this stadium deal, Selig, as both owner and commissioner, continued to counter players in their strike. In January, after the owners unilaterally instituted a salary cap at Selig's behest, the players filed unfair labor practice charges with the NLRB. On March 26, 1995, while spring training was underway with replacement players, the NLRB voted two to one, seeking a court injunction to force the owners to reinstate the provisions of the 1990–1993 CBA. Fehr quickly announced that the players would end the strike if the injunction was granted. On March 31, District Court Judge Sonia Sotomayor granted the injunction, ruling that "when a contract ends, the parties must not alter mandatory subjects until a new agreement is reached or a good-faith impasse is reached."[173] With this ruling, the 232-day strike ended, and the shortened 1995 and full 1996 seasons were played under the old CBA.

In November 1996 owners and players finally agreed to a new CBA. This contract included a raise in league minimum salaries to $150,000–$200,000 throughout the five-year contract period, the implementation of a luxury tax on team payrolls in place of a hard salary cap, a complex revenue sharing plan that would transfer roughly $39 million from the thirteen high-revenue clubs to the thirteen low-revenue clubs, and the joint request of players and owners to eliminate the antitrust exemption with respect to labor issues. This latter provision came into effect via the 1998 Curt Flood Act, which ended the exemption solely for major league players. The act expressly stated it did not apply to minor league players, franchise ownership/relocation, or the licensing and marketing of baseball products. Thus, while the act proved a victory for major league players, it in actuality did little to curb the antitrust exemption.

Conclusion

In light of this labor unrest and corresponding challenges to its antitrust exemption, MLB opened an office in Washington, DC, in 1993 for the purpose of lobbying members of Congress. Throughout the 1990s, MLB spent at least $1 million annually lobbying Congress—with individual owners spending more—to maintain their antitrust exemption and increase public subsidies for teams.[174] The ever-increasing monetary value of MLB teams and of their owners is both a product of their lobbying national and local governments and a means of obtaining greater control of America's public policies. It is essential for fans to finally discard the notion that these owners are stewards of the game without whom professional baseball could not exist and to reckon with the self-interest at the heart of these century-long battles over player rights and community contributions to teams.

At the heart of baseball is the relationship between the players and the fans, a relationship that is perfectly capable of existing without the presence of a multi-billion-dollar corporation that, throughout its history, has attempted to control both groups by pitting them against each other. To return to the question at the beginning of this chapter, it is evident that not only does a prioritization of liberal property rights not produce civic virtue, it also infringes on the rights it claims to protect. It may, then, be time for baseball fans and players to look more closely at the republicanism of William Manning as a potential solution for professional baseball's economic strife. If baseball is at all capable of promoting civic virtue, as I believe it to be, it is essential that communities and players, not owners or commissioners, decide the shape the game ought to take in America.

CHAPTER THREE

Equality and Economics

The Negro Leagues, Jackie Robinson, and Desegregation

> In baseball, democracy shines its clearest. The only race that matters is the race to the bag. The creed is the rule book. And color, merely something to distinguish one team's uniform from another's.
>
> —Former MLB play-by-play commentator Ernie Harwell

As has been documented by many writers, including W.E.B. Du Bois in his *Souls of Black Folk*, Black people's existence in America is riddled with contradictions stemming from the reality of their lives failing to match the mythic America constantly sold to them. Baseball is no exception to this truth, simultaneously promising racial equality while limiting Black people's participation in it. Sam Lacy, a sportswriter whose early career covering the Negro Leagues led him to lobby for MLB's desegregation, reflected on one such contradiction: "The Negro Leagues were an institution, but they were the very thing we wanted to get rid of because they were a symbol of segregation."[1] Once Jackie Robinson broke the color barrier in 1947, Black people's pride in the Negro Leagues turned to shame, and acceptance into white baseball required the destruction of Black baseball. This process involved a slew of arguments combining questions of personhood with those of economic and social advancement: To what degree and in what way should Black America assimilate into white America?

In this chapter, I uncover the origin of these questions by highlighting the liberal and republican arguments concerning slavery during the founding era that set the parameters of all future conversations about racial equality in America. I then demonstrate how these liberal-republican arguments wove their way into baseball by providing an overview of Black people's participation in the National Pastime, from amateur sport though the life of the Negro Leagues and the slow process of MLB's desegregation. I link this history to broader conversations on liberty and equality that took place in Black communities. By examining baseball's role in determining the parameters of Black liberty, we can better understand the problems posed by the liberal-republican conception of economic and civic freedom established during the founding era.

Founding-Era Slavery Debates

On their surface, both liberalism, with its foundation of self-ownership and contract rights, and republicanism, with its emphasis on self-rule and the common good, seem opposed to the existence of slavery. The founders, both liberal and republican, certainly understood the problem slavery posed for liberty. Their pre-revolutionary writings almost always discussed the colonists' relationship to England in terms of slavery, from John Adams's declaration in 1765 that the English wanted to "enslave all America," to Patrick Henry calling a potential revolution "a question of freedom or slavery."[2] The Declaration of Independence pronounced that "all men are created equal . . . with certain unalienable Rights, that among these are Life, Liberty and the pursuit of Happiness"; yet the Constitution offered protections for slave ownership in the form of the three-fifths clause and the fugitive slave clause. This apparent contradiction has been the subject of a great deal of scholarship, producing adamant defenses and strong condemnations of the founders.[3] The most helpful account of founding-era slavery arguments for this project belongs to François Furstenberg, who attributes chattel slavery to the combining of racism with a blended liberal-republican ideology that "linked freedom to resistance, grounding slavery in an act of individual choice."[4] This explanation offers insight into the seemingly contradictory nature of the founders' rhetoric and actions, while demonstrating the difficulty abolitionists faced in crafting a unified counterargument.

Liberal-Republican Pro-Slavery Arguments

Beginning with the popular framing of the American Revolution as an act of "heroic resistance by a people threatened with slavery," Furstenberg contends that the founding era viewed freedom as the ability to act, particularly to resist tyranny.[5] Thus, virtue was the maintenance of freedom and vice was the descent into slavery, not just of a society but of an individual. In this reading, individuals were responsible for their own virtue and could lift themselves out of slavery. George

Washington endorsed this articulation of freedom in his 1783 Circular to the States, writing, "At this auspicious period, the United States came into existence as a Nation and if their Citizens should not be completely free and happy, the fault will be intirely [*sic*] their own."[6] The argument was then that "just as white Americans acted to resist their enslavement, so it fell to chattel slaves to resist theirs."[7] That enslaved Black people did not mount a large-scale revolt meant that they had consented to slavery. Moreover, it meant that they were not virtuous enough to earn their freedom, and so the moral burden of slavery rested not on the slave owner, but on the enslaved.

This liberal-republican idea of freedom is most illuminated in discussions of enslaved people as both persons and property. The debates concerning the Constitution's three-fifths clause largely focused on the monetary value of an enslaved person, particularly versus that of a free laborer.[8] From these debates emerged a link between freedom and the acquisition of property.[9] William Patterson, a New Jersey representative and abolitionist, summarized this position in a critique of the three-fifths suggestion, stating of enslaved people, "They are no free agents, have no personal liberty, no faculty of acquiring property, but on the contrary are themselves property, and like other property, entirely at the will of the master."[10] The three-fifths compromise, though, was not simply about freedom but rather freedom in service of determining republican representation, linking civic personhood to free labor. James Madison, assuming the character of a Southern Gentleman, encapsulated the outcome of these arguments in *Federalist* 54, declaring that the Constitution recognized the enslaved person as possessing "the mixed character of persons and of property . . . as a moral person, not as a mere article of property."[11] Though many of these arguments were made for the sake of expedience in forming a union between North and South, their implication is that the full exercise of virtue necessary for civic participation is found in the exercise of free labor.

The pro-slavery justification that emerged from these principles was based on the contract theory of government and the cultivation of virtue. Essentially, if one's ability to participate in republican government is demonstrated through virtuous exercise of free labor, then the object of republican government is the protection of individual property rights. This framing of citizenship melded with racist beliefs in the natural inferiority of Black people to produce republican-based calls for the entrenchment of enslaved people as property. Bernard Romans, a Philadelphia-based Dutch explorer, claimed in his 1776 counter to abolitionism that slavery enabled America to utilize the "favorites of mankind (liberty and property)," and it therefore existed "for the good of the community."[12] The post-revolution flurry of state abolitions of primogeniture and entail laws governing the inheritance and sale of property also embodied these arguments. Allowing the sale of tracts of land and enslaved people would produce more equal and greater cultivation of the land, in the process crafting citizens with more "independent political judgment."[13] In essence, the subjugation of Black people was the means through which Southern white people could exercise their liberal-republican freedom.

Even the rise of scientific racism to explain away the hypocrisies of the American Revolution contained this liberal-republican synthesis. The rights and duties–based language of the founding increased the Southern fictional narrative of paternalism; if slaveowners had a right to their slaves, they had a corresponding duty to care for them. As part of this narrative, they contended that slavery offered the enslaved person many more comforts than the Northern industrial factories offered their poor free laborers.[14] This insidious myth allowed slaveowners to reduce the systemic violence inherent in slavery to the excessive cruelty of a handful of individual men. It also produced the argument that if left to their own devices, Black people would revert to their "natural" barbary. This latter argument allowed slaveowners to portray the free Black person as an individual exception rather than proof of natural racial equality.[15]

Liberal-Republican Abolitionist Arguments

Abolitionists faced the difficultly of placing their arguments within this liberal-republican framework. French American abolitionist Anthony Benezet, one of the founders of the Pennsylvania Abolitionist Society, offered one such example of the belief in obtaining virtue through economic participation. In his 1771 book, *Some Historical Account of Guinea*, he outlined an emancipation plan for Black people to become "industrious subjects" through working as "cheerful and willing-minded labourers" for planters and tradesmen. He argued that, although they are "undisciplined . . . in religion and virtue," through working as free laborers, they will "make proper use of their liberty" and "become interested" in the "safety and welfare" of the government.[16]

This gradual emancipation through property ownership and education in virtue characterized the position of the early abolitionist movement, which was mainly comprised of white elites who wanted to prove that enslaved people were capable of earning their freedom.[17]

Simultaneously, Black people were putting forth their own calls for abolition, many of which utilized the structure laid out by white abolitionist societies. Prince Hall, a Boston Methodist minister, founder of the first Black Masonic lodge in America, and former enslaved person, rested his abolitionist work on the foundation of natural property rights. In 1777 he helped draft a bill to abolish slavery in Massachusetts that stated its petitioners "have, in common with all other Men, a natural and unalienable right to that freedom, which the great Parent of the Universe hath bestowed equally on all Mankind, & which they have never forfeited by any compact or agreement whatever" and that slavery is therefore a "Violation of Laws of Nature and of Nations."[18] He expanded this natural rights argument in a 1788 petition to the General Court of Massachusetts urging the court to protect free Black seamen from being kidnapped and sold into slavery. In this petition, which was circulated in newspapers in New York, Pennsylvania, Vermont, and Virginia, he argued that the fear of such kidnappings prompts many Black men to "stay at home . . . and the one half of our time loiter about the streets, for want to employ," and that laws protecting them would thereby enable them to get a "handsome livelihood for themselves and theirs."[19] Hall, then, reaffirmed the centrality of property rights as the real foundation of freedom.

Venture Smith's 1798 autobiography, one of the earliest and few slave narratives in America, also emphasizes the link between property and freedom. In it, he recounts his life from his time in Africa as the son of a prince through working to earn his freedom in America. After being resold several times, Smith was able to buy his freedom through doing extra wage labor. He moved from Connecticut to Rhode Island, where he worked to buy his wife and three children's freedom. He concludes his autobiography by stating,

> My freedom is a privilege which nothing else can equal. Notwithstanding all the losses I have suffered by fire, by the injustice of knaves, by the cruelty and oppression of false hearted friends, and the perfidy of my own countrymen whom I have assisted and

> redeemed from bondage, I am now possessed of more than one hundred acres of land, and three habitable dwelling houses.[20]

His measure of success, of his fight to exercise freedom, is the amount of property he possesses. The original 1798 preface to the autobiography characterizes it as a story of "honesty, prudence, and industry" about a Black man who is "remarkable for size, strength, industry, fidelity, and frugality."[21] Hence, it has been interpreted as championing "liberty and equality" in the vein of "individualistic merchant capitalist" practices.[22] The autobiography itself, as well as the narrative surrounding it, exemplify emancipation as an individual pursuit of virtue through the use of labor to acquire property.

Other Black public figures of the time, such as Phillis Wheatley, Richard Allen, and Lemuel Haynes, advocated for a republicanism based on community rather than individual virtue. For instance, Lemuel Haynes in an 1801 sermon titled "The Nature and Importance of True Republicanism," states that a true republican government is one which "defend[s] and secure[s] the natural rights of men" and "where the people are free and view each other as brethren engaged in one common cause."[23] The true republican citizen must therefore be willing to "lend his heart, his sword, and his property" to defend his fellow citizens and these republican values. Yet even these articulations of republicanism rested on the notion that slavery had made Black people "despised, ignorant, and licentious," needing to be educated so that they could control "their purse, their property, and liberty."[24] The vast majority of Black abolitionists could not escape the framework established by the white founders, namely that they had to prove their ability to participate in American society.

The founding era debates on slavery placed strict divisions between white Americans and Black Americans, the logic of which stemmed from the liberal-republican justification of classifying enslaved Black people as both persons and property. The burden of crossing this divide rested on individual Black people asserting their civic equality through their industriousness, and entry into society was seen as the highest privilege and the highest exercise of freedom. Systemic moral and economic concerns were thereby reduced to individual relationships and choices. This view of slavery and Black participation in society established the framework for Black baseball both before and after Jackie Robinson's breaking of MLB's color barrier.

Early Black Baseball and the Negro Leagues

In the South, long before the Civil War, town ball was one of the few respites offered to enslaved people. Slave owners ordinarily allowed their slaves to practice only individual sports, such as boxing and wrestling, that were both violent and that they could win money on from bets placed on games against neighboring estates.[25] Some enslaved people, like John Finnley from Alabama, enjoyed these sports, while others viewed them as merely another form of enslavement.[26] Town ball, however, was regarded much more favorably, and although it is unclear why certain owners allowed enslaved people to partake in the purely recreational team sport, such instances often became one of the few positive memories from their enslavement.

Through testimonials of former enslaved people gathered by the Library of Congress in 1940, we can see the popularity of trap ball and baseball between the 1840s and 1860s.[27] Variations of baseball were played by enslaved people in Texas, Arkansas, Florida, Georgia, Missouri, and the Carolinas. In one of many similar accounts, Duncan Gaines of Florida recalls, "Most of the time of the slave children was spent in playing ball and wrestling and foraging in the woods . . . they were often joined in their play by their master's children."[28] Henry Baker of Alabama offers a more in-depth account of playing in the late 1850s, describing playing in large groups consisting of both enslaved children and white children and using a ball made out of rags, an example of the adaptability of the game.[29] Ed Allen of Arkansas reaffirms this account: "White boys and colored boys . . . we used to play base ball together. All had a good time. We never had to buy a ball or a bat. Always had 'em. The white boys bought them."[30] These records demonstrate the popularity of baseball and are early suggestions of its ability to help overcome racist divisions within society.

While the Civil War marked a monumental victory for the Union and baseball, it ushered in newer hardships for Black baseball. Although Black people were now technically free, they found themselves still barred from much of society, including white organized baseball. Segregation soon became the norm, seeping into baseball as it did all aspects of society. While white baseball thrived economically and cemented itself as America's Game, Black baseball led a more secretive life rarely recognized by white America. In fact, the first white reporting of Black baseball was accidental in nature: "On October 16, 1862, 'a sporting correspondent for the Brooklyn Eagle, discovering the game between two white teams that he was supposed to cover had been canceled, stumbled instead on the Weeksville Unknowns playing Brooklyn's Monitor team.'"[31] However, the knowledge that Black baseball did exist did little to persuade white newspapers to run the risk of legitimizing it by covering it.

On the eve of the professionalization of baseball in 1867, the National Association of American Base Ball Players "unanimously reported against the admission of any club which may be composed of one or two colored persons" on the basis that "if colored clubs were admitted there would be in all probability some division of feeling whereas, by excluding them no injury could result to anybody, and the possibility of any rupture being created on political grounds would be avoided."[32] What little coverage Black baseball received in white newspapers was dedicated to framing it as a conduit for criminal activity or portraying it as a spectacle akin to a circus act. In 1869 *The Memphis Public Ledger* wrote about a game between a Black team and a white team in Philadelphia, concluding, "The darkeys got the worst of the game, but they have won more than they lost by the social recognition they have gained."[33] In 1877, though, as civil rights protests strengthened throughout the country, the *Ledger* suggested turning in Black people for playing baseball on Sunday and thereby violating the Sabbath. The city police offered a reward of $3 per Black person arrested.[34]

Nonetheless, Black people did play baseball in both casual and organized ways. In his groundbreaking book *Black Baseball, 1858–1900: A Comprehensive Record of the Teams, Players, Managers, Owners and Umpires*, James E. Brunson argues that "Black baseballists" used the game for their own ends, often incorporating it into communal celebrations and other social functions that were distinctly Black in character.[35] Between 1858 and 1900, hundreds of amateur Black teams were formed throughout the country, with the majority of players being hotel employees whose play was sponsored by their hotels. Like their white semiprofessional counterparts, these employees often joined baseball teams both for their love of the game and for the potential it offered them for class mobility, something that white people greatly feared.[36] These early

Black teams demonstrate the natural equality and community-building elements of baseball, setting up Black baseball as a potential critique of white baseball's exclusivity.

Octavius Catto and Baseball as a Civil Rights Tool

The connection between baseball and civil rights was most apparent in this era to Octavius Catto, a Philadelphia-based abolitionist and Black baseball player and manager who attended and taught at the Institute for Colored Youth. Since the early 1830s when it got its first baseball club, the Olympics, Philadelphia had been one of the most baseball-obsessed cities in the country. On the eve of the Civil War, the city boasted over one hundred clubs and had erected its first real public ballpark with seating for sixty-five hundred fans. The demand for the sport quickly exceeded the ballpark's capacity, though, as an 1866 game between the Athletics—one of the first teams to start paying players—and the Atlantics had to be cancelled due to the thirty thousand fans who stormed the gate looking for entrance.[37] Although each of these teams was white, the city's growing Black population—which doubled in size from 1860 to 1880—coupled with its deep segregation (remarked upon by W.E.B. DuBois in 1898 and Curt Flood in 1969) made it ripe for Black baseball as a means of fighting for equality.[38]

After serving in the Pennsylvania National Guard during the Civil War, Catto returned to Philadelphia, and with Jacob C. White, cofounded the Pythian Base Ball Club, a team bringing together mixed-race Black middle-class professionals from Philadelphia, Washington, and New York. Catto first foreshadowed his hopes for this club in his address at the Institute for Colored Youth Commencement of 1864. He stressed the teachings of the school as all the "advantages of a Republican Government," those being "the principals of right, equity, and justice; the very ideas of an improved civilization . . . the very moral conception of individual and mutual rights of property, contract and government."[39] He stated that the best measure of success for the school is "the positions the graduates hold in the sphere of usefulness to their fellow-men, and the amount of intelligently directed labor they may be performing."[40] He added to this depiction of republicanism a year later in an address to the pro-suffrage Union League Association. Speaking about the end of the Civil War, he declared, "it is the duty of every man, to the extent of his interest and means, to provide for the immediate improvement of the four or five million of ignorant and previously dependent laborers . . .

It is for the good of the nation that every element of its people, mingled as they are, shall have a true and intelligent conception of the allegiance due to the established powers." Thus, Catto's conception of American government echoes both the liberal-republican understanding of property ownership as an expression of virtuous freedom and the grander sentiments of the "true republicanism" championed by Haynes. As such, the Pythians' constitution banned "all gambling, betting on games, and card playing" in an effort to instill virtue in its members and offer them as examples for the ever-growing Black population of Philadelphia.[41]

The Pythians went 9–1 in 1866, playing against more informal Black teams. By 1867, however, four other, more professional Black teams had been founded, including L'Overture, named after the Haitian revolutionary Toussaint L'Ouverture. In their first two games of the 1867 season, the Pythians beat L'Overture 62–7 and then the Excelsiors 39–16, quickly cementing their reputation as the best Black team in the region and perhaps in the country. Even more than a premier baseball club, the Pythians became an essential means of connecting Black people throughout the region. Through games against such teams as the Washington Alerts, whose 1870 roster included Frederick Douglass Jr., Pythian baseball brought together leading Black figures in society. Moreover, Catto required everyone on the Pythians to participate in various committees focused on securing playing grounds for the Pythians and other Black ballclubs and connecting the club to different Black organizations in the area. The games themselves were often secondary to the networking opportunities they provided.[42]

These opportunities and his ties to white businessmen led Catto to believe that the nation's growing attachment to baseball could be used to demonstrate physical and moral equality between Black people and white people. In October 1867 the Pythians applied to the Pennsylvania Association of Amateur Base Ball Players but withdrew their application when it was clear it would be rejected. Later that year, the National Association of Base Ball Players ruled against admitting clubs with even one Black player. These actions spurred Catto to challenge every white team in Philadelphia to a game. Although the Athletics refused invitation after invitation, several lower-tier but still very recognizable teams accepted the challenge on the belief that Black teams were inherently inferior and the contests would be easy wins.[43] The first of these games was played on September 3, 1869, against the Olympics, Philadelphia's oldest white team. The Olympics beat the Pythians handedly, 44–23, in front of a crowd of roughly four thousand Black and white fans. On the significance of this game, *The Wilkes' Spirit of the Times*, one of the premier sporting journals in the country, preemptively declared that "old-time prejudices are melting away in this country . . . now [that] the prejudice has been broken through here, it will be entirely swept away."[44] Two weeks later, the Pythians beat the white City Item club 27–17, proving that they could match the play of white ball clubs.[45] Despite closing the year by losing once again to the Olympics, the Pythians were applauded by *The Morning Post* for "having the manliness to grapple with our great social question in a practical way."[46] In only a few short years, Catto and the Pythians managed to carve out a place for "respectable" Black baseball in a deeply segregated city.

On February 3, 1870, the Fifteenth Amendment was ratified, granting Black men the right to vote. In light of Philadelphia's entrenched segregation, Catto and the Pythians recognized that inviting Black teams to play them in the city would be exposing these teams to violence, and so the team played very few games that year. The following year, the Pythians resumed play, but Catto himself did not, instead focusing on the upcoming election. He spent a great deal of time canvassing Philadelphia's Black districts to encourage Black men to vote for the first time. His efforts were successful in part, as Black people flocked to the polling stations on election day, but many were intimidated and assaulted by police officers and white vigilantes brought in by the police officers for assistance. Catto himself was caught up in the ensuing violence and was murdered by a white man who shot him multiple times as he attempted to cast his vote.[47]

A week after Catto's death, the Pythians printed a series of resolutions, declaring Catto the club's "most active and valued member" and one of Philadelphia's "most prominent and most intelligent citizens."[48] The club stated that Catto was killed in the pursuit of "truth, justice, and equality" and had lived his life struggling "faithfully against oppression and wrong . . . [and] carry[ing] out what was his life chosen work by striving earnestly to raise ourselves still higher above all vile calumny and unholy prejudice."[49] This was the club's last public statement as it disbanded shortly afterward and was not replaced with another such Black club. Catto was, undoubtedly, the face of Black baseball in the Reconstruction era, and his career demonstrated both baseball's ability to foster the common good and the massive obstacles in place for those Black players who want to participate in America's national game.

The Rise of the Negro Leagues

In his 1970 account of the Negro Leagues, author Art Rust called Black professional baseball "an empire built on poverty."[50] The foundation of this empire was laid in the 1880s after Black players were barred first from the major leagues and then the minor leagues. In the mid-1880s, upwards of two dozen Black players played on predominately white major league and minor league teams, but as white southerners grew wary of this push for greater equality, the number of Jim Crow laws increased, relegating Black people to second-class citizenship. By 1891 Black players were no longer allowed to play on white professional teams, and the first attempt at an all-Black league failed after it was designated purely minor league, blocking any path toward playing in the major leagues.[51] In 1892 the Cuban Giants—a merging of the Philadelphia and Washington teams—was the sole remaining "professional" Black team.

Barred from white professional baseball, Black communities and individual players turned to their own teams as objects of civic pride. In the North, Black players formed barnstorming teams that traveled all over the country, earning the bulk of their money from playing exhibition games against far wealthier white professional and semiprofessional teams, while also playing against Black professional and semiprofessional teams. These barnstorming teams afforded players like Cooperstown native Bud Fowler, one of the pioneers of Black baseball, the opportunity to play baseball, connect with southern Black communities, and develop the innovation necessary to make Black baseball financially viable.[52] These southern Black communities attempted to form an independent regional Black league in 1886 and 1887, but their extremely impoverished and predominately rural condition prevented them from being able to afford travel and ballpark rental fees. Thus, Black baseball in the final years of the nineteenth century was almost entirely a local game possessing far-reaching dreams.[53]

As both Black protests and baseball teams strengthened at the turn of the century, white political and news publications tried to regain control over them by characterizing them as lawless threats to society. In 1903 newspapers in St. Louis reported on an incident in which "negroes used baseball bats as weapons" after a game one day and attacked a "white peacemaker" who attempted to break up a riot.[54] In 1905 *The New Orleans Times-Democrat* wrote that the ballpark would serve as a "rendezvous and headquarters for negro loafers and hoodlums," thereby driving down the value of the neighborhood.[55] Similar stories appeared across the country over the next two decades. Some writers halfheartedly claimed they were looking out for the best interests of the Black players, like in Atlanta: "It was claimed that a white man was behind the project for the purpose of making money out of negroes and that such a park would cause lawless crowds to gather."[56] But the underlying motive was always apparent. White people viewed baseball as theirs and feared the ramifications of a "Black takeover"; if they lost baseball, there was no telling what else they could lose.

These fears were greatly exacerbated by the Great Migration, which saw over six million Black people move from the South to the North, Midwest, and West between the early 1910s and 1970. Spurred by the increased industrialization of the country during WWI and the decline in the number of European immigrants, Black people flocked to northern and western cities to fill factory jobs where they received a higher wage than what they earned primarily as sharecroppers in the South. In some cases, rural white communities in the South banded together to force out thousands of Black people and take over their land. In many cases, white northerners reacted with deep suspicion and resentment toward their new Black neighbors and coworkers. Black people were routinely excluded from labor unions and were often forced into predominately Black neighborhoods. These distinct neighborhoods did succeed in giving Black people the space to engage in their own entertainment, creating music halls, theaters, and baseball teams that rivalled their white counterparts, and in the process developing a deep sense of community.[57]

After several failed attempts to create a Black baseball league to rival Major League Baseball, the Negro National League was finally founded in 1920.[58] Initially comprised of eight teams, the Negro League saw such early success that a secondary league, the Eastern Colored League, was formed in 1923, and the two joined together in 1927 to become the Negro Leagues. Along with these teams came a boom in Black businesses like hotels and restaurants as each host city had to accommodate tens of thousands of fans annually. Among cities with a Negro Leagues team, there grew an entire Black economy and culture.[59] For many Black people, the success of these teams and their star players was proof of their equality with white people.

Central to the existence of the Negro Leagues and the corresponding Black communities was the constant interplay of two philosophies of Black existence in America. On one hand was the familiar philosophy championed by Booker T. Washington, which called for the slow accumulation of civil rights through sustained economic success and assimilation into white America. Washington summarized this position in an address at the 1895 World's Fair in Atlanta, warning that "our greatest danger is, that in the great leap from slavery to freedom we may overlook the fact that the masses of us are to live by the productions of our hands, and fail to keep in mind that we shall prosper in proportion as we learn to dignify and glorify common labor and put brains and skill into the common occupations of life," in essence declaring that social equality will be a result of gradual economic prosperity.[60] On the other hand was W.E.B. Du Bois's philosophy of socialism, which opposed Black participation in capitalism. He criticized Washington's position for "practically accept[ing] the alleged inferiority of the Negro races" and argued that it was impossible to achieve economic or political equality through embracing segregation.[61] To be sure, both Washington's and Du Bois's political thought is more complex than merely these two competing arguments, but they outline the broad political landscape to which the Negro Leagues was firmly affixed.

The majority of Negro Leagues owners recognized the unique cultural opportunity of an exclusively Black professional baseball league but also understood that it could not be financed with Black money alone and so often kept up appearances while incorporating white backers to fund things such as ballpark lights and team busses. The fact that these Black populations in urban areas were clustered tightly together—in Chicago, for instance, 92,000 of its 118,000 Black residents lived within a nineteen-block area—meant that any money coming into the community was distributed to a wide number of businesses, from saloons to beauty parlors and drugstores. [62] The substantial money from Negro Leagues teams went a great way to making these communities largely self-sufficient at a time when many white facilities refused to serve Black people or gave them lesser service.[63] Ed Bolden, a Black Philadelphia businessman and the founder of the Eastern Colored League, characterized the relationship between white and Black businessmen in much the same way as Du Bois, declaring in 1924 that "the Eastern Colored League is composed of colored and white owners, the co-operative efforts alone of this group should warrant immunity from the citation of the race question. Close analysis will prove that only where the color-line fades and co-operation instituted are our business advances gratified. Segregation in any form, including self-imposed, is not the solution."[64]

For Bolden, the Negro Leagues provided a great opportunity to combat segregation and enrich both the white and Black communities.

The relationship between Negro Leagues teams and their white backers was not harmonious, however, as they were still seen as second-class by many of these white backers. When the first few seasons of professional Black baseball in the early 1920s failed to attract sizeable enough crowds due to the disjointed nature of the schedules, teams and leagues turned to white booking agents to fix this issue. Many Black fans were irate with this switch, blaming the increased involvement of white businessmen for directing the teams' attention from the fans to the business aspect of baseball. In 1929, *The Pittsburgh Courier* wrote that "white capital is increasingly entering what has heretofore been known as strictly Negro fields. If we are to survive this competition, we must give as good service as the white business, reinvest more of our profits in our businesses."[65]

The economic hardships of the Great Depression intensified the political debates surrounding the Negro Leagues. Black people, suffering from higher rates of unemployment, had even less money to spend on entertainment, and teams had to work harder to persuade them to spend it on baseball. The relatively independent nature of Negro Leagues owners compared to their Major League counterparts worsened the economic instability of the leagues, prompting owners to search for new independent investors to share the costs, such as Pittsburgh racketeer Gus Greenlee, famous for supporting Black businesses. The league marketed these investors as morally superior men "who put their life earnings into the game," in contrast to the selfish capitalist millionaires running MLB teams.[66] Due to these new modest investors, the reduction of rosters to sixteen players, and several franchise relocations, the Negro Leagues survived the Great Depression when many Black businesses did not.

Also emerging from the Great Depression were two things that shaped the future of the Negro Leagues. The first was the northern migration of hundreds of thousands of Black southerners who had lost their jobs due to the mechanization of cotton production and were seeking employment in prewar industrial productions. The second was a growing belief that, in the words of National Negro Business League member John F. Perdue, it was time for Black people to integrate "into the business and industrial pattern of America" and leave behind "parasitic" Black enterprises.[67] The former turned the Negro Leagues into a prosperous industry while the latter ensured its ruin at the hands of an integrated Major League Baseball.

Setting the Stage for Jackie Robinson

In 1945, while playing with the Kansas City Monarchs of the Negro American League, Jackie Robinson was scouted by Branch Rickey, the General Manager of the Brooklyn Dodgers. After undergoing an interview with Rickey in which the GM told Robinson he was looking for a Black player who could withstand the racism he would face without losing his temper, Robinson signed a contract to play with the Dodgers' International League affiliate, the Montreal Royals.[68] On April 15, 1947, he made his Major League debut in front of a Brooklyn crowd that included fourteen thousand Black people eager to see how their superstar player would fare against an entirely white competition. The events of this game were fairly simple—Robinson walked and scored a run in a 5–3 victory—but the politics surrounding it were anything but.

Many thought the first Black MLBer would be Robinson's teammate on the Monarchs, pitcher Satchel Paige. He joined the Negro Leagues at the age of twenty in 1926 with the Chattanooga Black Lookouts, and by 1941, his skill and ability to entertain made him undeniably its star. League owners used his popularity to attract both Black and white fans, hiring him out to teams for individual games like the May 11, 1941, Yankees Stadium game between the Black Yankees and Philadelphia Stars, a doubleheader that attracted over twenty thousand fans, as well as members of the white press.[69] Following the success of this game, other MLB owners rented their stadiums to the Negro Leagues, and for the first time, the Negro Leagues became a million-dollar business.[70] Cognizant of his worth, Paige increasingly demanded larger revenue shares, receiving three or four times more than other players, who earned only $300 to $700 per month.[71] While Paige's individual success helped sustain the Negro Leagues, it brought greater white attention to the Black baseball as a product and Black people as consumers whose equality would be predicated on purchasing white entertainment products.

Thus, one of the most common understandings of Branch Rickey signing Robinson is that he was a maverick who did so purely for financial reasons.[72] The truth concerning this claim is much more complicated. It is true that Rickey was a staunch capitalist who loved the reserve clause and spent much of his life speaking against those he deemed to have "avowed Communist tendencies" in their opposition to it.[73] He invented the farm system, a way for major league teams to hold on to talented prospective players by stashing them on various minor league teams beyond the reach of other professional teams, giving each MLB team full control over hundreds of players.[74] Indeed, historian Robert Burk argues that "the more completely the white baseball industry committed itself to the farm system form of vertical integration, and in so doing rooted itself in the segregated towns and cities of the Jim Crow South, the more it apparently ruled out any future within it for players of color," because integration was seen as a far riskier economic practice than minor league consolidation.[75] This growth of the farm system enabled major league owners to collect ballpark rental, concession, and parking fees from Negro Leagues teams not only for their major league stadiums but also for the minor league teams they now owned.[76] Thus, during the Great Depression, much of MLB's financial success depended on segregation.

It was not until after WWII that Major League Baseball slowly came to see reintegration as economically beneficial. In 1945 Rickey said the Negro Leagues were "the greatest untapped reservoir of raw material in the history of the game" and he would "happily bear being called a bleeding heart and a do-gooder and all that humanitarian rot" that came with signing a Black player.[77] The unwillingness of MLB owners to pay the one thousand major leaguers and three thousand minor leaguers returning from war their full prewar salaries caused a great deal of labor unrest and left vacant many major league and minor league roster spots. Rickey, who was supposedly extremely sympathetic to the plight of Black Americans, seized on this opportunity to integrate both the major leagues and the minor leagues, acting against the wishes of the majority of his fellow owners.[78]

More so than any personal reason, though, Rickey was likely motivated to sign Robinson due to decades-long efforts by Black sportswriters and white labor reporters to make Black baseball a legitimate sport and demonstrate the sport's relationship with American politics. One of the papers most dedicated to the fight for desegregation was the communist paper *The Daily Worker*, led by Lester Rodney. Beginning almost immediately after Jesse Owens's display of antiracism at the 1936 Olympics, *The Daily Worker* published hundreds of baseball columns arguing for desegregation. The paper argued that desegregation would improve the quality of the game and would bring "Americanism . . . equal opportunities for Negro and white stars" to the sport.[79] Urged by these columns, labor unions began in 1940 to picket outside major league stadiums in New York and Chicago, calling for the end of Jim Crow laws in baseball.

These protestors collected more than a million signatures in favor of desegregation, earning the attention of MLB Commissioner Kenesaw Mountain Landis.

One of the most prominent Black sportswriters, Wendell Smith, dedicated his column in *The Pittsburgh Courier* to arguing for baseball's desegregation, in the belief that "the desegregation of baseball would give Blacks a new dignity and self-esteem . . . necessary components of the ultimate destruction of discrimination in this country."[80] Perhaps Smith's most significant contribution to the desegregation project was interviewing a number of major leaguers on the subject. Prior to these interviews, the common line among MLB executives, particularly National League President Ford C. Frick, was that it was not them but the players and the fans who would not tolerate baseball's desegregation.[81] Calling baseball's segregation "the great American tragedy," Smith worked tirelessly to disprove the notion built by the white press that Black players were physically and mentally inferior to their white counterparts. He interviewed both white players and coaches, the majority of whom could name at least several Negro Leagues players who could thrive in the majors if ownership would give them the opportunity. These interviews were not disinterested moral acts, however. Most of these people understood that desegregation would have to be seen as a financial victory for the owners. For instance, Boston Braves manager Casey Stengel named players like Paige and Josh Gibson before wondering "if it would be profitable to admit Negroes in the majors" and if Black fans would bother to pay to come to games.[82] Smith's series of interviews was reprinted by both Black and white newspapers in the years following its first printing in 1939, prompting MLB Commissioner Landis in 1942 to declare that there is "no rule in organized baseball prohibiting" the signing of Black players.[83] Now, baseball just had to wait for an executive and player brave enough to take the first step.

Jackie Robinson Breaks the Color Barrier

Jackie Robinson was not the most established Negro Leagues player but he was good, and Branch Rickey deemed him the most capable of having a major league career. Unlike the vast majority of Negro Leagues players, Robinson was college educated. He was well-spoken, humorous, and affable. In a word, he was unintimidating. The success of what was called Rickey's "great experiment" depended on Robinson's ability to be seen as "a great ball player and a fine gentleman."[84] Robinson must become the twentieth century's Venture Smith, ready to distinguish himself by his ability to succeed through adhering to the rules of white American society. In so doing, he must be both an individual and a community, a difficult feat no matter the stakes, and the stakes were high.[85] Roy Wilkins, future leader of the NAACP, declared that if Robinson could have a major league career, it would prove that Black people "should have their own rights, should have jobs, decent homes and education, freedom from insult, and equality of opportunity to achieve."[86]

Regardless of his gentlemanliness and what the testimonials gathered by Wendell Smith might indicate, Robinson faced swift, violent backlash for his daringness to insert himself into a white man's game. Robinson's teammate Dixie Walker was an early opponent, requesting to be traded rather than play with a Black man. Philadelphia Phillies manager Ben Chapman repeatedly referred to Robinson as "gorilla-like," and both the Pittsburgh Pirates and St. Louis Cardinals considered striking rather than being forced to play against the Dodgers.[87] Other teams instructed their players to throw at his head or spike him on the bases. While there were times that Robinson wanted to fight back or quit the team altogether and return to the Negro Leagues, he thought about what he believed Rickey had sacrificed to get him to this point—many friends and family members who disapproved of desegregation—and became determined to see the "great experiment" through.

The first measure of success was winning the respect of his team, the people closest to him and therefore most reliant on him and he on them. Of his relationship with his teammates, Robinson wrote, "some of the Dodgers who swore they would never play with a Black man had a change of mind, when they realized I was a good ballplayer who could be helpful in their earning a few thousand more dollars in world series money."[88] It was the liberal idea of enlightened self-interest that marked Robinson's first success and left open the door for further desegregation. As Robinson proved his baseball abilities throughout his 1947 rookie season, his teammates increasingly warmed to his presence and began to stick up for him against the more overtly racist opponents, like Chapman, who at one point got several Phillies players to point their bats at Robinson and pretend they were machine guns.[89] What was understood by his teammates within a month of the season—that Robinson was crucial to the team's success—was soon made apparent to the team's fans who were tired of watching their team lose and would largely support any player promising to bring them a World Series title.

Robinson's ability to bring together both white fans and Black fans resulted in a boom in attendance across the National League and reaffirmed his belief that he was "involved in something momentous" and had come to symbolize Black America's "hunger for opportunity."[90]

Although the Dodgers lost the World Series 4–3, Robinson's success—he won Rookie of the Year and came fifth in NL MVP voting—and thus the success of the team as a whole cracked open the door for more Black players. It took until 1959 for every MLB roster to have at least one Black player, but Robinson and the Dodgers proved that there was a new market to be exploited and much money to be made in signing Black players.[91] Larry Doby made his debut for Cleveland in July of 1947, becoming the first Black player in the American League. Just fifteen days later, the struggling St. Louis Browns debuted two Black players of their own, Willard Brown and Hank Thompson. By 1952 there were over 150 Black players in Major League Baseball, each of whom was likely attracted by the promise of greater salaries than those offered by Negro Leagues teams and the opportunity to play for a wider white audience. As with Branch Rickey, the owners of teams with Black players did not sign them for altruistic reasons, but rather "because they recognized . . . the competitive value of this new source of manpower."[92] Nonetheless, baseball's integration helped dispel the idea that Black people were inferior to white people, fortifying the national desegregation movement. For instance, President Truman's Committee on Civil Rights 1947 report relied on NL President Frick's defense of Robinson from racist attacks as proof of the possibility of integrating the military.[93]

Robinson's presence on the Dodgers allowed for the coming together of Black and white people and instilled in many a sense of hope for the future of America. Ira Glasser, former head of the ACLU, recalled his memory of that 1947 season:

> There was a sense of community between black and white that day at Ebbets Field, a meeting ground in a society that had banished most other meeting grounds, a place where black and white made common cause, both on the field and in the bleachers. It is quite possible that in those early years, Ebbets Field was the only fully integrated public accommodation in America.[94]

Of course, Robinson's presence in Major League Baseball did not single-handedly solve the problem of racism in American society, but baseball's special place in society gave great weight to the game's desegregation. It brought together diverse audiences that could equally enjoy the talents of a singular Black man.

Baseball's ability to integrate American society did not end with Jackie Robinson. In the early 1960s, many cities vied for a Major League Baseball team; one of these was Houston, which was awarded a team to begin play in 1962. One of the stipulations attached to Houston acquiring a team was an agreement for the owners to construct a covered stadium for the team. To win over Black voters, this potential stadium, the Houston Astrodome, nicknamed the "eighth wonder of the world" due to it being completely enclosed and air conditioned, was marketed as a fully desegregated space in the deeply segregated Harris County neighborhood. This marketing scheme successfully won over enough Black community leaders for the city to commit to $31 million in funding for the stadium and another $2.5 million in relocation fees paid to MLB. The promise of an MLB team proved essential in the city's overall desegregation efforts as Black leaders in Houston threatened a national Black boycott of MLB should the franchise fail to desegregate, and so the franchise was awarded to Houston with the stipulation that the Astrodome would be a fully desegregated space.[95] City officials further realized that the acquisition of an MLB team would require the full desegregation of the city as it would be a national embarrassment for Black stars like Willie Mays to have to stay at a segregated hotel. Ten days before the first MLB game at the Astrodome, all eleven of Houston's convention hotels desegregated.

Atlanta, too, in a bid to become a major American city, promised to build a new stadium in order to receive an MLB team, the then–Milwaukee Braves, which would become the first MLB team in the South. When the team's star player, Henry Aaron, was told of the move to a state which had banned integrated baseball teams in 1957, he told reporters in 1964, "I have lived in the South, and I don't want to live there again."[96] Several Black civil rights leaders in Atlanta reached out to him to remind him of the fact that Black leaders had "labored in the conviction that integrated pro teams would dramatically demonstrate what citizenship of color can accomplish given equal opportunities" in the South.[97] In short, these people believed that the presence of Henry Aaron on a Major League Baseball team would quicken the overturning of Jim Crow laws. Much of the push for the Braves came from Atlanta mayor Ivan Allen, who campaigned on a promise to bring professional sports to the city. He quickly amassed support for the stadium and oversaw its construction in 1964, stating that "the Negro feels the stadium belongs to him," as it was "the first new municipal building erected since the Negro has had full citizenship."[98] But the stadium was built with public tax dollars on land previously promised for low-income housing in the majority-Black Summerhill neighborhood, meaning that while the stadium itself was a point of integration on the field, in the stands, and in the front office, the land surrounding it became increasingly segregated and poverty stricken.

Indeed, though this liberal emphasis on the pursuit of individual good bolstered the desegregation movement across the country and led to many white people confronting their overt racism, it had disastrous consequences for many Black communities. Citing a belief in one's right to sell one's labor and one's freedom to enter into contracts, the vast majority of MLB teams refused to compensate Negro Leagues teams for the Black players they signed.[99] The few Negro Leagues teams who did receive compensation were akin to minor league teams in the early 1920s: selling players was the only way to keep teams afloat. Robinson's Monarchs in 1950 sold players for $21,750, offsetting the team's gate receipt decline and erasing the $1600 operating loss incurred in 1949.[100] The difference was that major league teams had no interest in absorbing Negro Leagues teams, only their best players.

Compounded by dwindling attendances as Black fans shifted toward the major leagues, this loss of star players led to the collapse of the Negro Leagues. Although Black men's and women's wages increased throughout the 1940s, resulting in a jump from earning 38.1 percent of white income to 52.2 percent by 1950, this money tended to be spent on white-owned businesses.[101] The affordability of television drew Black people further into the world of white baseball and white consumerism in general, and Black businesses that were slower to embrace desegregation came under fire for their outdated "race pride" language. Several of the remaining supporters of the Negro Leagues, such as Wendell Smith, viewed it not as a good in itself but as a feeder system for Major League Baseball that would ensure organized baseball's continued desegregation.[102]

MLB owners, however, increasingly opted to bypass the Negro Leagues altogether, signing Black players to contracts out of high school and college. The Negro Leagues attempted to combat this new pipeline by arguing that Black players would receive better pay and treatment in the Negro Leagues than in the minor leagues, but playing in the majors had become the goal for the vast majority of Black players, many of whom threatened to quit baseball if forced to play in the Negro Leagues.[103] The pride that had once left players such as Josh Gibson feeling as though they had "something to play for . . . besides just making a pay day" had been replaced with shame.[104] By the mid-1950s, the collapse of the Negro Leagues in the North and Midwest symbolized the regions' commitment to integration, and the continuation of Black professional baseball in the South was a reminder of its entrenched segregation.[105]

Although the Negro Leagues disbanded in 1949 and no professional Black team remained after 1962, integration proved a slow and divisive affair. There was an unofficial cap of three to four Black players placed on organized baseball teams in order to prevent them from being "top heavy," and owners were concerned about Black fans driving away racist white fans.[106] Organized baseball's desegregation allowed individual Black players to prosper with higher salaries, but it closed off the only "available outlet for blacks to participate in all aspects of the game—playing, managing, and owning."[107] Black umpires, officials, statisticians, and general stadium workers lost their jobs due to being unemployable by Major League Baseball. In 1948, *Pittsburgh Courier* writer William Webster spoke of the business side of baseball, declaring that "Negro baseball . . . needs preserving equally as much as Negro insurance companies, groceries, and bars."[108] The collapse of the Negro Leagues resulted in the marginalization of Black participation in professional baseball and the folding of bars and hotels and restaurants that had relied on Black baseball, thereby ending an entire way of life among Black people.[109]

This ending to the Negro Leagues demonstrates the crucial difference between desegregation and integration, in which the liberal emphasis on individualism and property rights leaves the wealthier, more established white businessmen and politicians in charge of dictating race relations at the expense of Black communities. Beset though it was by economic instability, the Negro Leagues provided a strong cultural tie for Black people in America. Writer Amiri Baraka characterized the Negro Leagues as being "like a light somewhere . . . connected to laughter and self-love."[110] Its collapse at the hands of "virtuous" economic individualism extinguished this light, and it became the job of Jackie Robinson and the oncoming civil rights movement to find some way to reignite it.

Jackie Robinson: Civil Rights Leader

After breaking MLB's color barrier, Robinson became a household name. He was somebody in whom Black people could find hope, and he was somebody white people were willing to listen to—up to a point. Upon his retirement, the NAACP awarded him the Spingarn Medal, given annually to the Black person who "made the highest achievement during the preceding year or years in any honorable field." Robinson considered this award to be a greater accomplishment than any baseball accolade he had received, stating that the NAACP "has stood out for me as the tireless champion of rights and the well-being of the Negroes of America. It is even more than that, because its cause is the cause of democracy, which makes it the champion of all Americans who cherish the principles on which this country was founded."[111] Along with this award, the NAACP offered him the opportunity to travel the country making speeches to various community groups, and he was given a weekly column in *The New York Post* and *New York Amsterdam News*. In the span of three years, Robinson moved from baseball player to full-fledged civil rights activist.

Robinson's impact on the civil rights movement became immediately apparent. When President Eisenhower gave a speech in 1957 following the "Little Rock Nine" in which he urged Black people to be patient, Robinson publicly responded, telling Eisenhower that Black people "want to enjoy now the rights that we feel we are entitled to as Americans."[112] This correspondence ultimately led to Eisenhower agreeing to meet with Martin Luther King Jr. to discuss his stance on civil rights. Moreover, Robinson's popularity among Black voters had both Richard Nixon and John F. Kennedy scrambling to earn his endorsement during the 1960 presidential election. After meeting with both candidates, Robinson—who to that point had avoided endorsing any specific parties or politicians—threw his support behind Richard Nixon because he thought Kennedy far too wealthy to be able to relate to Black Americans.[113]

For Robinson, the key to winning equal rights came down to what he called "the ballot and the buck."[114] In essence, he believed that Black people must assert their own political and economic freedom if they were to be free at all. In light of this position, and his overall approach of "Black capitalism," Robinson helped fundraise for the Freedom National Bank in New York City, a bank operated by Black people with the goal of addressing the shortage of affordable housing for Black people and the problem of redlining. As chair of this bank, he hoped to help Black people free themselves from discriminatory white institutions that offered them loans with higher interest rates. Speaking about the bank, Robinson declared that "we need to fight on the civil rights front, it is true, but it is just as important for us to make inroads on an economic level, if we are to solve some of our many problems."[115] He hoped this bank would give Black people "an economic unity so we can build an independent power base from which to deal with whites on a more equal basis."[116] This belief led Robinson to seek out support for the bank from the likes of Nelson Rockefeller, even after Rockefeller vetoed a federal minimum wage increase and refused to add more Black people to his staff. Although Rockefeller declined to support the bank on the belief that it would be a conflict of interest, Robinson maintained a close relationship with Rockefeller, who he believed was the only politician capable of uniting Republicans and Democrats.

As part of his liberal approach to politics, Robinson believed that individual liberty was the cornerstone of American democracy and was guaranteed in the Constitution. But his experiences as a Black man in America led him to recognize that his individual freedom gave him the responsibility to fight for the freedom of his community.[117] To this end, Robinson was particularly critical of politicians who refused to legislate equal rights for Black people. He believed that private individuals could potentially inculcate virtue among one another, but the social and moral effects of the Jim Crow laws could only be nullified by overturning each individual law.[118] Thus, we see that Robinson's civil rights activism was motivated by an adherence to the established liberal-republican synthesis, through which his efforts to build an interracial community rested on the economic participation of Black people and a deference to existing laws and political structures.

His championing of "Black capitalism" and belief in the promise of American democracy put Robinson at odds with other prominent civil rights leaders such as Huey P. Newton, Malcolm X, and, eventually, Martin Luther King Jr. Robinson criticized Newton and Malcolm X for desiring a separate Black society, calling Malcolm X in particular racist for his hatred of white people. Malcolm X, who had once reacted with joy over Robinson's first MLB game, responded to Robinson, charging him with letting himself be "used by the whites" like Branch Rickey and Nelson Rockefeller and criticizing him for testifying against opera singer and political activist Paul Robeson in front of the House Un-American Activities Committee.[119] Years later, Robinson came to regret testifying against Robeson, stating, "I have grown wiser and closer to the painful truth about America's destructiveness. And, I do have an increased respect for Paul Robeson who sacrificed himself, his career, and the wealth and confidence he once enjoyed because, I believe, he was sincerely trying to help his people."[120]

Although Robinson continued to distance himself from these other civil rights leaders, one of his last public acts further suggests he had grown to see a great deal of truth in their politics. In 1970, less than two years before his death, he founded a construction company in New York to build low-income housing for Black people. Speaking on his decision to found this company, he said:

> We talked about not having capital, but we needed to learn to take a chance, to be daring, to pool capital, to organize our buying power so that the millions we spent did not leave our communities to be stacked up in downtown banks. In addition to the economic security we could build with green power, we could use economic means to reinforce black power. How much more effective our demands for a piece of the action would be if we were negotiating from the strength or our own self-reliance rather than stating our case in the role of beggar or someone crying out for charity.[121]

Where earlier he tied himself to people like Nelson Rockefeller and Richard Nixon, he now believed that Black people could not sit around and wait for white people to give them their rights. Rather, achieving them would take deliberate economic and political organization at the community level. In other words, Robinson came to understand that the struggle for individual rights could not be won without a deep concern for civic virtue.

Central to this shift in his thinking was his disillusionment with the lack of progress in desegregating the country. By the late sixties, he began criticizing MLB for its refusal to hire Black coaches and managers, and he called out Black stars Frank Robinson and Willie Mays for refusing to speak openly about the sport's racism.[122] He accurately, yet ironically, labeled those associated with MLB "a narrow-minded, bigoted group" who only gave Black players opportunities if they promised not to "rock the boat."[123] This disgust with MLB propelled him to support Curt Flood's lawsuit against the reserve clause. In a February 1970 edition of *Jet*, the most popular Black magazine in the country, Robinson wrote of Flood that he "is doing a service to all players in the leagues, especially for the younger players coming up who are not superstars. All he is asking for is the right to negotiate. . . . He is a very sensitive man concerned about the rights of everybody."[124] His testimony as a witness in May of that year restated this endorsement of Flood's character and decried the reserve clause as preventing players from saying "I have a certain value and I can place it on myself." He did not call for its abolition but argued that players should become free agents "after a certain number of years."[125] He continued:

> Anything that is one-sided is wrong in America. The reserve clause is one-sided in favor of the owners and should be modified to give the player some control over his destiny. Whenever you have one-sided systems, in my view, it leads to serious, serious problems, and I think that unless there is a change in the reserve clause, that it is going to lead to a serious strike in terms of ball players.[126]

These two statements again summarize Robinson's conception of Black capitalism as a blend of liberalism and republicanism in which individual property rights lead to further freedoms. They also mark a change in Robinson, who in 1958 told a Senate subcommittee that he was "highly in favor of the reserve clause."[127]

Although his politics and his friendships with white politicians potentially afforded him protections not available to many of his fellow civil rights leaders, he was left deeply unsatisfied with the role he had played in igniting the civil rights movement. In 1968, reflecting on his hesitancy to support proposed boycotts of the upcoming Olympics, he said, "Maybe we, as negro athletes have 'been around' too long, accepting inequities and indignities and going along with the worn out promises about how things are going to get better."[128] His 1972 autobiography, written just prior to his death in October, was a frank discussion of his successes and failures as a civil rights leader, as well as a harsh critique of America. Reflecting on his first World Series game, he remarked, "As I look back on that opening game of my first world series, I must tell you that it was Mr. Rickey's drama and that I was only a principal actor. As I write this twenty years later, I cannot stand and sing the anthem. I cannot salute the flag; I know that I am a black man in a white world. In 1972, in 1947, at my birth in 1919, I know that I never had it made."[129] The resistance he faced from white America to his more gentle politics of "Black capitalism" left him feeling as though America would never truly achieve racial equality.

Black Participation in Baseball Post-Robinson

The destruction of the Negro Leagues and the economy built around them did not result in full integration but rather drove Black fans away from professional baseball. In cities like Chicago and Philadelphia that had once enthusiastically supported Black baseball, Black attendance at major league games in the 1980s and '90s hovered around 3 percent.[130] And despite Robinson's desire to see Black managers in MLB, since 1972 only 17 Black men have been hired for the position versus 224 white men.[131] In 1987, as part of MLB's fortieth anniversary of Robinson's debut, Dodgers General Manager Al Campanis did an interview with *Nightline* in which he was asked about the lack of Black managers and general managers in MLB. He replied that Black people don't have the "necessities" to be managers or general managers.[132] Campanis was fired because of the interview, but his answer nonetheless was revealing of MLB's attitude toward Black people.

Black players in the last three decades of the twentieth century fared a little better than Black fans and managers, but they, too, never achieved the equality Robinson hoped for. The 1970s through the mid-'80s served as the height of Black participation in Major League Baseball, both in terms of percentage of Black players (roughly 20 percent) and number of stars who were Black. In 1971 the Pittsburgh Pirates became the first team to field an all-Black starting lineup. In 1974 Henry Aaron, the last remaining MLBer who played in the Negro Leagues, broke Babe Ruth's career home run record. And in 1977 the NL and AL Rookie of the Year award winners, Andre Dawson and Eddie Murray, were both Black players. But Major League Baseball, as with other sports leagues, attempted to "depoliticize" itself in the 1970s, punishing Black players for being too outspoken. In 1970 Dick Allen was traded from the Phillies to the Cardinals for Curt Flood because of his divisive politics, prompting other Black players to remain silent in fear of losing out on contracts.[133] Furthermore, by the mid-'80s, MLB had abandoned Black communities in favor of Latin American ones, where they could control players from a younger age and therefore sign them to cheaper contracts than Black stars were demanding in post-1975 free agency.[134]

Black players, coaches, and fans had overwhelmingly abandoned baseball for basketball, which offered them greater "collective identity and civic pride."[135] While there was no singular cause of Black people's shift from baseball to basketball, a large part of it was due to MLB's abandonment of Black people. By the 1990s youth baseball had largely become a suburban sport played by middle-class white families who could afford the mounting registration, travel, and equipment fees. Basketball, meanwhile, began to flourish in inner cities where the majority of Black people lived. It was cheaper to play, NCAA scholarships were often full ride unlike with baseball, and there were more Black coaches and managers associated with the sport.[136] The myths that had kept Black people associated with professional baseball through much of the twentieth century were no longer enough; the mounting cost of all aspects of participation in baseball, from player to spectator, exposed the absurdity of baseball's democratic myth.

As Major League Baseball kept Black players, fans, and managers at arm's length, Jackie Robinson continued to be touted as a symbol of progress, not just on the ballfield but in American society, too. Reflecting on Robinson's position as civil rights icon, essayist Gerald Early wrote in 1998:

> If nothing else, Robinson, an unambiguous athletic hero for both races and symbol of sacrifice on the altar of racism, is our most magnificent case of affirmative action. He entered a lily-white industry amid cries that he was unqualified . . . and he succeeded, on merit, beyond anyone's wildest hope. And here the sports metaphor is a perfectly literal expression of the traditional democratic belief of that day: If given the chance, anyone can make it on his ability, with no remedial aid or special compensation, on a level playing field . . . Here was our democratic orthodoxy of color-blind competition realized. Here was an instance where neither the principle nor its application could be impugned. Robinson was proof, just as heavyweight champion Joe Louis and Olympic track star Jesse Owens had been during the Depression, that sports helped vanquish the stigma of race. . . . For the conservative today, Robinson is the classic, fixed example of affirmative action properly applied as

> the extension of opportunity to all, regardless of race, class, gender or outcome. For the liberal, Robinson is an example of the process of affirmative action as the erosion of white male hegemony, where outcome is the very point of the exercise.[137]

In Robinson, white America found a person into whom they could inject whatever political project best suited them. Because his reintegration of MLB necessarily separated him from his community and forced him to act as a single individual, he became the perfect representative for the success of liberal individualism as a solution to slavery and anti-Black racism.

Conclusion: Deconstructing the Myth of Equality

Although Robinson ended his life disillusioned with America and Major League Baseball, his image lived on as a celebration of the civil rights movement. Reverend Jesse Jackson, delivering Robinson's eulogy, spoke of Robinson's 1947 MLB debut as America "for a fleeting moment" trying democracy and becoming "one nation under God." He stated that Robinson "turned a stumbling block into a stepping stone" and integrated baseball not for himself but "for all of us."[138] Therefore, "No grave can hold his body down because it belongs to the ages."[139] Despite Jackson's obvious focus on Robinson's relationship to the Black community, he would soon be absorbed by the white community as a symbol of white belief in racial equality.

Rather than uphold this attachment to Robinson's image as a victory for equality, an analysis of this treatment of Robinson illustrates the problem of attempting to address the remnants of slavery through economic individualism. The fact that team owners were motivated by pursuit of profit meant that they did not understand or perhaps did not care about the ramifications of their actions. The ensuing integration was thus limited in scope and driven almost entirely by wealthy white men who were ignorant of the complexities of the Black communities surrounding the Negro Leagues. Moreover, Black people found themselves operating within this same framework, equating freedom and equality with the consumption of white businesses and products. While Black baseball during segregation provided a sense of community where Black people could learn from and celebrate one another, it could not withstand the civic-mindedness attached to greater Black participation in the white economy. When Jackie Robinson stepped onto the field for the Dodgers, he became caught between these two ideologies. On one hand, his success was the success of the Black community and vice versa, but on the other, he was divorced from his community and forced to become his own individual.

Although Robinson did emphasize the significance of community and civic virtue as the basis for American society, the systems in place in Major League Baseball and the American government forced the civil rights conversation toward economic individualism, and the pursuit of greater wealth became the means through which civil rights advancements were made. However, this framework also limited Robinson's effectiveness. His value was tied to his productivity on the field, and he knew that if he played poorly, he would lose his job and his ability to reach out to white fans.

In line with Furstenberg's liberal-republican synthesis concerning slavery, participation in government and civil society more broadly fell along economic lines; economic production remained the ticket to freedom and economic barriers remained in place. Thus, the civil rights progress Robinson made necessitated the destruction of a vibrant Black community whose existence was closed off to white America. Robinson and other Black people's adherence to "Black capitalism" demonstrates the limitations inherent within the liberal-republican conception of freedom cemented during the founding era. Robinson followed this model, achieving individual economic success as a measure of his ability to be a citizen, and yet he ended his life deeply unsatisfied with Black people's place in American society.

His legacy and the position of Black people in baseball—both organized and amateur—in the final decades of the twentieth century demonstrates the insufficiencies in conflating assimilation with equality. The former demands that the oppressed find freedom in conforming to the rules laid out by the oppressor: Black players and fans must make themselves palatable to white audiences, in the process destroying large swaths of Black culture. The latter achieves equality through a mutual respect in a diversity of culture in a process that is constructive rather than destructive—it is not swapping one culture for another, but rather creating a new culture together. Perhaps had white owners, players, and fans understood and respected the economic and civic value of the Negro Leagues to their Black communities, true equality could have been achieved through preservation of these communities and careful integration of white people into Black spaces, rather than almost exclusively the other way around.

CHAPTER FOUR

Bloomers and Beanball

Women's Involvement in America's National Pastime

> I love baseball. It's my life. I grew up not knowing anything else but baseball, so I'm gonna die not knowing anything else but baseball because I love it so much.
>
> —AAGPBL Player Maybelle Blair

In his 1888 baseball guide, John Montgomery Ward declared that "it would require an elastic imagination to conceive of little girls possessed of physical powers such as [baseball] demands."[1] He was far from alone in this sentiment as many, such as A. G. Spalding, worked hard to link baseball to the myth of American manliness and thereby preclude women from playing it. The essential argument was that women were neither physically nor mentally fit enough to play the game, which, when combined with the notion that participation in baseball was crucial for fostering citizenship via learning American values, meant that women could not become citizens in either the liberal sense, as property holders, or in the republican sense, as purveyors of civic virtue.

This tactic of linking baseball to manliness succeeded in barring women from the highest level of the sport, but women have remained staunch fans and players of the game since its development in the 1840s. Indeed, women have used their participation in the national pastime to assert their claim to equal rights, arguing that their capacity to enjoy the sport demonstrates their capacity to be equal citizens. However, in making the argument, white women have often distanced themselves from Black women, thereby equating their citizenship with their whiteness; white women are worthy of citizenship, the argument goes, insofar as they are capable of maintaining the subjugation of Black people that is so fundamental to the American way of life. Here, again, we see that the American founding era's blend of liberalism and republicanism falls short of producing equality because it ties white women's civic participation to a liberal individualist approach to politics that dissuades them from connecting their equality to the equality of the whole of American society.

In this chapter, I explore baseball's relationship to gender conflicts throughout America's history. I begin with a discussion of the role of women during the American founding era, in which many women developed a newfound interest in politics and an understanding of themselves as political actors. This interest in politics brought with it arguments about the role of women in society pertaining to both the cultivation of civic virtue associated with republicanism and the liberal argument for property rights as the foundation of political participation. I reveal how these conceptions of gender and citizenship have developed throughout women's participation in baseball. I argue that during the twentieth century, women relied on the sport's ability to foster community and provide individuals with economic success, all while continuously demonstrating their love for both playing and watching the game. But their efforts to participate in the national pastime have also demonstrated the extent to which gender inequality is embedded within American society.

Women's Rights in the Founding Era

Leading up to the American Revolution, white women in the colonies were increasingly appealed to as political actors. They were urged to take part in boycotting English-made goods after the English parliament enacted a series of taxes in the Sugar Act of 1764, the Stamp Act of 1765, and the Townshend Acts of 1767. A good example of this boycotting is the Edenton Tea Party, in which fifty-one white women in Edenton, North Carolina, signed an agreement to boycott British goods on the basis that it was "necessary, for the public good."[2] Women in other states boycotted in several ways, including refusing to marry men who applied for a stamped marriage license. In both Boston and Philadelphia, women publicly shamed men for not fully supporting the boycott, with one anonymous Pennsylvania woman publishing a poem declaring, "If the sons, so degenerate! The blessings despise / Let the Daughters of Liberty nobly arise!"[3]

This political inclusion marked a decisive contrast to the strict division between public and private that had characterized English and colonial society to that point. For centuries, the cornerstone of society had been the patriarchal family in which the man controlled the economic and political elements of the household, leaving his wife to tend to the strictly domestic elements like housework and child rearing. This arrangement was codified in the English common law doctrine of coverture, through which wives' legal status was subsumed by their husbands, meaning they became property of their husbands.[4] Through participating in these boycotts, however, women attempted to insert themselves into political life by reframing household economics as a component of civic virtue rather than a wholly private, individual concern.

White women in this era were not able to fully escape the domestic framework that shaped their lives, and it instead converged with the strain of republicanism present during the revolution to create what historian Linda Kerber termed "republican motherhood."[5] The American Revolution demanded a recontextualization of the domestic role of women, now recognized as a crucial conduit of civic virtue that Kerber calls the "fourth branch of government," alongside the legislative, executive, and judicial branches created by the Constitution.[6] Although this shift did not invite women into state legislatures, it broke down the previous distinction between public and private in acknowledging that the household served a fundamental political function.[7] It also carved out a specific political role for women in educating their sons in civic virtue, which required first for women to be educated en masse in literature, mathematics, and science, the latter two of which had previously been primarily restricted to boys and men.

This role for women was championed by Thomas Jefferson, who in a letter to Philadelphia socialite Anne Willing Bingham wrote that "our good ladies, I trust, have been too wise to wrinkle their foreheads with politics. They are contented to soothe and calm the minds of their husbands returning ruffled from political debate. They have the good sense to value domestic happiness above all other, and the art to cultivate it beyond all others."[8] As part of his belief in the inherent virtue of a republican, pastoral society, Jefferson contended that it was in the domestic sphere that women would embrace their natural equality, and such a thing could only be achieved in America with American women who were uncorrupted by European decadence.[9] Fellow founding father Benjamin Rush echoed Jefferson's sentiments in his 1787 speech "Thoughts upon Female Education" given to the Young Ladies' Academy in Philadelphia. In this speech, he listed five reasons for educating girls and women, including the necessity of education for being "stewards, and guardians of their husbands' property" and for "instructing their sons in the principles of liberty and government."[10] For Jefferson, Rush, and other proponents of "republican motherhood," the foundational fear was that granting women the right to vote would destroy the family structure upon which society was based.

Despite these republican efforts to confine women to the domestic sphere, the increased emphasis on natural rights in American society provided women the ammunition necessary to argue for a more direct inclusion in politics. In a letter to her husband John in March of 1776, four months before the signing of the Declaration of Independence, Abigail Adams wrote of the woman's place in the impending political project of a free United States. She urged her husband,

> in the new Code of Laws which I suppose it will be necessary for you to make I desire you would Remember the Ladies, and be more generous and favourable to them than your ancestors. Do not put such unlimited power into the hands of the Husbands. Remember all Men would be tyrants if they could. If perticuliar care and attention is not paid to the Laidies we are determined to foment a Rebelion, and will not hold ourselves bound by any Laws in which we have no voice, or Representation.[11]

Although this letter was never intended to be public and her sentiments were dismissed by her husband, they foreshadowed women's oncoming critiques of the contradictions of the natural rights basis for American government.

Other women made more public appeals to natural rights as the basis for their inclusion in the political realm. Judith Sargent Murray's 1790 work *On the Equality of the Sexes* plainly states that "our souls are by nature equal to yours" as part of a critique of the predominant biblical and educational arguments for the superiority of men.[12] English philosopher Mary Wollstonecraft's *A Vindication of the Rights of Woman*, published in England in 1792, furthered this conversation, becoming one of the most widely distributed works in America by the end of the decade.[13] In part a response to Thomas Paine's *Rights of Man*, published one year prior, Wollstonecraft argued for women's rights from both a Lockean natural rights perspective and a republican position.[14] In her dedication, she outlines her republicanism, stating:

> Contending for the rights of woman, my main argument is built on this simple principle, that if she be not prepared by education to become the companion of man, she will stop the progress of knowledge and virtue; for truth must be common to all [. . . and] if children are to be educated to understand the true principle of patriotism, their mother must be a patriot; and the love of mankind, from which an orderly train of virtues spring, can only be produced by considering the moral and civil interest of mankind; but the education and situation of woman, at present, shuts her out from such investigations.[15]

In short, providing women with an education equal to that of men is essential for ensuring the cultivation of virtue not only in their children but in society as a whole. This argument is an amending of Jefferson's and Rush's, positing that women have a direct relationship with civil society rather than one strictly through their male children.

Wollstonecraft extends this republican argument to incorporate liberal conceptions of natural rights. She argues that if the foundation of republican government is liberty, then the enslavement of women at the hands of men undermines this foundation because "how can a being be . . . virtuous, who is not free?"[16] What Wollstonecraft means by liberty is the Lockean natural rights conception whereby rights precede government. In the dedication to *Rights of Woman*, she reiterates Locke's emphasis on reason as a fundamental characteristic of human beings, stating, "if women are to be excluded, without having a voice, from a participation of the natural rights of mankind, prove first . . . that they want reason."[17] She further extends Locke's argument, declaring it is from the English unequal distribution of property which "most of the evils and vices" flow.[18] This problem of property is due to the fact that women cannot own it and are therefore "absolutely dependent on their husbands," preventing them from exercising virtue.[19] The solution, then, is a more equal distribution of property rights that would enable both men and women to exercise their rights and corresponding duties toward one another. In other words, Wollstonecraft combined the liberal foundation of government with its republican ends to point out the hypocrisy of the subservience of women to men.

Although Wollstonecraft never discussed the subject directly, this link between property and citizenship manifested itself in arguments about voting rights in America. Article 1 section 4 of the Constitution counted white women as "free persons" for the purpose of apportioning House representatives, and the vast majority of state constitutions contained gender neutral language when discussing voting, but all contained property qualifications, therefore disenfranchising the vast majority of women. New York Senator Samuel Mitchill explained the issue thusly: "In the theory of our Constitution women are calculated as political beings. They are numbered in the census of inhabitants . . . and the Representatives are apportioned among the people according to their numbers, reckoning the females as well as the males. Though, therefore, women do not vote, they are nevertheless represented in the national government to their full amount."[20] White women were both political and not political, and although the Constitution did not expressly disenfranchise them, it left each individual state to determine the extent of their political participation.

Recognizing the limitations of gender neutral language in a society that customarily excluded women from the vote, New Jersey in 1790 began the process of enfranchising women, altering previously gender-neutral language to specifically include women: "No Person shall be entitled to Vote in any other Township or precinct, than that in which he or she doth actually reside at the time of the Election."[21] Speaking of this change, a Trenton newspaper declared that it was enacted "from a principle of justice, deeming it right that every free person who pays a tax should have a vote."[22] However, because voting was tied to ownership of property, this enfranchisement of women extended only to the several hundred widows who had inherited their husbands' estates. Nonetheless, the majority of men in New Jersey found women's enfranchisement so unacceptable that in October of 1807 the state legislature passed a bill restricting voting to "free, white, male citizens" on the basis that doing so would reduce electoral corruption.[23]

While white women were largely unsuccessful in integrating themselves into the political community during the founding era, the parameters within which they would continue to fight for political equality were drawn. Their efforts were largely thwarted by both republican arguments concerning the centrality of the domestic realm in inculcating civic virtue and the liberal emphasis on property as the qualification for political participation. The framework was therefore set: The future success of women's rights movement must rest on women's abilities to mitigate the concerns of men embedded within these two pervasive political theories, namely the fear that women entering into male-dominated elements of society would cause society to collapse, whether through impeding the development of civic virtue or further illustrating the contradictions at the heart of liberal individualism that had begun to be exposed through abolitionist movements.

Women and Baseball in the 1800s

With the advent of industrialization in the late 1700s, women began entering the workforce, leaving behind lives of pure domesticity. Throughout the 1800s, groups of women formed various labor unions and political groups, intent on not only proving they were capable of the same things as men but on ushering in a total civil rights movement, linking anti-slavery with women's rights, an effort welcomed and supported by many abolitionist leaders. The progress toward both was languid, though, hampered by a strong resistance and a growing belief among white women that they should focus on less radical concepts, restricting their efforts to domestic equality and rebuking the strong language and policies of Susan B. Anthony.[24] By the mid-1850s, six years after the Seneca Falls Convention, women in various states had won equal divorce rights and began entering educational institutions in greater numbers.[25] In the few years prior to the Civil War, however, women's rights movements ceded prominence to abolition efforts, which they believed would also lead to women's suffrage.

Over four hundred women, many of whom disguised as men, fought in the Civil War, and those who remained home experienced more freedom and amassed more power than they ever had before. Following the Civil War, women were disappointed to learn that their efforts were for naught, as the Fourteenth and Fifteenth Amendments applied only to men. This stinging loss emboldened the women's rights movement, pushing it further toward total economic and social equality, with the main goal being suffrage.[26] Many women, both white and Black, refused to return to domestic lives, instead clamoring for increased freedoms and rights.

Men quickly sought to counter these movements, asserting that women belonged in no place but the home. Activities from which they wished to bar women were labeled "masculine" and assigned the potential to crush feminine sensitivities and invite evil into the family dynamic. Men stressed the need for women to return to their homes and not engage in activities geared toward "manly virtues," to instead fulfill their "feminine duties" in rebuilding the country.[27] Women's rights movements were viewed by many, including a number of well-to-do women, as selfish acts bent on destroying America for good.[28] Now, more than ever, it was crucial for women to embrace their femininity, to put away hopes of being like men, to eschew bloomers in favor of full skirts and dainty corsets. All aspects of women's lives were scrutinized and women in large part were pushed toward quiet, feminine activities that left no room for politics.

Unsurprisingly, women's involvement in baseball during this time followed a similar pattern. Since the sport's popularization in the 1830s, women have played it, but with the creation of organized teams and the professionalization of the game, men began asserting it as something masculine, far too difficult for women to play. Nonetheless, women continued playing it, and in 1866, the newly formed Vassar College instituted the first two organized women's teams. Created in 1861, Vassar was one of the seven Ivy League equivalent schools for women that sprouted up in New York and New England throughout the decade. At the behest of his niece, Matthew Vassar established Vassar with the goal of strengthening women's bodies so they could participate in rigorous academic disciplines formerly believed to be too strenuous for delicate feminine bodies. As part of this goal, he instituted physical education courses and morning calisthenics. From this emphasis on physical strength sprang the establishment of a number of sporting clubs, including one for baseball.[29]

The first baseball teams, Laurel and Abenakis, were created in 1866, each featuring nine women. One of the creators, valedictorian Annie Glidden, wrote to her brother John about the creation of these teams, joking that "we think after we have practiced a little, we will let the Atlantic Club play a match with us," demonstrating at the same time the seriousness with which they viewed their participation in the game.[30] While the women were allowed to form baseball teams, the sport was considered to be far too manly to be overly beneficial for them. The players had to provide their own equipment, and the field was rough and hidden from the rest of the school. Women were allowed to play baseball, but only barely. The next year, both Laurel and Abenakis had disbanded, and no woman on either team was present on their replacement, the Precocious club. This kind of turnover continued until the early 1870s, when the school buckled under public pressure and finally parroted the falsity that the sport was far too manly for these women of high society to play.[31]

The initial teams in 1866, though, were pioneers of a larger trend that saw the creation of over twenty women's teams across the country in the ensuing three years. In 1867 a team popped up at Miss Porter's School in Connecticut. Called Tunxis after the Indigenous people who had inhabited the state, the team played several games but was ultimately shut down after the school received a number of letters from parents calling for a stop to this "strenuous exercise." The women at Mills College experienced a similar series of events. It was already controversial enough to have women's colleges and allowing them to play baseball was a step too far, a play for more independence than society was willing to grant. Once news of these teams circulated, they each faced a swift backlash from parents and then the general public in the form of newspapers.[32]

The papers first assumed an informative tone that then gave way to incredulity. Initially, newspapers simply asserted that their city or town now included a women's baseball team. But among these reports were ones that commented on the absurdity of women playing baseball. *The Utica Morning Herald and Daily Gazette* wrote in 1867 that while women technically had the right to play, doing so was laughable: "Imagine a fair creature arrayed in all the paraphernalia of dress, hoop skirts, and sun bonnet making a home run! . . . Who would wish to see his sweetheart's eye done in mourning for a week or her fair hand battered and bruised and soiled by a 'foul' ball, or her fair hair all pulled out or her ankle swathed in bandages."[33] Other newspapers wrote much the same thing, equating the idea of women playing baseball to the equally fanciful notion of them practicing law or medicine.[34]

But the backlash did not stop girls and women from playing, and those who were not members of these exclusive schools also created teams. In 1867 both Michigan and Florida got teams and the rest of the country quickly followed suit. Peterborough's team is the best-documented of the bunch, having as participants several women closely associated with the women's rights movement, including Elizabeth Cady Stanton and Nannie Miller, the daughter of the inventor of bloomers, Elizabeth Smith Miller. The most notable accounts of the team stem from several letters written by Stanton, one of which notes "it was a very pretty sight to see the girls . . . in full possession of the public square . . . while the boys were quiet spectators."[35] For these women, though, the sport was less about furthering the women's rights movement than about simply achieving physical fitness. Never was baseball a component of Susan B. Anthony's message, and though it was in a sense a political act, it was not viewed as such by these women; they just assumed baseball was open to them as a physical activity.

Some men bought into the spectacle of women's teams and, like the owner of Crab Orchard in Louisiana, promoted them as means of boosting business.[36] But as it became clear that women would not give up the sport, the sentiment dramatically shifted. Newspapers quickly attributed playing baseball to the feminist agenda, politicizing the game and radicalizing its participants. The more professionalized the men's teams became, the less acceptable the women's teams grew. Just prior to these attacks, though, newspapers struck at the relatively common notion that it was healthy for women to play baseball. The climax of this trend occurred in late 1867, when several newspapers asserted that a woman in Michigan died after "over-exerting herself" playing it.[37] From this point, the majority of men and upstanding women took the physical weakness of women as truth.

In 1873 renowned doctor Edward H. Clarke published *Sex in Education; or a Fair Chance for the Girls*, in which he posited that physical exertion, like playing baseball, caused uterine damage and hysteria. After the circulation of this book, few men were willing to defend women's universities and larger participation in baseball. For society, allowing women to participate in the sport would be permitting it to injure women physically and morally.[38] The more embedded the sport became in American society, the less acceptable it was for girls and women to play it.

More subtle means of demeaning women baseball players also entered the fray. If newspapers did not outright condemn the act, they sought to undercut its significance by focusing on the women's appearance. In 1876 Philadelphia added a women's team, which *The Reading Times* declared would wear "the finest [uniform] that ever graced the ball field."[39] Likewise, Springfield's teams, the Blondes and the Brunettes, would wear new uniforms that "enable[d] them to travel on their shape."[40] Since women could not be prevented from playing baseball, society was determined to refuse them legitimacy, reducing teams to spectacles and games to places where men could pick out their future wives.

But women continued to play it and take seriously their participation in the game. It made a resurgence at Vassar College in 1875, thanks to two women employees, school physician Dr. Helen Webster and Director of the Department of Physical Training Lilian Tappan. This resurgence, though, was not widely reported, was only open to the most fit students, and was explained as a means of getting students better motivated to exercise during their mandatory daily hour of fitness.[41] Even fewer students than were qualified participated, many of whom preferred croquet or sailing, both of which would avoid the "'cold world's' sneer" attracted by baseball.[42] Yet there were enough participants to form two teams of twelve, and interest sustained baseball for four years, long past the point of propriety, until it was finally abolished in favor of the more socially acceptable tennis.[43]

Despite the best efforts of men to exclude women from baseball, they continued to flock to it in various capacities for much of the late 1800s. In addition to the resurgence of college baseball at Vassar, Smith, Wellesley, and Holyoke, which lasted into the 1890s, women of lesser education created teams in their towns and cities, and Black women organized teams of their own, particularly in Philadelphia, when they were barred from white women's teams.[44] Baseball appealed to women as it did to men, and the more American it became, the more women used it to dig out a space for themselves in the social realm. Men forced women's participation in the sport to be politicized, and women of the 1800s responded, setting up a long battle for generations ahead.

The Bloomer Girls

Beginning in the 1890s with the increased acceptance of Social Darwinism, the concept of the "New Woman" took center stage in discourse concerning gender and women's role in society. Contrary to the Victorian Era woman who was meek and proper, this "New Woman" was characterized by her confidence, robustness, ambition, and penchant for wearing bloomers. Central in many ways to this change in women's perceptions of themselves and their place in society was baseball. Essayist Charles Dudley Warner noted that society by and large has "ceased to be astonished at finding women in unexpected places," and it had been "more shocked some years ago by the appearance in the field of female baseball clubs than it would be now by the advent of female football teams."[45]

Women's involvement in baseball expanded rapidly in the 1890s, with the formation of amateur and school-based teams in twenty-five states.[46] These teams comprised women from all social classes and featured both married and single women. Although no team was interracial, there were plenty of white women's and Black women's teams throughout the country. The newfound emphasis on physical health enabled these teams to market themselves not as spectacles but as legitimate sources of talent, allowing more women to earn money playing amateur and semi-pro men's teams, as well as other women's teams. Of course, these women also received a great deal of pushback, and for the first time, women's involvement in the sport was linked to the suffrage movement. In 1892 *The Atchison Daily Globe* wrote that "equal rights means an equal right to dress up in stripes and tear over a field after a ball, as well as it means the right to vote."[47] This relationship between baseball and women's rights was cemented when various teams adopted the nickname Bloomer Girls, linking them to suffragist Amelia Jenks Bloomer, who popularized bloomers, loose fitting pants that allowed women to have a far greater rage of mobility than while wearing skirts.

Between 1890 and 1934, hundreds of women's teams were formed in both large cities and small towns across the country, featuring white women, Black women, and the occasional man. In 1910 and 1911, for instance, the St. Louis Black Bronchos, consisting of twelve Black women and four Black men, traveled throughout the South, drawing crowds of up to five thousand for their games.[48] These teams most frequently lasted two or three years before collapsing and being replaced by other women's teams, but three teams of white women—the Boston Bloomer Girls, the Star Bloomers, and the Western Bloomer Girls—spanned several decades, providing consistency for the women's baseball movement. These teams in particular benefitted greatly from their relationship with Maud Nelson, whose forty years in baseball included stints as player, scout, manager, and owner.

Born in Italy as Clementina Brida, Nelson emigrated with her family to America when she was a young child. Taking up baseball as a child allowed her to become "Americanized" and to carve out a place for herself in her new country. She began her baseball career at age twelve in 1892 when she joined a New York women's team, but it was not until her signing with the Boston Bloomer Girls in 1896 that she began to receive attention for her pitching ability.[49] After a game against the San Bernardino Bloomer Girls in 1897, the local paper declared that Nelson was the star of the game: "Miss Maud Nelson in the box [pitchers' mound] did great work and called out great applause. At the bat, too, she proved a star, she being the only one that gave the fielders any trouble."[50] As the main attraction, Nelson had to pitch every single game, but she proved particularly resilient, pitching in various capacities until the age of forty-one.

In 1911 Nelson and her husband, John B. Olsen Jr., purchased the Western Bloomer Girls, transforming them into the premier women's barnstorming baseball team. Determined to field only the best players, Nelson personally scouted every single one, ensuring they would put talent over spectacle. For the most part, her efforts paid off, as the team gained a reputation for being "a first-class outfit, respectable in every way" that drew large crowds wherever it toured.[51] After her husband's death in 1917, Nelson returned to the Boston Bloomers for a brief stint before assuming control of the Chicago Athletic Club and creating the All Star Ranger Girls. Almost every single noteworthy women's player of the Bloomer era played with or for Maud Nelson.[52]

Perhaps the second-most notable woman player of this era, Lizzie Arlington, had a much different encounter with professional baseball. In 1898, after playing for women's teams for eight years, Arlington was approached by William J. Connor, who offered her $100 per week to play on various men's teams in the Philadelphia area. Connor figured that Arlington would draw large crowds who wanted to see a woman player, and so he marketed her as such. Throughout the 1898 season, Arlington's competent play was overshadowed by her gender, as she was made to wear a distinct uniform consisting of a skirt, while her contemporaries—both men and women—wore pants. After her debut on July 5, making her the first woman to play in a professional men's game, *The Reading Eagle* declared, "for a woman, she is a success."[53] Shortly after her debut, the Atlantic League president, unsatisfied with the small crowds she attracted, cut her loose. As was often the case with racial and gender minorities, Arlington's quest for equality was reduced to her economic prospects. Once her contract was terminated, she returned to the Boston Bloomer Girls and continued to play baseball for years, but the media stopped caring about her once she was no longer novel.

When there was no means of profiting from women's baseball, men for the most part condemned the phenomenon, fearing the "feminization" of American society. Inspired by historian Frederick Jackson Turner's 1893 paper, "The Significance of the Frontier in America History," in which he argued that the manly pursuit of civilizing the "savage wilderness" gave shape to America's democratic institutions, men attached their fears of decline to women's supposed assault on masculinity.[54] If women were allowed to play professional baseball, one of society's proudest fixtures, society as a whole would be weakened by the fairer sex, and the fundamental distinctions between America and Europe would cease to exist. Limiting women's involvement in baseball to school fitness activities, then, was essential for the preservation of American democracy.

As part of this project to protect baseball from women, by 1900 all baseball involving women was called "women's baseball," thereby distinguishing it from the "regular" baseball played by men. The sexism inherent in coverage of women's baseball increased in the 1900s in conjunction with the efforts to amateurize it and distinguish it from men's baseball. One newspaper wrote of a game in 1909, "In short, the Bloomer Girls knew as much about baseball—professional baseball—as the average man knows about crocheting a peek-a-boo shirt waist, which is less than nothing."[55] Then, in the 1910s and 1920s, baseball became essential to the development of boys, entrenching within the game a masculine purpose.[56] In his widely read book published in 1913, *Training the Boy*, William McKeever asserted that "no boy can grow to a perfectly normal manhood today without the benefit of at least a small amount of baseball experience and practice."[57]

The gender conservatism that emphasized masculinity also praised femininity in women. As baseball become more associated with boys and men, women's baseball was demonized as the cultivator of predatory "mannish lesbians" who corrupted innocent, feminine women.[58] Girls and women, then, were increasingly funneled into "indoor baseball," the precursor to softball. Indoor baseball was slower, more controlled, and thus more "ladylike" than regular baseball. While both men and women played indoor baseball and softball, its designation as an amateur sport lent itself to women's involvement. Gladys Palmer's 1926 book, *Baseball for Girls and Women*, contained rules for a modified, less strenuous version of baseball with shorter basepaths and a smaller outfield.[59] In 1927 the National Committee on Women's Athletics adopted these rules as the official baseball that girls and women would play.[60]

Nonetheless, women throughout the 1920s and into the '30s continued to play the same version of baseball that men played. In Chicago, Madame H. Caldwell assembled a predominately Black Bloomer team, declaring, "Our women are voting now, so why not be able to play a real game of baseball?"[61] The team traveled to Michigan and other close states, charging 25 cents per ticket to watch them play teams of all genders, races, and ages. Margaret Nabel's New York Bloomer Girls consistently fielded a team from 1913–1933, drawing crowds large enough for players to earn between five and twenty dollars per game from 1926–1929, although they never made more than thirty-five dollars per week.[62] Nabel particularly relished the opportunity to play other women's teams, traveling all over the east coast of Canada and America to play factory teams and other semiprofessional barnstorming teams. As star player and the first woman MLB scout Edith Houghton put it, the joy of playing baseball for these women "was never the money."[63]

In 1931, following an exhibition game between the minor league Chattanooga Lookouts and the New York Yankees in which seventeen-year-old Jackie Mitchell struck out Lou Gehrig and Babe Ruth, MLB Commissioner Landis voided Mitchell's contract and banned her from major and minor league baseball, declaring the game "too strenuous" for women to play.[64] The advent of the farm system in 1930, through which major league clubs assumed ownership of minor league clubs, further precluded women from playing professional baseball as they could no longer offer their services to individual teams without the consent of the major leagues.[65] Devoid of paths to playing in major or minor league baseball and in the throes of the Great Depression, women's professional baseball collapsed. Citing the steep financial costs associated with providing women players their own dressing rooms and hotel rooms, many communities barred women from professional and semiprofessional baseball.[66] The final assault against the Bloomer Girls era came in 1939 when the newly formed Little League Baseball organization unofficially banned girls from participating, almost entirely cutting off their access to the sport.[67]

Ladies' Days and the Suffrage Movement

As women began making their mark on the field in professional baseball in the late 1800s, they also sought to exert their influence in the stands. In order to increase attendance, Major League Baseball began advertising to women in the 1880s with Ladies' Day promotions, wherein women accompanied by a man received discounted or free tickets to a designated Ladies' Day game. Now with the opportunity to attend games, women did so with such vigor that *The Washington Sunday Herald* asserted in 1891, just three years after the first Ladies' Day, that "it is now fashionable for ladies to make up a party and go without the usual male escort."[68] Moreover, women's attendance at games was applauded for its civic function, which Pittsburgh Athletics owner J. Earl Wagner described as providing "a higher and more dignified tone to the sport."[69] While many accounts of Ladies' Day belittled the women fans, claiming they only attended to watch good-looking players, it quickly became undeniable that women simply loved baseball as much as men and were capable of being the same caliber of fan.[70]

Indeed, women's presence at baseball games became so notable that it was the subject of a 1908 song, "Take Me Out to the Ball Game." The song opens with a description of one woman's eagerness to watch baseball:

> Katie Casey was baseball mad,
> Had the fever and had it bad.
> Just to root for the home town crew
> Ev'ry sou
> Katie blew.
> On a Saturday her young beau
> Called to see if she'd like to go
> To see a show, but Miss Kate said "No,
> I'll tell you what you can do."

The song was instantaneously popular, becoming the number one song in the country for seven weeks. In addition to demonstrating women's love for baseball, the lyrics foreshadow the relationship between baseball and women's suffrage as they were based on the life of Trixie Friganza, a famous actor and suffragist who was having an affair with Jack Norworth, the song's writer. Although it was not played at a ballgame until the 1930s, the song's popularity indicates women's love for baseball and refusal to be barred from it.

As the women's suffrage movement gained traction in 1900 with the strengthening of the National American Woman Association through appealing to women in all classes (though not all races—many white suffragists sought white male approval by arguing their votes would counter Black ones, while Black suffragists touted a far more racially inclusive platform), the National League outlawed Ladies' Day. Men utilized numerous publications to craft an image of female fans as both dangerous and insincere; not only did they obtain nothing from their visits to the park, they ruined the experience for the serious male fans in attendance.[71] When the ban became official in 1909, the NL claimed it was due to the fact that women no longer required a special day to attend games as they had become full-fledged fans. This ban came on the heels of the American Association's failed ban the year prior, which was enacted unilaterally by league President Joseph O'Brien after no owner agreed to it. Though the less-established American League continued to profit from and therefore hold Ladies' Days, this ban drove away scores of female fans who no longer felt welcome at ballparks.[72]

This desertion lasted only a handful of years, though, as women once again turned their heads toward gaining the vote and thought to use baseball as a means to drum up support for women's enfranchisement. In 1911 Helene Hathaway Britton inherited ownership of the St. Louis Cardinals from her father and uncle, becoming the first woman MLB owner in history. One of her first acts of business was to reinstate Ladies' Day, stating that "my whole outlook has been broadened and my enjoyment of life multiplied manifold" since becoming involved with baseball, and she hoped to do the same for other women.[73] She criticized women for spending "too much time in the home" and argued it would be good for them to "have their blood stirred up once in a while."[74] This "New Woman" outlook of Britton's extended to the issue of suffrage, where her passive support of it saw her labeled by newspapers as a "militant suffragette."[75] The men who had long been stewards of the game believed Britton's ownership of a professional team to be as equally absurd and dangerous as the women's suffrage movement, and the linking of the two sought to demonize both endeavors.

Although Britton loved being involved in baseball, the constant pushback she faced from her male counterparts, combined with her failing marriage, forced her to sell the team in 1917 to an ownership group that brought Branch Rickey on board.[76] Her team had moderate success under her ownership, finishing third in the NL in 1914, but coming in last place the majority of the remaining seasons. The team had fared even more poorly in the final years under her father and uncle, though, and so her six years as owner proved that a woman could be no worse than a man at the job. Nonetheless, it took twenty-two years for another woman to become team owner, this time Grace Comiskey with the Chicago White Sox, who also inherited the team from her father.

Over the same timespan as Britton's ownership, women throughout the country latched onto the relationship between baseball and suffrage that had been pointed out by her detractors. They initially did so by advertising women's suffrage in the ballpark without attending the games themselves. In 1912 the Oregon Equal Suffrage League placed a large sign next to the local ballpark in Eugene, reading "Votes for Women—Next November." It is estimated that over one million people saw the banner in the run up to the vote's passage and subsequent enfranchisement of white women throughout the state.[77] Likewise, a few women's suffrage organizations in New York placed large billboards outside local ballparks advertising women's suffrage where several thousand men would see them over the course of the 1913 season.[78] This passive equating of women's suffrage and baseball acted as a test of men's willingness to cede the space to women before women suffragists entered the ballpark themselves.

On May 18, 1915, Polo Grounds, home of the New York Giants, hosted the first the first of fourteen "Suffrage Day" games played across America between 1915 and 1919. To make the link between women's enfranchisement and baseball as alluring and memorable as possible, the ballpark was festooned with banners and ribbons urging the players and fans in attendance to vote for women's suffrage in the state that following November. In the months prior, anti-suffrage movements had increased their presence throughout the country, also using baseball as a medium to relay their message about the impropriety of women's involvement in politics.[79] Sponsored by the state's Votes for Women Baseball Committee, suffragettes sold over 8,000 individual tickets and 125 boxes, filling the stadium with men whose votes they wanted to earn and women suffragettes and baseball fans who would try to persuade them.[80] Although the players themselves were against suffrage, the event was so successful that the suffragettes were invited back the following year for another Suffrage Day, this time sponsored by the club.[81] New York did not pass women's suffrage until 1917, but the success of Suffrage Day led to other suffrage groups throughout the country using baseball as a vehicle for achieving women's rights.

The May 18 game was followed by a July 7 Suffrage Day game in Philadelphia against the Giants, for which suffragists sold thousands of tickets. Then, on September 16, the Pirates held a Suffrage Day game, also against the Giants. As part of this game, the suffragists pledged to give $5 to any Pirates player who scored a run, which was four players to the Giants' eight. Present at all of these games was a mapping of baseball jargon onto women's suffrage. Slogans like "Make a Home Run for Suffrage!" and "Be a 'Good Sport,' Vote 'Yes' for the Woman's Suffrage Amendment" were printed onto signs and pamphlets distributed to those in attendance. The aim of these slogans was to "counter such basic fears about woman suffrage's effect on social order and personal identity" by latching onto "familiar symbolism, non-threatening rhetoric, and arguments more subtle than rational debate."[82] In essence, baseball was such a part of national consciousness that affixing women's suffrage to its language offered the potential for support for women's suffrage to be a subconscious emotional response tied to men's appreciation for the game.

The most direct example of the success suffragists had in using baseball to promote their cause occurred in Tennessee. In 1915 the Tennessee General Assembly passed a constitutional amendment granting white women a partial right to vote in presidential and municipal elections, but the amendment still needed to be ratified by Tennessee voters. To drum up support, the Nashville Equal Suffrage League partnered with Clyde Shropshire, a member of the state House and owner of the Nashville Vols baseball team. On July 23, the team threw a Suffrage Day, adorning the stadium with a banner that read "Votes for Women. You believe in fair play. You've had your innings—we want ours. Score a home run for equal suffrage."[83] As with the Giants, the game was a roaring success, spawning future Suffrage Days throughout Tennessee in which women grew to participate more and more in the actual game, sometimes playing their own game beforehand and other times presenting prizes to fans and players (such as "handsomest player" and "ugliest player") during half-innings.[84] These events won over players, turning them into "confirmed suffragettes," as one newspaper put it, and the endorsement of professional players went a long way to changing the minds of baseball fans and writers over the ensuing five years it took to grant women the right to vote.[85]

As America became drawn into World War I, the war effort overshadowed the suffrage movement, and Suffrage Days were replaced with Red Cross donation days. Nonetheless, these women demonstrated once again the special place baseball occupies in American society, suggesting that their participation in the sport is fundamental to their participation in society at large and their advancement toward full political equality. Though they were forced out of many jobs assumed during the war, their efforts piqued the interest of Chicago Cubs' President Bill Veeck, who saw them as an untapped market. In defiance of the 1909 ban, Veeck established the first Ladies' Day of the 1919 season on June 6. He assumed that drawing in women would enable entire families to attend games, creating a continuous stream of fans for decades to come. The promotions proved successful, as Chicago women on Ladies' Day outdrew a number of other teams' total season attendance.[86]

The tale from here on out is much the same as baseball's first foray into Ladies' Day: Other teams eventually clambered aboard the bandwagon, women faced male backlash, and Ladies' Day was eventually cancelled. But this time, the promotion lasted decades as a result of the need for female fans to maintain the sport during the Great Depression. Though several teams in the 1930s and 1940s welcomed female fans by holding baseball clinics at various points, the majority of advertising was steeped in sexism and consumerism. Most ads focused on the female fan in relation to her male relatives, suggested a particularly handsome player to lure in women, or offered a free beauty product, like stockings and lipstick. Even those ads that acknowledged the adeptness of female fans did so condescendingly, voicing surprise "pretty young things" could be so manly.[87] Moreover, as Jean Hastings Ardell points out, MLB Commissioner Landis used the existence of women fans to further justify segregation: white women mingling with Black players might produce mixed-race children, which would be unacceptable.[88] Although women as spectators helped secure themselves the vote, it did not free them from the whims of male baseball fans and executives, who once again saw them purely as a means of securing their own economic and social interests.

The All-American Girls' Professional Baseball League

While the Great Depression saw women sidelined from baseball, World War II afforded them the chance to once again participate in the national pastime. When Major League Baseball lost scores of players to the war effort in the 1940s, Cubs owner Philip K. Wrigley sought to fill the entertainment and economic void by creating the first women's professional baseball league, the All-American Girls' Professional Baseball League (AAGPBL). The league, initially consisting of four teams, selected fifteen white women apiece from over six hundred who had attended tryouts at Wrigley Field. Cognizant of society's history of preventing women from paying baseball, the league's owners sought to ensure its success by molding its players into women who could be seen as role models. Thus, the players were not only tested on their baseball skills but also on their ability to appear feminine.[89]

When the players signed their contracts, they gave their teams the right to regulate their behavior on and off the field. Players were not allowed to participate in "male" activities such as drinking, smoking, and staying out late, and at no point were they allowed to wear shorts or pants or go without makeup. In essence, no player could appear to be "manly" or a lesbian. Their off-field image was meant to model their on-field one, which consisted of them wearing uniforms consisting of skirts and knee-length socks, designed to be feminine without being sexual in any way. As league secretary Maxine Keenan put it, "We do not want our uniforms to stress sex, but they should be feminine, with emphasis on the clean American sports girl."[90]

For the most part, the women accepted the dress code and etiquette lessons as something that needed to be done in order for them to do what they loved. Faye Dancer, fielder for the Fort Wayne Daisies, said that the players knew they were more than just athletes: "We had a product to sell, women's baseball, and we did sell it. We were in competition with women's softball, which was well organized in the Midwest. A lot of softball women were very mannish, had men's haircuts, and dressed like men."[91] As the league progressed, the players realized that so long as they maintained their public image of the moral, feminine "All-American girl," they could act how they pleased privately. Women began to wear pants on bus rides and in hotels, as they did not have to actually *be* ladies, but rather *look like* ladies. In this aspect, at least, the republican concern for civic virtue was used as a tool by both the owners and the players to further their liberal pursuits of individual glory and moneymaking.

While this combination of legitimate skill and marketing ploy benefited white players to various degrees, it was used to prevent Black women from joining the league. One Black woman, Toni Stone, wrote to the executives of the Chicago Colleens in 1948 requesting a tryout but never heard back from them. In 1951 AAGPPL declared during its postseason board meeting that any Black woman wishing to join the league would have to display "exceptional ability," a barrier that white women repeatedly faced in their individual efforts to join men's professional teams.[92] Moreover, the stereotyping of Black women as both manly and hypersexual conflicted with the league's image of white feminine innocence.[93] Signing Black women would challenge the racial and gender hierarchies embedded within professional baseball at a time when the reinforcement of these hierarchies was thought to be crucial for the perpetuation of America's values and political institutions.

Shut out from women's baseball, Stone worked her way through the semiprofessional ranks, first with the San Francisco Sea Lions of the short-lived West Coast Negro Baseball Association and then with the

New Orleans Creoles.[94] While with the Creoles, she caught the eye of Syd Pollock, owner of the Negro Leagues Indianapolis Clowns, who signed her to a contract for the 1953 season. Unlike the women of the AAGPBL, Stone convinced Pollock to allow her to wear pants instead of a skirt. While Pollock promoted her image based on gender at least as much as on her playing ability, she became an inspiration to many Black girls and women who desired to become professional baseball players. She was soon joined by two of these women, Mamie "Peanut" Johnson and Connie Morgan, the former of whom had also been turned away from the AAGPBL.[95] While the hiring of these three women was often described as a last-ditch marketing stunt by the Negro Leagues to stave off the NL's inevitable death, the opportunity to play meant a great deal to them and the scores of Black women who attended their games.[96]

While Stone was making her way through semiprofessional baseball, the AAGPBL executives capitalized on the white "All-American girl" to forge new relationships between baseball and the community. In response to Commissioner Landis asking whether he intended baseball to continue during the war, President Roosevelt stated in the affirmative:

> I honestly feel that it would be best for the country to keep baseball going. Baseball provides a recreation which does not last over two hours or two hours and a half, and which can be got for very little cost . . . If 300 teams use 5,000 or 6,000 players, these players are a definite recreational asset to at least 20,000,000 of their fellow citizens – and that in my judgment is totally worthwhile.[97]

As the MLB seasons during the war comprised fewer games and many minor league teams shut down, AAGPBL teams stepped up to fill this civic engagement void. Indeed, Wrigley had strategically chosen smaller industrial cities like Rockford and South Bend that would appreciate the distraction from the war effort provided by these teams.[98] The entire league began as a nonprofit, with each city contributing $20,000 to the team and Wrigley and his investors contributing the rest. Each team's profit was designed to fund various projects in each city, such as the creation and maintenance of parks.[99]

To accommodate work schedules, games were occasionally played at night, with lights installed in stadiums for the first time. Furthermore, exhibition games were played near military bases and veteran hospitals in order to cement the league's patriotic reputation and involve veterans in the community. The league sought to be as accessible as possible to everyone in each community, drawing in both middle-class and poor people and providing entertainment for the whole family through playing games and partnering with local orchestras and bands to throw free musical events.[100]

However, after Wrigley (who never attended an AAGPBL game) became once again too occupied by men's baseball, he sold the league to a management corporation that turned it into a for-profit enterprise. This shift was initially imperceptible as teams continued to draw large numbers of fans: After expanding to eight teams in 1946, the league drew upwards of 800,000 fans, almost doubling the previous year's attendance number.[101] Marketing during this time shifted from the league as a whole to individual players, emphasizing not the patriotism inherent in the league but instead the ways the league has improved these players' lives. For instance, in 1948 over a dozen articles were written about Kenosha Comets' outfielder Audrey "Doc" Wagner, who was able to use her salary to fund her medical school expenses.[102]

Nonetheless, the rise of television and the emphasis on the nuclear family—with the wife as homemaker—that emerged during the 1950s led to a sharp decline in attendance for the AAGPBL, just as it had for minor league baseball and the Negro Leagues. The management corporation sold the league to individual cities, decentralizing it and leaving ill-equipped local executives to market individual teams on their own. As a result, national coverage of the league dwindled and the viability of women as professional baseball players slipped from the national consciousness, replaced by a return to the "traditional" idea of the woman based on her domesticity.[103] The league folded in 1954 after every single team reported a financial loss.

In its twelve years of existence, the league offered its players a sense of legitimacy and independence, as well as the opportunity to demonstrate to the country that they could equal men even in one of society's most sacrosanct elements. They were willing to accept all of Wrigley's character stipulations so long as they were provided the opportunity to do what they loved: play baseball. Not every player received high praise, but the play of some caught the eye of even the most discerning critics. For instance, Dorothy "Dotty" Kamenshek, first baseman for the Rockford Peaches, was called "the fanciest fielding first baseman I've ever seen, man or woman" by former all-star first baseman for the Yankees, Wally Pipp.[104] Kamenshek was offered a minor league contract after the

AAGPBL folded, but she did not take it because she did not want to be reduced to a spectacle. Although she did not continue her baseball career, Kamenshek spoke favorably of the AAGPBL's role in preparing her for a variety of potential careers: The league "gave a lot of us the courage to go on to professional careers at a time when women didn't do things like that."[105]

Most of the players were from poor and working-class families, and their time in the league afforded them some degree of social mobility. Throughout the league's twelve-year existence, weekly salaries ranged from $50–$125, far more than many trade jobs paid men at the time.[106] This money allowed upward of 35 percent of the players to earn college degrees and 14 percent to earn graduate degrees, a significant increase form the national average of 8.2 percent and 0.8 percent respectively.[107] This financial independence enabled these women to forego marriage during a time in which marriage rates were on the rise, affording them a great deal of independence while placing them in opposition to societal norms.

Far more valuable than the economic benefits, however, was the enduring strength of the community created by these women who shared this remarkable experience of playing professional baseball. Immediately after the league folded, most players returned to their lives and lost touch with one another, but by the 1980s the league had become an area of scholarship, and efforts to piece together its history reconnected the women. Since then, the players created a newsletter, *Touching Bases*, in which recipients are notified of players' needs for financial assistance, opportunities to attend public events, and the naming of public parks and schools after various players.[108] Maybelle Blair, pitcher for the Peoria Redwings in 1948, summarized the importance of baseball's community-building as she watched young girls take the field in a 2015 Baseball For All event: "This right here is the most important thing to come out of the league. Maybe, just maybe, our real legacy is them. Not what we did on the field in those years we played, but this. We helped build this."[109]

Women's Baseball Post-AAGPBL

Over two decades after Landis informally banned women from professional baseball, in 1952 the new commissioner, Ford C. Frick, made the unofficial ban on women official after Eleanor Engle signed with the minor league Harrisburg Senators, hoping to become the first woman since Lizzie Arlington to play professionally with and against men. Minor League Baseball President George Trautman immediately voided her contract and put out a joint statement with Frick, declaring that "it is just not in the best interest of baseball that such travesties be tolerated."[110] This ban, coupled with the end of the AAGPBL, led to a decline in girls and women's participation in the sport. Still, women never disappeared entirely from baseball.

Unwilling to witness women's professional baseball die out, former Rockford Peaches coach Bill Allington assembled two barnstorming teams, called Allington's All-Stars. Between 1955 and 1958, these teams played one hundred games across the country, offering a select few women the opportunity to prolong their careers. Although conditions were tough and crowd sizes dwindled by 1958, the women looked back favorably upon these years. Pitcher Jeneane Lesko summarized her experience in a poem:

> We stick together not for money alone
> For we can all get jobs if we return home.
> But, we love the game and deep down inside
> There's a glowing warmth and a heartfelt pride
> There may be no trophy for winning the game
> But the pressure's there just the same.
> We must make the catch or hit the long drive
> For these are the things on which we thrive.
> So we'll travel around from pillar to post
> Go without sleep and live on toast.
> For our love of the game, we'll give our best,
> After the season, then we'll rest.[111]

For these women, money was not the reason they played baseball. Rather, they played it because they loved it and it gave them a sense of community and a joint feeling of pride that extended to future generations of women baseball players.

After the passage of Title IX in 1972, a number of women and girls sued the National Association of Baseball Leagues and Little League Baseball on the basis of gender discrimination.[112] The cases largely focused on whether baseball is considered a contact sport and therefore outside of the purview of Title IX, as well as whether allowing girls would prohibit Little League from fulfilling its charter promise to instill in boys "citizenship, sportsmanship, and manhood." Opponents of allowing girls to play Little League baseball relied on many absurd arguments, such as the possibility of girls getting breast cancer if they get tagged in the chest or the violation of privacy that would occur if a coach needed to check them for injuries.[113] After the courts ruled in favor of the girls, one girls' baseball advocate likened the backlash to that of *Roe v. Wade*, as thousands of Little League teams refused to play with or against girls.[114] Due to this backlash, some parents refused to allow their girls to play baseball for fear of them being intentionally injured.[115] In 1973, while the lawsuits were making their way through the courts, parents in Rhode Island created a girls' baseball league called the Slaterettes, in which over one hundred girls participated, demonstrating that girls will play baseball if provided the opportunity. Finally in 1978, Little League Baseball ended its ban on girls, and although girls continued to be funneled into softball, the door was theoretically ajar for women to play professional baseball.

In 1984 former Atlanta Braves executive Bob Hope attempted to use minor league expansion to establish a women's team as part of the Class-A Florida State League (FSL). He viewed this potential team as essential for women who want to play in the majors: "In baseball a woman will never make it to the big leagues if she has to depend on her own tenacity. 'Hey I want to try out for the boys team.' The pressure is on her as an individual in an awkward situation."[116] As such, he wanted the team to give women "a legitimate chance to play and be comfortable in baseball. No gimmickry."[117] Henry Aaron—who in 1977 declared that "there is no logical reason" women should not play professional baseball because "baseball is not a game of strength . . . The game needs a special kind of talent, thinking and timing . . . a ball going 90 miles an hour can be knocked over the fence by anyone sticking a bat out and making perfect contact"—served as the team's VP.[118] Sixty women tried out for the team, and scouts rated the six of them who had played baseball rather than softball growing up as immediately ready to play, but the FSL refused to take the team seriously. League executives initially proposed a sixty-game half schedule consisting entirely of exhibition games before ultimately awarding the expansion team to a team from Tennessee. Hope, who had once said he was "90 percent certain" the Sun Sox would be admitted, called the decision to exclude women once again from professional baseball "a vote for tradition" and "a meaningful human rights issue."[119]

The tryouts, which took place at Georgia Tech, were heavily covered by the media and attracted the opinion of major and minor league executives and players, many of whom belittled the women. Miami Marlins third baseman Dave Dunlap declared, "Men are just better as a whole . . . I'd look at the women like they were just somebody trying to take bread out of my mouth."[120] Barry Foote, manager of the Class-A Fort Lauderdale Yankees, said that if the team was admitted, he would "knock 'em on their butt every chance I'd get to see if they're man enough to play a man's game." Minor league pitcher Mark Rexrode concurred, stating he would try "twice as hard to get them out . . . you don't want to get hit or beat by a girl."[121] Despite Aaron's characterization of baseball, people once again clung to it as not simply a sport but as a means of enforcing strict gender roles. The question of skill was superseded by a focus of "aesthetics and role identity" that attributed the correct functioning of society to the entrenchment of physical and mental distinctions between men and women.

In 1993, capitalizing on the 1992 release of *A League of Their Own*, Hope tried once again to establish a professional women's team, this time succeeding in fielding a team from 1994 to 1997. This team, the Colorado Silver Bullets, received a $2.6 million sponsorship deal from Coors, who hoped to sell more beer to women. The team was an independent member of the AA Short Season Northern League, playing fifty games against minor league, semiprofessional, and college teams, for a salary of $20,000 per player, much more than other minor leaguers made. Over eighteen hundred women, most of whom had been forced to become softball players once they aged out of Little League, tried out for the twenty-four available roster spots. The team lost its inaugural game against the Northern League All-Stars 19–0, and finished its first season with a 6–38 record, which manager Phil Niekro attributed to the players' lack of experience, stating "if these players had the training that men had," some of them would already be in the minors or majors.[122] In 1997, the team's final year of existence, it posted a winning record, 23–22, playing against semiprofessional teams, but it was not enough to draw in crowds large enough to finance the team once Coors pulled its sponsorship due to fears of being known as a "women's beer."[123]

Illustrating the difficultly of being a woman baseball player, the team's first baseman, Julie Croteau, spoke of what the team meant to her. Summarizing the barriers she faced in high school and college, from outright discrimination to the more subtle sexism of "locker-room speak," Croteau felt she had "spent more time fighting and being emotionally destroyed by baseball" than enjoying playing the game.[124] Although she was forced to retire in 1995 after injuring her shoulder, her time with the Silver Bullets helped her become "comfortable with who I am" and gave her the opportunity to become the first woman to coach a men's Division I team after UMass Amherst hired her in 1996.[125] The existence of the Silver Bullets also prompted more people to question the designation of softball as a baseball-equivalent sport and advocate for greater access to baseball for girls and women. Yet, the twentieth century ended with zero professional women's teams.

For Ila Borders, a minor league pitcher from 1997–2000 who was the first woman to start and win an integrated men's professional game, the story was much the same. She loved baseball, as she wrote in her autobiography, but "the stress of having to prove myself game by game, season by season, had worn me down. The game was no longer fun."[126] These accounts reveal both the damage done to the players and the relative futility of their sacrifices when the burden of solving systemic gender discrimination is placed on the individual.

Conclusion: Toward Gender Neutrality

Women's participation in baseball provided them with opportunities for civic participation outside of the domestic sphere and economic freedom through earning salaries independent of their fathers or husbands. These gains were not achieved easily, however, and so the history of women's baseball is also an account of the continuous reinforcement of societal gender norms. Thus, baseball in its "purest" form breaks down gender stereotypes by being a sport anyone can play, regardless of size and strength. But the exclusion of women from men's professional baseball highlights the centrality of gender divisions and the subservience of women to white men, as well as the use of white femininity to further America's political project of the subjugation of Black people. This analysis of women's baseball, then, demonstrates the faulty assumptions embedded within the liberal-republican foundations of society and the difficulty in achieving gender equality in a society in which the economic and political structures necessitate gender inequality.

Furthermore, when the goal of women in baseball is merely to break into the male world of baseball, women's participation will always be limited and at the whim of the odd wealthy man willing to experiment with them for a brief moment. Instead, it is perhaps time to imagine a new approach to baseball, no longer beholden to the American founding myth of manliness that routinely reinforces gender distinctions and therefore the inferiority of women. Rather, what may be necessary for liberating both women and the sport from these patriarchal foundations is reconceiving it as a genderless sport in which everyone might participate at all levels, thereby finally orienting baseball toward a genuine conception of civic virtue that takes into account the whole of American society.

Conclusion

> It seems to me that through baseball I came to understand and experience patriotism in its tender and humane aspects, lyrical rather than martial or righteous in spirit, and without the reek of saintly zeal, a patriotism that could not quite so easily be sloganized, or contained in a high-sounding formula to which one had to pledge something vague but all-encompassing called one's "allegiance."
>
> —Philip Roth

The professionalization of baseball in the late 1800s entangled the sport in fundamental questions of property rights, citizenship, and the public good that emerged from liberal and republican theories of government. A. G. Spalding positioned professional baseball as the antidote to the moral ills of the Gilded Age's rapid industrialization and creation of the working class. As such, professional baseball became a medium through which American society debated the civic role that people marginalized by class, race, and gender should occupy, conversations that were restrained by society's need to uphold myths of the American founding. Those in charge of professional baseball argued that the sport was a means of inculcating civic virtue in the ever-expanding working class, fostering racial unity and bringing about the end of the Jim Crow era, and re-entrenching gender roles based on masculinity and femininity. Their project of linking baseball with American values helped ingrain in American society a conception of liberalism and republicanism that defines civic virtue in terms of consumerism, simultaneously reducing morality to individual economic participation and granting moral superiority to the actions of monopolies like Major League Baseball. Those who wanted to gain greater freedoms through their participation in baseball were stuck within this liberal-republican framework in which their civic participation was tied to their economic output; if Black teams, women's teams, and individual Black and women players did not sell enough tickets, they were understood to be unworthy of existing.

By the end of the twentieth century, major league players had obtained some degree of individual freedom of contract, but the expansion of MLB's antitrust exemption kept minor league wages stagnant and communities on the hook for the cost of stadiums, Black participation in professional baseball was steadily declining, and women were still banned from men's professional baseball. The question these failures bring to the forefront is whether it is possible for professional baseball to solve the economic, racial, and gender-based problems it has helped create. In other words, is it possible to separate baseball from liberal-republican consumerism and provide a different, real, community-oriented blueprint for American society? To begin to answer this question, we must turn to a brief discussion of baseball's position in the early twenty-first century.

The "Baseball as America" Exhibit

In March 2002 the National Baseball Hall of Fame and Museum launched a touring exhibition titled "Baseball as America," starting in New York's Museum of Natural History and concluding in Boston's Museum of Science in September 2008. The exhibit contained five hundred items, divided into seven sections: "Our National Spirit," "Ideals & Injustices," "Rooting for the Team," "Enterprise & Opportunity," "Sharing a Common Culture," "Invention & Ingenuity," and "Weaving Myths." Hall of Fame chairman Jane Forbes Clark stated of the exhibition, "In bringing this exhibition to people across the country, it is our hope that we can learn more about *ourselves as a people* with shared values, as reflected in our national game."[1] The press release for the exhibition hinted at these shared values, declaring that "one can glimpse our entrepreneurial spirit, our values and self-image, and the tensions and triumphs of embracing diverse traditions while forging a sense of community."[2] According to Professor Michael L. Butterworth, "the exhibition narrated a lesson in citizenship that spoke only to America's noblest purposes," those being its assumed commitment to democracy and justice.[3]

In conjunction with this exhibition, the Hall of Fame and Museum published a collection of short pieces that further explained each of the exhibition's seven sections. The explanations included historical documents and contemporary analyses from players and scholars. In the book's introduction, Jackie Robinson biographer Jules Tygiel provides a brief overview of the history of baseball, writing that the exhibition "reminds us at every turn of why, across the broad historic sweep of American experience, baseball maintains its hold on our imagination and reality and remains, above all other activities and institutions, our enduring national pastime."[4]

Both the exhibition and the book cover the Doubleday myth, Curt Flood, FDR's "green light" letter to Landis, Jackie Robinson, and the AAGPBL, as well as things like *Field of Dreams* and baseball cards. While the book provides more in-depth discussions of baseball's history, both aim to explain baseball as having "an enduring connection to the idea of America because it really is an extension of democracy."[5] Thus, both are designed to celebrate baseball rather than fully critique it. In his introduction to "Ideals & Injustices," Tygiel mentions the lack of women in professional baseball but argues that "if freedom implies an openness of opportunity unimpeded by artificial barriers or obstacles, baseball has achieved that ideal as well as any other American institution"[6] The overall sense is that the problems of baseball belonged to the twentieth century and that the twenty-first offers nothing but unencumbered possibility.

Much of this possibility is attributed to baseball's economic opportunities for players and fans. The exhibition and the book present baseball as "a beacon of social mobility" offered to impoverished Black and Latin American players.[7] They also argue that fans benefit from the corporatization and commercialization of baseball by receiving a more "diverse, immersive, and entertaining" ballpark experience.[8] Moreover, the "Sharing a Common Culture" section of the exhibition primarily discusses baseball's shaping of culture in terms of movies and television, like *The Natural* and *A League of Their Own*, as well as product advertisements for cereal, cars, and cigarettes. The biggest draw of this part of the exhibition is a Honus Wagner baseball card, supposedly the most valuable baseball card in existence, ironically because he halted its production after learning it would be used to sell tobacco.[9] This presentation of baseball reduces fans to consumers and systemic problems of poverty to individual actors. Baseball provides a means for individuals to escape poverty, but there is no mention of the causes of this poverty or the ways that professional baseball has exacerbated it.

One reviewer praised the exhibition for not stating "exactly how baseball has shaped our values or aspirations or exactly how it has helped us as a society grapple with social and economic issues" but instead providing "the right amount of suggestive text to make us ponder" the influence of baseball on American society.[10] Others have critiqued the exhibit as celebrating "capitalism in excess" and taking on a "triumphant" tone that presents the past as "something we feel superior to."[11] Butterworth concludes that the exhibition is a "resilient, yet incomplete and arrogant, reproduction of the imagined community in the United States."[12] Collectively, these reviews bring up the distinction between exploring the relationship between baseball and patriotism and exploiting this relationship, an important debate to be had given the exhibition's context: the aftermath of 9/11.

Baseball's Consumerist Response to 9/11

The United States' domestic response to the September 11 terrorist attacks made explicit the relationship among baseball, consumerism, and American patriotism that had developed throughout the twentieth century. The first mass public gathering post-9/11 was the Braves-Mets game on September 17, 2001, which immediately connected baseball with the recovery of a "sense of normalcy."[13] Then, most famously, President George W. Bush threw out the ceremonial first pitch before game three of the World Series on October 30 at Yankee Stadium, throwing a perfect strike while the crowd around him chanted "USA! USA!" Former New York Mayor Rudy Giuliani later remarked, "Something about [the World Series] games helped restore hope. They gave a sense of being able to come back against extreme odds— exactly the metaphor the city needed."[14] Alice M. Greenwald, president of the Hall of Fame and Museum, said baseball was used to bring out "that authentic sense of, 'We're in this together, we are one, this is one team. Yes, we play games against each other, but what really matters is the fabric of our society and who we are' . . . [baseball] does that better than anything else in our society. It just does it in ways that everybody can relate to."[15]

The Hall of Fame and Museum exhibition and companion book emphasized this link between baseball and nationalism. MLB Commissioner Bud Selig included a section titled "Baseball in a Time of Crisis," in which he discusses the role baseball has played in "the healing of our great nation." He refers to baseball as a "much-loved and much-needed social institution," the stoppage of which would have gone "against the ideals of our great nation."[16] The exhibition reinforced this connection by either beginning or ending with "Our National Spirit," depending on the participating museums' setup. This section included photographs of players in uniform during World War II but not the Vietnam War, videos of presidents throwing the first pitch at games, the playing of the national anthem, and an abundance of American flags.[17] This section of the exhibition, then, presents baseball and America as uniquely and uncomplicatedly good entities that combine to promote democracy at home and abroad.

Beyond this exhibition, the most striking example of baseball's connection to post-9/11 America is the Montreal Expos' relocation to Washington in 2005. From 1901–1960, the city had been home to the Washington Senators, a team that was almost routinely at the bottom of the league and played second fiddle to the Negro Leagues Homestead Grays, whose roster (including Josh Gibson and James "Cool Papa" Bell) won nine championships between 1938 and 1948. The news of the Expos' relocation to Washington, which hinged on the creation of an entirely publicly funded stadium, received immediate backlash from poor Black residents whose neighborhoods had long been underfunded. Many such residents—and a number of economists—critiqued the demonstrably false argument that the team would spark a complete economic revival of the 92 percent Black Anacostia neighborhood and pointed out that the government was willing to spend money on a baseball stadium while the neighborhood still lacked a hospital.[18] In late 2005 the district government invoked eminent domain to seize $84 million in property from sixteen businesses, ranging from art studios to trash transfer stations.[19] This move began the lengthy project of turning the entire area into a tourist-friendly destination by closing Black-owned businesses and community spaces and erecting new apartments, hotels, and shopping complexes in their place. While these changes appear to have positively transformed the neighborhood by reducing visible signs of poverty and crime and increasing residential income, they have priced out former Black residents in favor of catering to wealthier white business owners, residents, and tourists.[20]

Nonetheless, this false argument was parroted by avid baseball fan and former owner of the Texas Rangers, George W. Bush, who said of the relocation, "I also subscribe to the theory that a new ballpark will help lift up a neighborhood and provide a lot of entrepreneurial opportunities for people" and that "it's good for baseball to come back to the nation's capital."[21] The team's new stadium, completed in 2008, was an enormous success for everybody who understood American freedom to be synonymous with liberal consumerism. Post 9/11, President Bush urged Americans to show their lack of fear by going shopping and taking their families to Disney World.[22] With its numerous luxury boxes, restaurants, and food stands and the massive television screen in center field bombarding fans with advertisements, Nationals Park embodied this mentality.

The idea for the stadium was to "create 'neighborhoods' within [it]" that appealed to fans' differing tastes.[23] The stadium also features glass walls along South Capitol Street, designed to "offer a 'transparency' that reflects the nation's capital."[24] Washington's mayor at the time, Adrian Fenty, said that the construction project "represents the true greatness of Washington, D.C."[25] Sportswriter Thomas Boswell concurred, writing of the stadium, "A metropolitan area of nearly 6 million people that is not supposed to possess a 'sense of place' now has a park that epitomizes that very virtue, using its central location and panoramic views to unify the major threads in the region's complex fabric."[26] Yet the best seats were reserved for the wealthy and came with many exclusive perks: the ability to watch players take indoor batting practice, programs and notes for each game, and a free parking space right next to the stadium. The cheaper seats, though farther away from the field, were celebrated for having great views of the whole field, as well as the Capitol, a building in which poor DC residents have no representation. Thus, while the idea of unity is a noble one, the particular factors involved in the construction of Nationals Park have precluded it from achieving this goal in any tangible way.

The entire project of Nationals Park illustrates the association of civic virtue with consumerism. The stadium was not only seen as a good for the team, but as a good for DC and the country as a whole in the aftermath of 9/11. It brought the purity and simplicity of baseball to the nation's capital at a time when America required a strong national symbol, as had been the case during WWII and the Cold War. In ignoring the concerns of the neighborhood's Black residents, MLB, the team's owners, and the municipal government reduced civic participation to consumerism, as fans were encouraged to demonstrate their patriotism and unity through purchasing tickets and concessions at the games.

The Future of Baseball

The baseball mythology that began with Spalding linking Abner Doubleday and the invention of baseball to the Civil War has expanded to present the history of professional baseball as one of progression toward the constitutional aims of liberty and equality. The problem is that the founding era did not contain a singular theory of liberty and equality and was instead characterized by a division among several strands of liberalism and republicanism that sometimes blended together and were other times completely contradictory. Theoretical conceptions of liberty and equality were further muddled by the practical problems of slavery, industrialization, and the family structure. What actually emerged from this era, then, was a general blended conception of liberalism and republicanism in which ownership of property determined civic participation and established the parameters of the public good, and civic virtue required the elimination of particular groups of people from the political sphere.

The naturally liberal and republican elements of baseball endeared the sport to all groups of people in America, from white aristocratic men to enslaved Black men, women, and children. It was a simple sport that could be played virtually anywhere and allowed individuals to show off their skills while building communal bonds. It is unsurprising, then, that it quickly became a way for businessmen and public figures to reach a wide and diverse audience with their political projects. The genuine love American people have had for baseball made it easy for these figures to present baseball as an antidote to whatever moral ills characterized the time, from labor unrest to segregation to women's rights. What emerged throughout the twentieth century, then, was the use of baseball as a moral arbiter and the association of those in charge of baseball with civic virtue. Professional baseball's owners were therefore able to portray their economic investment in their monopoly over baseball as the solution to social inequality. By the end of the twentieth century, Jacques Barzun's claim that "whoever wants to know the heart and mind of America had better learn baseball, the rules, and reality of the game" was undoubtedly correct.[27]

While this paints a bleak picture of baseball as inseparable from a political theory fundamentally incapable of producing liberty and equality, there is room for hope. Much of the monopolization of baseball is due to the mythologizing of the sport and the mythologizing of the American founding. The first step in rescuing baseball from this conundrum is to reveal these myths as myths and to explain their origin and purpose. Baseball scholarship has done a tremendous amount of work in breaking down the Doubleday myth, but baseball has nonetheless clung to it because it is part of an entire web of myths surrounding the sport. Addressing the Doubleday myth, then, must be part of a project that uncovers "the reality of the game" as being central to the development of a liberal-republican theory that links civic virtue and commercial capitalism. Through demythologizing baseball, fans and the general American public can begin to understand the ways in which their attempts at creating community paradoxically further liberal individualism.

Baseball, fundamentally, is a game concerned with communal experiences of joy and grief. It allowed Black men, Black women, and white women to carve out spaces for themselves in which they could, for a few hours a week, bond over a shared interest and shared life experiences when such opportunities were few and far between. It offers individual and communal triumphs along with long periods of anguish. It also offers the cautionary tale of attempting to divorce the good and the bad, of attempting to see only the good in the professionalization of the sport. If, on one hand, the history of baseball tells the story of corporate greed, it also tells the story of love of the game blossoming into love of the public good. It tells the story of individuals finding success through recognizing the political bonds of community. It is in this latter truth that we might be able to find the desire for a civic virtue that is not subservient to corporate capitalism.

It is up to us in the twenty-first century to decide the role we want baseball to play in our lives. We must determine whether we are content with our money subsidizing tax breaks for MLB's billionaire owners, with Jackie Robinson's image being used to paper over MLB's continued racism, with women players being barred from the sport's highest league. We must look at Major League Baseball for what it is—for how far it has strayed from the inherent joy of grabbing a bat, a ball, and a glove, and heading to the neighborhood ballpark to play until it is too dark to continue—and for what we want it to be. If, as Roger Angell says, baseball teaches us the importance of "caring deeply and passionately, really caring" about something, understanding all the ways that baseball affects our lives will allow us to extend this deep and passionate caring to a great number of people in a great number of communities.[28] In determining what baseball should be, then, we will learn what civic virtue really is and why we must choose it over corporate consumerism. The contents of this book have been but one step in this process that must occupy the whole life of a baseball fan.

Notes

INTRODUCTION

A. Bartlett Giamatti, interview with *The Hartford Courant*, April 15, 1984.

1. Thomas Gift and Andrew Miner, "DROPPING THE BALL: The Understudied Nexus of Sports and Politics," *World Affairs* 180, no. 1 (2017): 127–61.

2. Horace Traubel, *With Walt Whitman in Camden*, vol. 1 (Small, Maynard, 1906).

3. A. Bartlett Giamatti, *Take Time for Paradise: Americans and Their Games* (Bloomsbury, 2011), 93.

4. For a discussion of myth in baseball, see: Robert F. Lewis, *Smart Ball: Marketing the Myth and Managing the Reality of Major League Baseball* (University Press of Mississippi, 2010); Brian Martin, *Baseball's Creation Myth: Adam Ford, Abner Graves and the Cooperstown Story* (McFarland, 2013); Steven Riess, "Baseball Myths, Baseball Reality, and the Social Function of Baseball in the Progressive America," *Stadion* 3, no. 2 (1977): 273–311. For a discussion of myth in American politics, see: Richard T. Hughes, *Myths America Lives By: White Supremacy and the Stories That Give Us Meaning* (University of Illinois Press, 2018); Kevin M. Kruse and Julian E. Zeiler, *Myth America: Historians Take on the Biggest Legends and Lies About Our Past* (Basic Books, 2023).

5. Richard Slotkin, *A Great Disorder: National Myth and the Battle for America* (Belknap Press of Harvard University Press, 2024), 4.

6. Slotkin, *Great Disorder*, 8.

7. Steven J. Overman, *The Protestant Ethic and the Spirit of Sport: How Calvinism and Capitalism Shaped America's Games* (Mercer University Press, 2011).

8. Thomas David Bunting, *Democracy at the Ballpark: Sport, Spectatorship, and Politics* (State University of New York Press, 2021).

9. Paul Heike, *Myths That Made America: An Introduction to American Studies* (Transcript Verlag, 2014), 407.

CHAPTER 1

John Thorn, "Why Baseball: An American Eden of the Mind," *Our Game*, October 19, 2018, https://ourgame.mlblogs.com/why-baseball-8849e118519c.

1. John Thorn, *Baseball in the Garden of Eden: The Secret History of the Early Game* (Simon & Schuster, 2012), 11.

2. Jennifer Ring, *Stolen Bases: Why American Girls Don't Play Baseball* (University of Illinois Press, 2009), 81–82.

3. Jeffrey Orens, *Selling Baseball: How Superstars George Wright and Albert Spalding Impacted Sports in America* (Rowman & Littlefield, 2025).

4. Peter Levine, *A. G. Spalding and the Rise of Baseball, the Promise of American Sport* (Oxford University Press, 1985).

5. Albert Goodwill Spalding's Hall of Fame plaque (National Baseball Hall of Fame, 1939).

6. Thomas W. Zeiler, *Ambassadors in Pinstripes: The Spalding World Baseball Tour and the Birth of the American Empire* (Rowman & Littlefield, 2006), 22.

7. As part of the book's marketing, copies were sent to a variety of influential figures such as President Taft, Pope Pius X, and the crown prince of Sweden. Although none of these people provided a review of the book, it received glowing reviews from other sources and sold at least ninety thousand copies in the first six months of publication, with many more Americans reading it via excerpts printed in over two hundred newspapers. Levine, *A. G. Spalding and the Rise of Baseball*, 119–20. See also: *Birmingham News*, January 4, 1912, 10; *Boston Globe*, April 4, 1912, 7; *Daily Missoulian*, December 26, 1911, 8.

8. A. G. Spalding, *America's National Game: Historic Facts Concerning the Beginning, Evolution, Development and popularity of Base Ball* (American Sports Publishing Company, 1911), 3.

9. Spalding, *America's National Game*, 6.

10. Spalding, *America's National Game*.

11. Spalding, *America's National Game*, 9.

12. Mitchell Nathanson, *A People's History of Baseball* (University of Illinois Press, 2012), 2. Trinidadian historian and journalist C.L.R. James wrote an excellent account of cricket's use as an imperialist cultural tool in Trinidad and Tobago. See: Cyril Lionel Robert James, *Beyond a Boundary* (Duke University Press, 2013).

13. Kenneth Cohen, *They Will Have Their Game: Sporting Culture and the Making of the Early American Republic* (Cornell University Press, 2017).

14. David P. Sentance, *Cricket in America, 1710–2000* (McFarland, 2006), 6.

15. Sentance, *Cricket in America*, 8.

16. Sentance, 12.

17. Sentance, 8.

18. Indeed, this conception of cricket caught on enough such that in the 1789 Senate debates over the title Washington should hold as head of state, John Adams and Oliver Ellsworth—Connecticut senator and John Jay's successor as chief justice of the Supreme Court—rejected the House proposal of "President" on the grounds that it was too democratic as "even fire companies and cricket clubs" had presidents. Sentance, 9.

19. Sentance, 45.

20. Thorn, *Baseball in the Garden of Eden*, 54–64.

21. Rather than baseball skills, the admittance requirement for team membership was to be a "gentlemen of standing, wealth and intelligence, the very Corinthian column of the community." The club thus consisted solely of the upper class and played only teams of equal social standing, eschewing the more physical New England town ball style of play for a leisurely approach in which the game came a distant second to socializing. Nathanson, *People's History*, 13.

22. *Porter's Spirit of the Times*, September 13, 1856, 28.

23. "How Baseball Began," *San Francisco Examiner*, November 27, 1887, 14.

24. *New York Daily Herald*, October 16, 1859, 1. *The New York Daily Herald* published its first paper in 1835 and by 1860 it circulated eighty-four thousand copies, making it the most widely read newspaper in America.

25. Jacob Morse, *Sphere and Ash: History of Base Ball* (Camden House, 1984); George B. Kirsch, *The Creation of American Team Sport: Baseball and Cricket, 1838–1872* (University of Illinois Press, 1989); Gunthar Barth, *City People: The Rise of Modern City Culture in Nineteenth-Century America* (Oxford University Press, 1980).

26. Spalding, *America's National Game*, 30–37.

27. His belief that children "delight in the exploitation of ownership" is akin to Locke's discussion of dominion in *Some Thoughts Concerning Education*, in which he claims that children from a very early age demonstrate a natural desire to dominate others. Locke offers two solutions to this problem of dominion. Firstly, this natural desire must be channeled into physical education, namely working the land so as to hold dominion over it instead of over people. Secondly, children must be encouraged to share by being taught that sharing always amounts to possessing more and then by being put into competition with one another to see who can share the most. John Locke, *Some Thoughts Concerning Education*, ed. Ruth W. Grant and Nathan Tarcov (Hackett, 1996), 81–83.

28. Virginia Declaration of Rights, 1776, Art 1. See also: Pennsylvania, 1776, Art. 1; Vermont, 1777, Art. 1; Massachusetts, 1780, Art. 1; New Hampshire, 1784, Art. 2; Delaware, 1792, Preamble.

29. Aristotle begins book 1 of his *Politics* with the statement that "man is by nature a political animal." Aristotle, *Aristotle's Politics*, trans. Carnes Lord (University of Chicago Press, 2013).

30. Oscar Handlin and Mary Handlin, eds., *The Popular Sources of Political Authority: Documents on the Massachusetts Constitution of 1780* (Harvard University Press, 1966), 444.

31. Carli N. Conklin, *The Pursuit of Happiness in the Founding Era: An Intellectual History* (University of Missouri Press, 2019), 107–9.

32. Dr. Robert N. McMurry, head of the Chicago office of the Psychological Corporation, used similar reasoning in 1938 when he declared that baseball would keep the United States out of World War II. Unlike in America, where man can hash out their differences on the ballfield, "in Central Europe, they have no sports compared to baseball, no harmless emotional safety valves for the people of their countries.

As a result, many of them take out their aggressions in politics." *Bakersfield Californian*, October 4, 1938, 18.

33. Spalding, *America's National Game*, 533.

34. A. G. Spalding, *Spalding's Official Base Ball Guide* (A. G. Spalding & Bros., 1889), 9.

35. The working-class subjects of this moral panic were most frequently European immigrants and Black people, adding racist components to this class antagonism. Nicola Beisel, "Class, Culture, and Campaigns Against Vice in Three American Cities, 1872–1892," *American Sociological Review* 55, no. 1 (1990): 44–62; W. Jett Lauck and Edgar Sydenstricker, *Conditions of Labor in American Industries* (Funk & Wagnall, 1917); Marcy Sacks, "'To Be a Man and Not a Lackey': Black Men, Work, and the Construction of Manhood in Gilded Age New York City," *American Studies* 45, no. 1 (2004): 39–63.

36. Spalding, *America's National Game*, 5.

37. Spalding, *America's National Game*, 9.

38. Spalding, *America's National Game*, 5.

39. Spalding, *America's National Game*,10.

40. Spalding, *America's National Game*, 11.

41. Spalding, *America's National Game*, 561.

42. Spalding, *America's National Game*, 10.

43. Spalding, *America's National Game*, 13.

44. Spalding, *America's National Game*, 542.

45. Previously, the only way to record a strike was a swing and miss, so batters could wait for good pitches at which to swing. This rule frequently led to losing teams prolonging at-bats by refusing to swing at pitches until it became too dark to play, thus preventing the game from reaching its conclusion.

46. Spalding, *America's National Game*, 408.

47. Spalding, *America's National Game*, 406.

48. Theodore A. McKee, "Judges as Umpires," *Hofstra Law Review* 35, no. 4 (2007): 1709.

49. As a potential solution to this problem, MLB has been testing robo-umpires in the minor leagues. Zach Helfand, "Invasion of the Robot Umpires," *New Yorker*, August 23, 2021, https://www.newyorker.com/magazine/2021/08/30/invasion-of-the-robot-umpires.

50. Paul Finkelman, "Baseball and the Rule of Law," *Cleveland State Law Review*, 46, no. 2 (1998): 240. For more from Finkelman on baseball and American laws, see: Paul Finkelman, "Baseball Is a Civics Education," *Atlantic*, October 24, 2019.

51. Finkelman, "Baseball and the Rule of Law," 243.

52. Spalding, *America's National Game*, 534.

53. Spalding, *America's National Game*, 534.

54. Spalding, *America's National Game*, 536–37.

55. Michael Kimmel, *The History of Men: Essays on the History of American and British Masculinities* (State University of New York Press, 2005), 67.

56. Michel-Guillaume Jean de Crèvecœur, *Letters from an American Farmer; and, Sketches of Eighteenth-Century America*, ed. Albert E. Stone (Penguin Books, 1981), 70.

57. In their poem "The Rising Glory of America," Philip Freneau and Hugh Henry Brackenridge describe America as a new and perhaps perpetual Garden of Eden: "No dangerous tree with deadly fruit shall grow / No tempting serpent to allure the soul / From native innocence. A *Canaan* here, / Another *Canaan* shall excel the old." Philip Freneau and Hugh Henry Brackenridge, "A Poem on the Rising Glory of America," in *The Poems of Philip Freneau*, ed. Fred Lewis Pattee (University Library, C.S. Robinson & Co. University Press, 1902), 82. See also: Richard Hofstadter, *The American Political Tradition and the Men Who Made It* (Knopf, 1951); James L. Machor, "The Garden City in America: Crevecoeur's Letters and the Urban-Pastoral Context," *American Studies*, 23, no. 1 (1982): 69–83; Henry Nash Smith, *Virgin Land: The American West as Symbol and Myth* (Harvard University Press, 2007); and Paul Heike, *The Myths That Made America: An Introduction to American Studies* (Transcript Verlag, 2014), 317–20. For Jefferson's quotation, see Thomas Jefferson, *Notes on the State of Virginia*, ed. William Peden (1954), xxi.

58. Thomas Jefferson to John Jay, August 23, 1785, in *The Papers of Thomas Jefferson*, vol. 8, ed. James P. McLure, (Princeton University Press, 2019), 427.

59. The strongest of Jefferson's critiques of industrialization comes from a letter written to James Madison in 1787. In it, Jefferson writes, "I think our governments will remain virtuous for many centuries; as long as they are chiefly agricultural; and this will be as long as there shall be vacant lands in any part of America. When they get piled upon one another in large cities, as in Europe, they will become corrupt as in Europe." Thomas Jefferson, "From Thomas Jefferson to James Madison, 20 December 1787," in *The Papers of Thomas Jefferson*, vol. 12, *7 August 1787–31 March 1788*, ed. Julian P. Boyd (Princeton University Press, 1955), 438–43.

60. Christopher Michael Curtis, *Jefferson's Freeholders and the Politics of Ownership in the Old Dominion* (Cambridge University Press, 2012), 8.

61. For more on Jefferson's conception of agrarianism and pastoralism in relation to republicanism, see: Alley M. Jordan, *Virgil in Virginia: Eighteenth-century Pastoralism and the Novus Ordo Seculorum* (University of San Diego Press, 2016).

62. Frederick Jackson Turner, *The Significance of the Frontier in American History* (Penguin Books, 2008), 22.

63. Turner, *Significance of the Frontier*, 3.

64. Turner, 261.

65. Richard Slotkin, "Nostalgia and Progress: Theodore Roosevelt's Myth of the Frontier," *American Quarterly* 33, no. 5 (1981): 612.

66. Lawrence Buell, "Pastoral Ideology Reappraised," *American Literary History* 1, no. 1 (1989): 2.

67. J.G.A. Pocock, *The Machiavellian Moment: Florentine Thought and the Atlantic Republican Tradition* (Princeton University Press, 2016), 539.

68. Richard Hofstadter, *The Age of Reform: From Bryan to F.D.R* (Knopf Doubleday, 1955), 23.

69. Henry Chadwick, "Baseball in the South," *Outing: An Illustrated Monthly Magazine of Recreation* 12, no. 6 (1888): 538.

70. Allen Guttmann, *Essays on Sport History and Sport Mythology* (University of Texas at Arlington Press, 1990), 57; "Voices from the Stands," *Civil War Times Illustrated*, May 1998, 33; Isaac Johnston, "Baseball in the Masculine Age: Sport and Popular Media as a Means of Revolution," *Ezra's Archives* 8, no. 1 (2018): 63–78.

71. Christopher H. Evans, "The Kingdom of Baseball in America: The Chronicle of an American Theology," in *Faith of 50 Million: Baseball, Religion and American Culture*, ed. Christopher H. Evans and William R. Herzog II (Westminster John Knox, 2002), 38.

72. Robert F. Lewis, *Smart Ball: Marketing the Myth and Managing the Reality of Major League Baseball* (University of Mississippi Press, 2010), 23; and Kimmel, *History of Men*, 61–77.

73. Steven M. Gelber, "Working at Playing: The Culture of the Workplace and the Rise of Baseball," *Journal of Social History* 16, no. 4 (1983): 6–7.

74. Kevin Baker, "At the Park," *Creative Nonfiction*, no. 34 (2008): 8–20.

75. George Grella, "Baseball and the American Dream," *Massachusetts Review* 16, no. 3 (1975): 550–67.

76. David McGimpsey, *Imagining Baseball: America's Pastime and Popular Culture* (Indiana University Press, 2000), 66.

77. "Archeology of Baseball," *New York Sun*, May 2, 1905.

78. *Reading Times*, June 7, 1907, 1.

79. Andrew J. Schiff, *"The Father of Baseball": A Biography of Henry Chadwick* (McFarland, 2008), 205.

80. Spalding, *America's National Game*, 25.

81. Spalding, *America's National Game*, 7.

82. Spalding, *America's National Game*, 367.

83. Spalding, *America's National Game*, 92–93.

84. George B. Kirsch, "The War's Legacy," in *Baseball in Blue and Gray: The National Pastime During the Civil War* (Princeton University Press, 2003), 113–30.

85. *Chicago Inter Ocean*, March 29, 1908. This connection may have been made because William Henry Harrison once proposed marriage to—and was rejected by—Hannah Cooper, sister of James Fenimore Cooper and daughter of Congressman William Cooper, who founded Cooperstown. Rosemarie Zagarri, *Revolutionary Backlash: Women and Politics in the Early American Republic* (University of Pennsylvania Press, 2007), 89.

86. *Wichita Eagle*, April 4, 1909.

87. Kenesaw Mountain Landis, "Address at the Dedication Ceremony for the National Baseball Hall of Fame & Museum," June 12, 1939, https://www.americanrhetoric.com/speeches/kenesawlandisbaseballcentennialceremony.htm.

88. David Vaught, "Abner Doubleday, Marc Bloch, and the Cultural Significance of Baseball in Rural America," *Agricultural History* 85, no. 1 (2011): 4–5.

89. Lewis, *Smart Ball*, 11.

90. Craig Calcaterra, "Shocker: Bud Selig Believes That Which Has Been Thoroughly Debunked," *NBC Sports*, November 8, 2010.

CHAPTER 2

Roger Angell, *Five Seasons: A Baseball Companion* (Open Road Media, 2013).

1. R. Terry Furst, *Early Professional Baseball and the Sporting Press: Shaping the Image of the Game* (McFarland, 2014), 94.

2. Gordon S. Wood, *The Radicalism of the American Revolution* (Alfred A. Knopf, 1992), 269.

3. For scholarship articulating the liberal argument, see: Louis Hartz, *The Liberal Tradition in America: An Interpretation of American Political Thought Since the Revolution* (Harcourt, Brace, 1955); John McGowan, *American Liberalism: An Interpretation for Our Time* (University of North Carolina Press, 2007); Helena Rosenblatt, *The Lost History of Liberalism: From Ancient Rome to the Twenty-First Century* (Princeton University Press, 2020); Rogers M. Smith, *Civic Ideals: Conflicting Visions of Citizenship in U.S. History* (Yale University Press, 1999). For scholarship on the liberal-republican position, see: Gregory S. Alexander, *Commodity and Propriety: Competing Visions of Property in American Legal Thought, 1776–1970* (University of Chicago Press, 2008); Clement Fatovic, *America's Founding and the Struggle over Economic Inequality* (University Press of Kansas, 2015); Drew R. McCoy, *The Elusive Republic: Political Economy in Jeffersonian America* (University of North Carolina Press, 2012); Joseph Postell, "Regulation During the American Founding: Achieving Liberalism and Republicanism," *American Political Thought* 5, no. 1 (2016): 80–108; Carroll Smith-Rosenburg, "Fusions and Confusions," in *This Violent Empire: The Birth of an American National Identity* (University of North Carolina Press, 2010), 55–87; Clement Fatovic, *America's Founding and the Struggle over Economic Inequality* (University Press of Kansas, 2015); Drew R. McCoy, *The Elusive Republic: Political Economy in Jeffersonian America* (University of North Carolina Press, 2012); Joseph Postell, "Regulation During the American Founding: Achieving Liberalism and Republicanism," *American Political Thought* 5, no. 1 (2016): 80–108; Carroll Smith-Rosenburg, "Fusions and Confusions," in *This Violent Empire: The Birth of an American National Identity* (University of North Carolina Press, 2010), 55–87.

4. John Locke, "Of Property," in *Two Treatises of Government*, ed. Lee Ward (Hackett, 2016), 135.

5. C. B. Macpherson, "Locke on Capitalist Appropriation," *Western Political Quarterly* 4, no. 4 (1951): 550–66.

6. Alexander Hamilton, *The Papers of Alexander Hamilton*, vol. 4, *January 1787–May 1788*, ed. Harold C. Syrett (Columbia University Press, 1962), 219.

7. John R. Nelson, *Liberty and Property: Political Economy and Policymaking in the New Nation, 1789–1812* (Johns Hopkins University Press, 1987), 26.

8. "Alexander Hamilton's Final Version of the Report on the Subject of Manufactures, [5 December 1791]," *The Papers of Alexander Hamilton*, vol. 10, *December 1791–January 1792*, ed. Harold C. Syrett (Columbia University Press, 1966), 242.

9. Nelson, *Liberty and Property*, 29–30. See also: John Ferling, *Jefferson and Hamilton: The Rivalry That Forged a Nation* (Bloomsbury, 2014); Carey Roberts, "Alexander Hamilton and the 1790s Economy: A Reappraisal," in *The Many Faces of Alexander Hamilton: The Life and Legacy of America's Most Elusive Founding Father*, ed. Douglas Ambrose and Robert W. T. Martin (NYU Press, 2006), 211–30; Robert E. Wright and David J. Cowen, *Financial Founding Fathers: The Men Who Made America Rich* (University of Chicago Press, 2006).

10. "John Adams to James Sullivan, 26 May 1776," *The Adams Papers*, vol. 4, *February–August 1776*, ed. Robert J. Taylor (Harvard University Press, 1979), 208–13.

11. Mark Struges, "Enclosing the Commons: Thomas Jefferson, Agrarian Independence, and Early American Land Policy, 1774–1789," *Virginia Magazine of History and Biography* 119, no. 1 (2011): 42–74.

12. Thomas Jefferson, *Notes on the State of Virginia* (Wells and Lilly, 1966), 183. For a longer discussion of Jefferson's linking of agrarianism with virtue, see: Dean Caivano, "The Question of Sharing: Thomas Jefferson and the Idea of Communal Property,"*Histories* 1, no. 3 (2021): 85–99.

13. Thomas Jefferson, "Autobiography," in *The Writings of Thomas Jefferson*, ed. Paul Leicester Ford (G. P. Putnam's Sons, 1892), vol. 1, 49, 68.

14. Fatovic, *America's Founding*, 251.

15. Fatovic, 253.

16. William Manning, *The Key of Liberty* (Manning Association, 1922), 14.

17. Manning, *Key of Liberty*, 61.

18. Alex Gourevitch, "William Manning and the Political Theory of the Dependent Classes," *Modern Intellectual History* 9, no. 2 (2012): 331–60.

19. Andrea Tone, "The Politics of Labor Reform," in *The Business of Benevolence: Industrial Paternalism in Progressive America* (Cornell University Press, 1997), 25–26.

20. Pamela Grundy and Benjamin G. Rader, *American Sports: From the Age of Folk Games to the Age of Televised Sports* (Taylor and Francis, 2016), 61; "Prospect Park and Its Varied Opportunities," *Brooklyn Daily Eagle*, March 28, 1886, 8; Scott Cline, "'To Foster Honorable Pastimes': Baseball as a Civic Endeavor in 1880s Seattle," *Pacific Northwest Quarterly* 87, no. 4 (1996): 171–79; Debra A. Shattuck, "1865–1879: Contesting a National Pastime: The Amateur Game," in *Bloomer Girls: Women Baseball Pioneers* (University of Illinois Press, 2017), 27–61.

21. Warren Jay Goldstein, *Playing for Keeps: A History of Early Baseball* (Cornell University Press, 2014), 26.

22. Bryan Di Salvatore, *A Clever Base-Ballist: The Life and Times of John Montgomery Ward* (Pantheon Books, 1999), 85–87.

23. David Q. Voigt, *American Baseball* (Pennsylvania State University Press, 1983), 69–73.

24. Michael Haupert, "William Hulbert and the Birth of the National League," *Baseball Research Journal* 44, no. 1 (2015): 83–92; Glenn Moore, "Ideology on the Sportspage: Newspapers, Baseball, and Ideological Conflict in the Gilded Age," *Journal of Sport History* 23, no. 3 (1996): 228–55.

25. "The Diamond Squared," *Chicago Tribune*, February 4, 1876, 5.

26. For instance, Boston's pitcher Tommy Bond, despite being the best pitcher in the league in 1878 and 1879, saw his salary drop from $2,200 to $1,500 for the 1880 season. Dorothy Seymour Mills and Harold Seymour, *Baseball: The Early Years* (Oxford University Press, 1989), 116.

27. "Owners justified these moves": Michael Haupert, "Major League Baseball's Salary Leaders, 1874–2012," *Business of Baseball Research Committee Newsletter*, Fall 2012; "when the general working population": Krister Swanson, *Baseball's Power Shift: How the Players Union, the Fans, and the Media Changed American Sports Culture* (University of Nebraska Press, 2016), 7.

28. Benjamin G. Rader, *Baseball: A History of America's Game* (University of Illinois Press, 2018), 43.

29. Michael N. Danielson, *Home Team: Professional Sports and the American Metropolis* (Princeton University Press, 2021), 92.

30. *The Sporting Life*, December 12, 1883, 2.

31. Swanson, *Baseball's Power Shift*, 10.

32. Harold Seymour, *Baseball: The Early Years* (Oxford University Press, 1960), 164.

33. Edward T. O'Donnell, *Henry George and the Crisis of Inequality: Progress and Poverty in the Gilded Age* (Columbia University Press, 2015).

34. Tim McNeese, *The Labor Movement: Unionizing America* (Facts on File, 2007), 76–77.

35. J. R. Sovereign, *Preamble and Declaration of Principles of the Knights of Labor* (Knights of Labor, 1890).

36. Seymour, *Baseball*, 164.

37. *Chicago Tribune*, April 19, 1885, 11.

38. Robert B. Ross, *The Great Baseball Revolt: The Rise and Fall of the 1890 Players League* (University of Nebraska Press, 2016), 30.

39. Moore, "Ideology on the Sportspage," 235. When McCormick refused to play for his new team, the Pittsburgh Alleghenys, they locked him in the reserve clause, effectively ending his career. "No Ball for McCormick," *Boston Globe*, March 30, 1888, 3.

40. For instance, *The Cincinnati Enquirer* wrote in 1879 that "the Buffalo agreement is acknowledged already to be a gigantic wrong and a flat failure" (November 24, 1879, 5), and when the reserve clause was reaffirmed in 1880, *The Buffalo Morning Express* declared that "the baseball slavery act once more became a reality" (October 7, 1880, 1). In 1884 *The Cincinnati Enquirer* again issued a scathing critique of the reserve clause as "the sacrifice of all honorable and business practices"

(*Cincinnati Enquirer*, February 24, 1884, 10). Also in 1884, *The St. Louis Critic* called it "the white slave rule" (*St. Louis Critic*, February 22, 1884, 3).

41. John Montgomery Ward, "Is the Base Ball Player a Chattel?" *Lippincott's Monthly Magazine: A Popular Journal of General Literature, Science and Politics* 40 (1887): 312–13.

42. Ward, "Is the Base Ball Player a Chattel," 317.

43. Ward, "Is the Base Ball Player a Chattel," 319.

44. John Montgomery Ward, "Notes of a Base-Ballist," *Lippincott's Monthly Magazine: A Popular Journal of General Literature, Science, and Politics* (J. B. Lippincott, 1886), 217.

45. *New York Times*, November 6, 1887, 3.

46. *Chicago Tribune*, November 25, 1888, 10.

47. Di Salvatore, *Clever Base-Ballist*, 145.

48. A. G. Spalding, *America's National Game: Historic Facts Concerning the Beginning, Evolution, Development and Popularity of Base Ball* (American Sports Publishing Company, 1911), 273.

49. Spalding, *America's National Game*, 272.

50. "In Hostile Territory," *Sporting Life*, November 13, 1889.

51. Ross, *Great Baseball Revolt*, 74.

52. "How It Started," *Sporting Life*, November 6, 1889. Johnson was joined by Edwin McAlpin, a tobacco manufacturer and former general in the New York National Guard; Wendell Goodwin, a Brooklyn-based realtor; Arthur "Hi Hi" Dixwell, furniture store owner and son of a wealthy banker; and Cornelius Van Cott, New York postmaster and former New York state senator. Ross, *Great Baseball Revolt*, 76–77.

53. Ross, 78.

54. Charles C. Alexander, *Turbulent Seasons: Baseball in 1890–1891* (Southern Methodist University Press, 2011), 30–31.

55. Spalding, *America's National Game*, 198.

56. Moore, "Ideology on the Sportspage," 244.

57. *New York Clipper*, November 23, 1889, 5.

58. James R. Devine, "Baseball's Labor Wars in Historical Context: The 1919 Chicago White Sox as a Case-Study in Owner-Player Relations," *Marquette Sports Law Review* 5, no. 1 (1994): 20–21.

59. P. J. Carlino, "Bleacher Bugs and Fifty-Centers: The Social Stratification of Baseball Fans Through Stadium Design, 1880–1920," *Buildings and Landscapes: Journal of the Vernacular Architecture Forum* 28, no. 1 (2021): 7–8. The NL Boston Braves advertised their new stadium in 1888 as containing pavilion seating that no "patron of the outside seats" could "by any subterfuge" obtain. *Boston Globe*, September 16, 1887, 5.

60. Dean A. Sullivan, "Faces in the Crowd: A Statistical Portrait of Baseball Spectators in Cincinnati, 1886–1888," *Journal of Sport History* 17, no. 3 (1990): 354–65.

61. Sullivan, "Faces in the Crowd," 362.

62. *Buffalo Commercial*, March 8, 1884.

63. Robert P. Gelzheiser, *Labor and Capital in 19th Century Baseball* (McFarland, 2006), 75.

64. Moore, "Ideology on the Sportspage," 242.

65. Moore, 243; "Sympathy from Organized Labor," *Sporting Life*, December 18, 1889.

66. "To Aid the Brotherhood," *New York Times*, November 5, 1889, 8.

67. "In Hostile Array," *Sporting Life*, November 13, 1889; Swanson, *Baseball's Power Shift*, 25.

68. Swanson, 108–10.

69. *Philadelphia Times*, May 1, 1890, 5.

70. Ross, *Great Baseball Revolt*, 184.

71. *New York Clipper*, November 8, 1890, 7.

72. Robert Twombly, "Cuds and Snipes: Labor at Chicago's Auditorium Building, 1887–1889," *Journal of American Studies* 31, no. 1 (1997): 79–101.

73. Swanson, *Baseball's Power Shift*, 52.

74. Swanson, 53.

75. Robert Obojski, *Bush League: A History of Minor League Baseball* (Macmillan, 1975).

76. William L. Letwin, "Congress and the Sherman Antitrust Law: 1887–1890," *University of Chicago Law Review* 23, no. 2 (1956): 221–58.

77. David T. Searls, "Trade or Commerce Among the Several States or with Foreign Nations," *Section of Antitrust Law* (1953): 58–59.

78. Clayton Antitrust Act of 1914, §6, 38 Stat. 731 (1914).

79. Since the 1890s, many newspapers and other publications referred to baseball as a trust. *Munsey's Magazine* declared, "The sport of baseball has become as closely knit a trust as has ever defied the Sherman Act." *The San Francisco Chronicle* remarked that the NL was among "the most highly perfected trusts in the country." After the collapse of the Players League in 1890, professional baseball was routinely called "nothing more or less than a baseball trust." See: *San Francisco Chronicle*, July 31, 1890, 2; *New York Times*, March 4, 1890, 3; *Pittsburgh Dispatch*, November 9, 1890, 16; *San Francisco Examiner*, March 4, 1890, 2; *Kansas City Gazette*, December 19, 1891, 4; *Salt Lake Tribune*, August 1, 1890, 1; *Chicago Tribune*, July 31, 1890, 6.

80. *New York Times*, April 11, 1914, 11.

81. Nathaniel Grow, *Baseball on Trial: The Origin of MLB's Antitrust Exemption* (University of Illinois Press, 2014), 65.

82. Grow, *Baseball on Trial*, 65.

83. Grow, 65.

84. Hanlon, player-manager for the Players' League's Pittsburgh Alleghenys, had experience combatting the reserve clause.

85. Quoted in Mitchell Nathanson, "Who Exempted Baseball, Anyway? The Curious Development of the Antitrust Exemption That Never Was," *Harvard Journal of Sports and Entertainment Law* 4, no. 1 (2013): 11.

86. Stuart Banner, *The Baseball Trust: A History of Baseball's Antitrust Exemption* (Oxford University Press, 2013), 69.

87. Banner, *Baseball Trust*, 72–73.

88. Federal Baseball Club v. National League, 259 U.S. 200 (1922).

89. Nathanson, "Who Exempted Baseball, Anyway?" 20.

90. In *Direct Marketing Association v. Brohl*, the 10th Circuit's Neil Gorsuch cited *Federal Baseball* in his concurrence, declaring it one of the "precedential islands [that] manage[s] to survive indefinitely even when surrounded by a sea of contrary law."

91. Robert F. Lewis, *Smart Ball: Marketing the Myth and Managing the Reality of Major League Baseball* (University of Mississippi Press, 2010), 50–51.

92. Kenneth C. Land, Walter R. Davis, and Judith R. Blau, "Organizing the Boys of Summer: The Evolution of U.S. Minor-League Baseball, 1883–1990," *American Journal of Sociology* 100, no. 3 (1994): 781–813.

93. G. Edward White, "The Enterprise, 1923–1953," in *Creating the National Pastime: Baseball Transforms Itself, 1903–1953* (Princeton University Press, 1996), 280.

94. *Minneapolis Star*, July 12, 2929, 24.

95. White, *Creating the National Pastime*, 284.

96. *Oshkosh Northwestern*, December 2, 1924, 12.

97. *Buffalo Times*, April 4, 1930, 30.

98. "Cheap Labor in South Is Fatal to Its Progress," *The President's Report to the Board of Regents for the Academic Year* (University of Michigan Press, 1929), 30. Excerpts from the report were published in Pennsylvania's *The Daily Notes* (May 6, 1930, pg. 2); *Fort Lauderdale News* (May 2, 1930, pg. 1); and *Oregon Labor Press* (June 27, 1930, pg. 2), among others.

99. *The Textile Worker: Official Journal of the United Textile Workers of America*, vols. 18–19 (United Textile Workers of America, 1930–31), 97–99.

100. Jacquelyn Dowd Hall, *Like a Family: The Making of a Southern Cotton Mill World* (University of North Carolina Press, 1987).

101. Edgar F. Wolfe, "The Benevolent Brotherhood of Baseball Bugs," *Literary Digest*, 1923.

102. Wolfe, "Benevolent Brotherhood."

103. Robert Elias, "The National Pastime Trade-Off: How Baseball Sells US Foreign Policy and the American Way," in *Mapping an Empire of American Sport: Expansion, Assimilation, Adaptation and Resistance*, ed. Mark Dyreson, J. A. Mangen, and Roberta Park (Routledge, 2013), 96.

104. James Edward Miller, *The Baseball Business: Pursuing Pennants and Profits in* Baltimore (UNC Press, 1990), 71.

105. Rather ironically, in 1937, Wisconsin Congressman Raymond Cannon, a former semiprofessional ballplayer, argued for a congressional inquiry into organized baseball's labor practices, declaring the professional ballplayer's "constitutional rights are flagrantly violated without recourse" and claiming it to be "a national problem" because "the whole country is affected by the activities" of organized baseball. His resolution did not gain much traction in Congress, but it did open up questions about Congress and the courts when it came to antitrust legislation. "Baseball Inquiry Is Urged on House," *New York Times*, May 5, 1937, 11.

106. "Club Asks Milwaukee to Pay for Braves Shift," *Boston Globe*, March 16, 1953, 10; "Playing the Game," *Wisconsin State Journal*, May 27, 1953, 23.

107. Ron Briley, "Danny Gardella and Baseball's Reserve Clause: A Working-Class Stiff Blacklisted in Cold War America," in *Sport and the Law: Historical and Cultural Intersections*, ed. Samuel O. Regalado and Sarah K. Fields (University of Arkansas Press, 2014), 70.

108. Banner, *Baseball Trust*, 99–104.

109. United States Congress, *Report* (US Government Printing Office, 1952), 8–10.

110. United States Congress, *Report*.

111. United States Congress, *Report*, 228–31.

112. Banner, *Baseball Trust*, 112.

113. Banner.

114. Banner, 113–14.

115. Banner, 120.

116. Toolson v. New York Yankees, Inc., 346 U.S. 356 (1953).

117. Radovich v. National Football League, 352 U.S. 445 (1957).

118. Michael Sokolow, *Bush League, Big City: The Brooklyn Cyclones, Staten Island Yankees, and the New York-Penn League* (State University of New York Press, 2023), 12.

119. James R. Walker and Robert V. Bellamy, *Center Field Shot: A History of Baseball on Television* (Bison Original, 2008), 107–9.

120. Rebecca S. Kraus, *Minor League Baseball: Community Building Through Hometown Sports* (Haworth Press, 2003), 92.

121. Steven Riess, *City Games: The Evolution of American Urban Society and the Rise of Sports* (University of Illinois Press, 1991).

122. Thomas S. Hines, "Housing, Baseball, and Creeping Socialism: 'The Battle of Chavez Ravine, Los Angeles, 1949–1959,'" *Journal of Urban History* 8, no. 2 (1982): 123–44.

123. Swanson, *Baseball's Power Shift*, 100–101.

124. Owners attempted to sabotage Miller's campaign by presenting him to players as a radical labor figure whose presence would ruin baseball. This tactic worked particularly well with the Los Angeles Angels, whose owner, Gene Autry, a television and radio owner, was a notorious opponent of Hollywood unions. As a result of Audry's propaganda campaign, the entire team voted against Miller. Swanson, 112–13.

125. John Florio and Ouisie Shapiro, *One Nation Under Baseball: How the 1960s Collided with the National Pastime* (University of Nebraska Press, 2017), 106.

126. Charles C. Alexander, *Our Game: An American Baseball Story* (Macmillan, 1991).

127. Florio and Shapiro, *One Nation Under Baseball*, 173.

128. Michael Lomax, "'Curt Flood Stood Up for Us': The Quest to Break down Racial Barriers and Structural Inequality in Major League Baseball," *Culture, Sport, Society* 6, no. 2–3 (2003): 44–70.

129. Florio and Shapiro, *One Nation Under Baseball*, 175.

130. David L. Snyder, "Anatomy of an Aberration: An Examination of the Attempts to Apply Antitrust Law to Major League Baseball Through *Flood v. Kuhn* (1972)", *DePaul Journal of Sports Law* 4, no. 2 (2008): 193–94.

131. Snyder, "Anatomy of an Aberration," 194.

132. Florio and Shapiro, *One Nation Under Baseball*, 179.

133. Abraham Iqbal Khan, *Curt Flood in the Media: Baseball, Race, and the Demise of the Activist Athlete* (University Press of Mississippi, 2012), 96.

134. Curt Flood and Carter Richard, *The Way It Is* (Trident Press, 1971), 16–17.

135. *New York Daily News*, February 4, 1970, 28.

136. *New York Times*, December 8, 1970, 43. See also: *Arizona Republic*, December 8,1971, 42; *Cincinnati Enquirer*, December 8, 1971, 47; *Decatur Herald*, December 12, 1971, 19; *Louisville Courier-Journal*, December 9, 1971, 2; *Salt Lake Tribune*, December 8, 1971, 25.

137. *Los Angeles Times*, April 4, 1971, 30. In his career, Murray was a fourteen-time recipient of the "America's Best Sportswriter" award.

138. Khan, *Curt Flood in the Media*, 100–106.

139. Robert F. Burk, *Marvin Miller, Baseball Revolutionary* (University of Illinois Press, 2015), 156.

140. Banner, *Baseball Trust*, 194.

141. Banner, 194.

142. Justice Lewis Powell recused himself from the case due to owning stock in Anheuser-Busch, the owner of the St. Louis Cardinals.

143. *Flood v. Kuhn*, 407 U.S. 258 (1972). Both White and Burger refused to join this part of the opinion due to its sentimentality and seeming irrelevance to the ruling. The only regret Blackmun had in including it, however, was that he accidentally omitted Giants' legend Mel Ott from his list of players. For the rest of his career, he kept a Mel Ott bat on his wall as a reminder. Banner, *Baseball Trust*, 209–10.

144. Flood v. Kuhn.

145. Burk, *Marvin Miller*, 168.

146. Swanson, *Baseball's Power Shift*, 221.

147. Burk, *Marvin Miller*, 180.

148. Burk, 230.

149. Voigt, *American Baseball*, 280.

150. *Boston Globe*, July 3, 1977, 8.

151. Arthur T. Johnson, "Professional Baseball at the Minor League Level: Considerations for Cities Large and Small," *State and Local Government Review* 22, no. 2 (1990): 90–96; William G. Colclough, Lawrence A. Daellenbach, and Keith R. Sherony, "Estimating the Economic Impact of a Minor League Baseball Stadium," *Managerial and Decision Economics* 15, no. 5 (1994): 497–502; John Charles Bradbury, Dennis Coates, and Brad R. Humphreys, "Public Policy Toward Professional Sports Stadiums: A Review," *Journal of Policy Analysis and Management* 43 (2024): 899–937.

152. Selig became acting commissioner in 1992 after the owners fired Commissioner Fay Vincent in response to his handling of 1990 CBA negotiations between

owners and players in which he dropped the salary cap to get players to promise not to strike. Jon Pessah, *The Game: Inside the Secret World of Major League Baseball's Power Brokers* (Little, Brown, 2016), 11–13.

153. From 1985–1989, MLB owners colluded to limit player salaries—and thereby reduce the amount of money paid to players who were no longer in the league by the end of their contracts—by agreeing to not offer contracts to free agents. After the MLBPA filed a grievance, arbitrators ruled the owners had to pay these players $280 million they had lost due to this collusion. For a fuller account of this collusion, see: Maury Brown, "1985–1988—Collusions I, II . . . and III (A Hard Lesson Learned)" in *The Big Book of Baseball Blunders*, ed. Rob Neyer (Simon and Schuster, 2006).

154. Ballpark attendance reached 56.9 million in 1991, a 3.1 percent increase over 1990 attendance. Andrew Zimbalist, *Baseball and Billions: A Probing Look Inside the Big Business of Our National Pastime* (HarperCollins, 1992), 49.

155. Pessah, *The Game*, 14–15.

156. Gerald W. Scully, "Player Salary Share and the Distribution of Player Earnings," *Managerial and Decision Economics* 25, no. 1 (2004): 77–86.

157. Paul D. Staudohar, "The Baseball Strike of 1994–95," *Monthly Labor Review* 120, no. 3 (1997): 21–27.

158. Staudohar, "Baseball Strike," 24.

159. Athelia Knight, "The Fans Go to Bat vs. Strike," Washington Post, August 18, 1994; Christopher R. Martin, "News for the Everyfan: The 1994–95 Baseball Strike," in *Framed!: Labor and the Corporate Media* (Cornell University Press, 2004), 147.

160. The first of these two quotes can be found in Martin, *Framed!* 142. For the second, see Rachel Alex, "Central Springfield Wins, 2–1," *Washington Post*, August 23, 1994.

161. Martin, *Framed!* 143.

162. Mark Maske, "CONGRESS TO ENTER BASEBALL DISPUTE," *Washington Post*, December 24, 1994.

163. Bill Clinton, "Message to the Congress Transmitting Proposed Legislation to Settle the Major League Baseball Labor Dispute," February 9, 1995.

164. John B. Lord, "Era of Unrest: The Strike of 1994 and the 1996 Collective Bargaining Agreement," in *Bill Giles and Baseball* (Temple University Press, 2014), 103.

165. Elaine Halchin, Justin Murray, Kathleen Ruane, and Jon Shimabukuro, "Congressional Responses to Selected Work Stoppages in Professional Sports," U.S. Library of Congress, Congressional Research Service, R40160 (2013), 22.

166. Halchin et al., 26.

167. Martin, *Framed!* 127.

168. Bush, who was friends with Fay Vincent, dreamed of becoming commissioner after Vincent was fired in 1992. He initially believed he had Selig's backing, but after it was made clear that Selig wanted the job for himself, Bush chose to run for governor of Texas. Pessah, *The Game*, 6–7.

169. Allan H. Selig, Thomas J. Ostertag, and Matthew J. Mitten, "Baseball's Antitrust Exemption for Franchise Decisions: Its Justifications and Antitrust Law Implications for Other Professional Leagues," *Wisconsin Law Review* 3 (2019): 433.

170. Peter Schmuck, "Milwaukee's Selig Plays Role of Villain and Hero Strike Three! Baseball Calls off the Season," *Baltimore Sun*, September 14, 1994.

171. Pessah, *The Game*, 74. After two failed votes, the Senate narrowly passed the bill by one vote. George Petak, the swing voter, was recalled seven months later, in April of 1996, after a local committee using the slogan "No More P-Tax" gathered an overwhelming number of signatures to initiate a vote. He was the first Wisconsin legislator in history to be recalled. In the fall of 1995, a poll found that 80 percent of Americans disapproved of using taxpayer funds on sports stadiums. "GOP Tax Lesson," *Wall Street Journal*, June 24, 1996.

172. Andrew Zimbalist, *In the Best Interests of Baseball?: The Revolutionary Reign of Bud Selig* (Wiley, 2006), 176.

173. Staudohar, "Baseball Strike," 26.

174. Jerold J. Duquette, *Regulating the National Pastime: Baseball and Antitrust* (Praeger, 1999), 114–17.

CHAPTER 3

Former MLB play-by-play commentator Ernie Harwell, "The Game for All America," *The Sporting News*, April 13, 1995

1. Frank Litsky, "Sam Lacy, 99, Sportswriter Who Fought Against Racism," *New York Times*, May 11, 2003.

2. John Adams, *The Political Writings of John Adams*, ed. George W. Carey (Regnery, 2000), 20; Patrick Henry, "Give Me Liberty or Give Me Death," speech to the Virginia convention, March 23, 1775.

3. Scholars defending the founders tend to argue that the tension between the Declaration of Independence and the Constitution is more superficial than practical, and the Constitution was ultimately designed to end slavery. See: Bernard Bailyn, *Faces of Revolution: Personalities and Themes in the Struggle for American Independence* (Knopf, 1990); Herbert J. Storing, "Slavery and the Moral Foundations of the American Republic" in *The Moral Foundations of the American Republic*, 3rd ed., ed. Robert H. Horwitz (University Press of Virginia, 1986), 313—32; Paul A. Rahe, *Republics Ancient and Modern* (University of North Carolina Press, 1992); Thomas G. West, *Political Theory of the American Founding: Natural Rights, Public Policy, and the Moral Conditions of Freedom* (Cambridge University Press, 2017). More critical accounts of the founders, such as Matthew Mason, argue that they viewed slavery as a necessary evil, while others posit that the Constitution was deliberately and completely a pro-slavery document. See: Mason, *Slavery and Politics in the Early American Republic* (University of North Carolina Press, 2006); Alan Gibson, *Understanding the Founding: The Crucial Questions*, 2nd ed. (University of Kansas Press, 2010); Paul Finkelman, *Slavery and the Founders: Race and Liberty in the Age of Jefferson* (M. E. Sharpe, 2014). Duncan J. MacLeod, *Slavery, Race, and the American Revolution* (Cambridge University Press, 1974); William W. Freehling, "The Founding Fathers and Slavery," *American Historical Review* 77 (1972): 81–93; Sean Wilentz, *No Property in Man: Slavery and Antislavery at the Nation's Founding* (Harvard University Press, 2018); Finkelman, *Slavery and the Founders.*

4. François Furstenberg, "Beyond Freedom and Slavery: Autonomy, Virtue, and Resistance in Early American Political Discourse," *Journal of American History* 89, no. 4 (2003): 1295–330.

5. Furstenberg, "Beyond Freedom and Slavery," 1301–2.

6. George Washington to Meschech Weare, et al., June 8, 1783, "Circular Letter of Farewell to Army," in *The Writings of George Washington from the Original Manuscript Sources, 1745–1799*, ed. John C. Fitzpatrick (39 vols., Washington, 1931–44), 484–85.

7. Furstenburg, "Beyond Freedom and Slavery," 1302.

8. Edward J. Larson, James Madison, and Michael P. Winship, *The Constitutional Convention: A Narrative History from the Notes of James Madison* (Random House, 2011), 89–92.

9. Gia Phan Hoang, "Bound by Law: Apprenticeship and the Culture of "Free" Labor," in *Bonds of Citizenship: Law and the Labors of Emancipation* (New York University Press, 2013), 24–62.

10. James Madison, *Notes on the Debates in the Federal Convention of 1787* (W. W. Norton, 1987), 259.

11. James Madison, "No. 54," in *The Federalist*, ed. George W. Carey and James McClellan (Liberty Fund, 2001), 282–86.

12. Bernard Romans, *A Concise Natural History of the East and West of Florida* (R. Aitken, 1776), 105–7.

13. After the American Revolution, six states fully abolished primogeniture and entail laws: Georgia (1777), North Carolina (1784), Virginia (1785), New York (1786), Kentucky (1796), and Mississippi (1812). The remaining states either restricted these laws or did not have them in the first place. See Paul Starr, "Aristocracy and Inherited Wealth," in *Entrenchment: Wealth, Power, and the Constitution of Democratic Societies*, 32–55 (Yale University Press, 2019), 51; and Claire Priest, "The End of Entail: Information, Institutions, and Slavery in the American Revolutionary Period," *Law and History Review* 33, no. 2 (2015): 277–319.

14. Lacy K. Ford, *Deliver Us from Evil: The Slavery Question in the Old South* (Oxford University Press, 2009).

15. Clive Webb and David Brown, "Slavery, Race, and the American Revolution," in *Race in the American South: From Slavery to Civil Rights* (Edinburgh University Press, 2007), 63–87.

16. Anthony Benezet, *The Complete Antislavery Writings of Anthony Benezet, 1754–1783: An Annotated Critical Edition*, ed. David L. Crosby (Louisiana State University Press, 2014), 71.

17. Paul J. Polgar, "'To Raise Them to an Equal Participation': Early National Abolitionism, Gradual Emancipation, and the Promise of African American Citizenship," *Journal of the Early Republic* 31, no. 2 (2011): 229–58.

18. Sidney Kaplan and Emma Nogrady Kaplan, *The Black Presence in the Era of the American Revolution* (University of Massachusetts Press, 1989), 26, 202; Loretta J. Williams, *Black Freemasonry and Middle-Class Realities* (University of Missouri Press, 1980), 12; and William Cooper Nell, *The Colored Patriots of the American Revolution: With Sketches of Several Distinguished Colored Persons: To Which Is*

Added a Brief Survey of the Condition and Prospects of Colored Americans (R. F. Wallcut, 1855), 47..

19. Prince Hall, "Petition of Prince Hall to the Massachusetts General Court, 27 February 1788," Massachusetts Historical Society, available at https://www.masshist.org/database/670.

20. Venture Smith, *A Narrative of the Life and Adventures of Venture, a Native of Africa: But Resident Above Sixty Years in the United States of America. Related by Himself* (Printed by C. Holt, at The Bee-office, 1798), 31.

21. Rio Bergh, "Blackness in the 'Grey Area': Representations of Virtuous Labor in Venture Smith's Narrative," *Early American Literature* 56, no. 2 (2021): 424.

22. Robert E. Desrochers, "'Not Fade Away': The Narrative of Venture Smith, an African American in the Early Republic," *Journal of American History* 84, no. 1 (1997): 40–66; and J. B. Stewart, *Venture Smith and the Business of Slavery and Freedom* (University of Massachusetts Press, 2010).

23. Lemuel Haynes, *Preacher to White America: The Collected Writings of Lemuel Haynes, 1774–1833* (Carlson, 1990), 81.

24. Haynes, *Preacher to White America*, 84.

25. Sergio Lussana, "To See Who Was Best on the Plantation: Enslaved Fighting Contests and Masculinity in the Antebellum Plantation South," *Journal of Southern History* 76, no 4 (2010): 2.

26. WPA Federal Writers Project, *Slave Narratives: A Folk History of Slavery in the United States from Interviews with Former Slaves*, vol. 16, *Texas, Part 2, Easter-King* (Library of Congress, 1941), 37.

27. The first documented instance of enslaved people playing town ball is from a 1773 memo from Beaufort, South Carolina: "We present as a growing Evil, the frequent assembling of Negroes in the Town on Sundays, and playing games of Trap-ball and Fives, which is not taken proper notice of by Magistrates, Constables, and other Parish Officers." Then, in 1797, the North Carolina *Minerva* reported a penalty of fifteen lashes to "negroes, that shall make a noise or assemble in a riotous manner in any of the streets [of Fayetteville] on the Sabbath day; or that may be seen playing ball on that day." See: WPA Federal Writers Project, *Texas, Part 2, Easter-King*, 37; WPA Federal Writers Project, *Slave Narratives: A Folk History of Slavery in the United States from Interviews with Former Slaves*, vol. 1, *Alabama, Aarons-Young* (Library of Congress, 1941), 28.

28. WPA Federal Writers Project, *Slave Narratives: A Folk History of Slavery in the United States from Interviews with Former Slaves*, vol. 3, *Florida, Anderson-Wilson* (Library of Congress, 1941), 134.

29. WPA Federal Writers Project, vol. 1, Alabama, *Aarons-Young*, 28.

30. WPA Federal Writers Project, *Slave Narratives: A Folk History of Slavery in the United States from Interviews with Former Slaves*, vol. 2, *Arkansas, Part 1, Abbott-Byrd* (Library of Congress, 1941), 40.

31. Lawrence D. Hogan, *The Forgotten History of African American Baseball* (Praeger, 2014), 16.

32. Robert B. Ross, *The Great Baseball Revolt: The Rise and Fall of the 1890 Players League* (University of Nebraska Press, 2016), 21.

33. *Memphis Public Ledger*, September 18, 1869, 1.

34. *Memphis Public Ledger*, July 23, 1877, 3.

35. James E. Brunson, *Black Baseball, 1858–1900: A Comprehensive Record of the Teams, Players, Managers, Owners and Umpires* (Jefferson, N: McFarland, 2019), 18.

36. Brunson, *Black Baseball*, 4.

37. Ryan A. Swanson, *When Baseball Went White: Reconstruction, Reconciliation, and Dreams of a National Pastime* (University of Nebraska Press, 2014), 46–47.

38. Du Bois found Philadelphia's segregation so severe that he dedicated an entire book, *The Philadelphia Negro*, to its causes and ramifications.

39. Octavius Catto, "Our Alma Mater: An Address," May 10, 1864 (C. Sherman, Son, & Co. Printers, 1864).

40. Catto, "Our Alma Mater."

41. "Reports and Minutes," *Papers of the Pythians Baseball Club, American Negro Historical Society Collection 1790–1905* (microfilm, American Historical Society of Pennsylvania, 1867), roll no. 7, frame no. 1116.

42. Swanson, *When Baseball Went White*, 55–56.

43. Swanson, 76.

44. *Wilkes' Spirit of the Times*, September 11, 1869, 55.

45. Jerrold Casway, "Octavius Catto and the Pythians of Philadelphia," *Pennsylvania Legacies* 7, no. 1 (2007): 5–9.

46. *Morning Post*, September 25, 1869, 4.

47. Swanson, *When Baseball Went White*, 119–22.

48. *New National Era*, October 19, 1871, 3.

49. *New National Era*, October 19, 1871, 3

50. Art Rust, *Newsweek* 75, no. 25 (1970): 109.

51. Robert F. Burk, *Never Just a Game: Players, Owners, and American Baseball to 1920* (University of North Carolina Press, 2001).

52. Richard White, "Baseball's John Fowler: The 1887 Season in Binghamton, New York," *Afro-Americans in New York Life and History* 16, no. 1 (1992): 7–17; Jules Tygiel, *Extra Bases: Reflections on Jackie Robinson, Race, and Baseball History* (University of Nebraska Press, 2002), 52–55.

53. Thomas Aiello, "A Case for the Negro Southern League," *Black Ball* 3, no. 2 (2010): 37–45.

54. *St. Louis Republic*, June 1, 1903.

55. *New Orleans Times-Democrat*, April 22, 1905.

56. *Atlanta Constitution*, April 3, 1912.

57. James R. Grossman, *Land of Hope: Chicago, Black Southerners, and the Great Migration* (University of Chicago Press, 1989).

58. In 1910 there was another attempt to create a Black baseball league, but it failed when the owners refused to allow only Black owners and their teams into the league. Over the next decade, Black baseball players were largely confined to

amateur teams or made members of the traveling All Nations team that played Black and white teams across the country.

59. Neil Lanctot, *Negro League Baseball: The Rise and Ruin of a Black Institution* (University of Pennsylvania Press 2008).

60. Roberta J. Newman et al., *Black Baseball, Black Business: Race Enterprise and the Fate of the Segregated Dollar* (University Press of Mississippi, 2014), 16.

61. Newman et al., *Black Baseball, Black Business*, 18.

62. Christopher Robert Reed, *The Rise of Chicago's Black Metropolis, 1920–1929* (University of Illinois Press, 2011), 28.

63. Newman et al., *Black Baseball, Black Business*, 34.

64. *Baltimore Afro-American*, April 11, 1924, 7.

65. *Pittsburgh Courier*, September 7, 1929, 4.

66. Lanctot, *Negro League Baseball*, 76.

67. Lanctot, 98.

68. Jackie Robinson and Alfred Duckett, *I Never Had It Made: An Autobiography of Jackie Robinson* (Harper Collins, 2013), 33.

69. Lanctot, *Negro League Baseball*, 105.

70. Lanctot, 127–28.

71. Lanctot, 189; Newman et al., *Black Baseball, Black Business*, 110.

72. Robert Fredrick Burk, *Much More Than a Game: Players, Owners, and American Baseball Since 1921* (University of North Carolina Press, 2001); Arthur William Mann, *Branch Rickey: American in Action* (Houghton Mifflin, 1957); Robert Kuhn McGregor, *A Calculus of Color: The Integration of Baseball's American League* (McFarland, 2015).

73. *New York Times*, April 14, 1949, 33.

74. In his biography of Branch Rickey, legendary *New York Daily News* columnist Jimmy Breslin wrote that the farm system "was modeled somewhat after the Southern system of slavery, but that was all right because it was baseball and the sport had its own quaint beliefs." Breslin, *Branch Rickey* (New York: Viking, 2011), 72.

75. Burk, *Much More Than a Game*, 63.

76. Burk, *Much More Than a Game*, 77.

77. Jules Tygiel, *Baseball's Great Experiment: Jackie Robinson and His Legacy* (Oxford University Press, 1997), 52.

78. Rickey was supposedly shaken by an incident he witnessed as a college baseball coach in which his sole Black player, Charles Thomas, frantically rubbed at his skin one day while crying out, "If only I could make [it] white!" After witnessing Thomas's despair, Rickey said he "vowed to do whatever I could to see that other Americans did not have to face [this] bitter humiliation," but Rickey also repeated often in his career that he never meant to "be a crusader." Chris Lamb, *Conspiracy of Silence: Sportswriters and the Long Campaign to Desegregate Baseball* (University of Nebraska Press, 2012), 86. For an account of the position of other owners on integration, see Burk, *Much More Than a Game*, 97–99.

79. Burk, *Much More Than a Game*, 84.

80. Lamb, *Conspiracy of Silence*, 84.

81. When asked if it would be possible to segregate players in areas other than on the field, Frick replied, "A ball club must be a unit. The only way a manager can develop team spirit is to keep his men together as much as possible, especially on the road. It would also mean that ball players who were not broadminded would take advantage of the situation and use it to further their own cause. It might go so far as to demoralize a winning team." Lamb, *Conspiracy of Silence*, 36.

82. Chris Lamb, "Baseball's Whitewash: Sportswriter Wendell Smith Exposes Major League Baseball's Big Lie," *Nine* 18, no. 1 (2009): 8.

83. Lamb, "Baseball's Whitewash," 10.

84. Breslin, *Branch Rickey*, 165.

85. After signing with the Montreal Royals, Robinson said, "If I make the [Dodgers], I will not forget that I am representing a whole race of people who are pulling for me." Echoing the weight of this signing, another Black sportswriter wrote that it would be "a step toward a broader spirit of democracy in baseball and will do much to promote a friendlier feeling between the races." Lamb, *Conspiracy of Silence*, 290.

86. Lamb, *Conspiracy of Silence*, 290–91.

87. Patrick Joseph Harrigan, *The Detroit Tigers: Club and Community, 1945–1995* (University of Toronto Press, 1997), 26.

88. Robinson and Duckett, *I Never Had It Made*, 33.

89. Laurie Collier Hillstrom, *Jackie Robinson and the Integration of Baseball* (Omnigraphics, 2001), 41.

90. Hillstrom, *Jackie Robinson and the Integration of Baseball*, 49.

91. Although they tried out Robinson, Hank Aaron, Willie Mays, and Ernie Banks, the Boston Red Sox were the last team to integrate, doing so only after be pressured by local newspapers and the general public. See: Mcgregor, *Calculus of Color*, 162–78.

92. Hillstrom, *Jackie Robinson and the Integration of Baseball*, 53.

93. The Report of the President's Committee on Civil Rights, "To Secure These Rights" (1947), https://www.trumanlibrary.gov/library/to-secure-these-rights.

94. Ira Glasser, "Branch Rickey and Jackie Robinson: Precursors to the Civil Rights Movement," in *World and I*, 18, no. 3 (2003): 257.

95. David Berman and Thomas R. Cole, *The Strange Demise of Jim Crow: How Houston Desegregated Its Public Accommodations, 1959–1963* (California Newsreel, 1998).

96. *Michigan Chronicle*, October 31, 1964, 4.

97. Whitney Young, "To Be Equal," *Michigan Chronicle*, November 21, 1964, 8.

98. "Improved Racial Climate Had Big Role in Getting Braves to Atlanta, Ga.," *Philadelphia Tribune*, April 26, 1964, 6.

99. One of very few people who demanded compensation from MLB teams was Newark Eagles Effa Manley, the only woman owner in the Negro Leagues. For more on Manley, see: Shakeia Taylor, "Effa Manley's Hidden Life," *SB Nation*, April 20, 2020, https://www.sbnation.com/2020/4/30/21238190/effa-manley-hall-of-fame-negro-league-newark-eagles.

100. Lanctot, *Negro League Baseball*, 357.

101. Newman et al., *Black Baseball, Black Business*, 176.

102. Lanctot, *Negro League Baseball*, 361–64.

103. Lanctot, 367.

104. Lanctot, 153.

105. Lanctot, 369–70.

106. Lanctot, 380.

107. Richard Ian Kimball, "Beyond the 'Great Experiment': Integrated Baseball Comes to Indianapolis," *Journal of Sports History* 26, no. 1 (199): 156.

108. Kimball, 158.

109. Newman, et al., *Black Baseball, Black Business*, 150–60.

110. Lanctot, *Negro League Baseball*, 394.

111. Jackie Robinson, "Acceptance Address at Special Luncheon Honoring Him on Presentation of 41st Spingarn Medal" (New York, December 8, 1956).

112. Hillstrom, *Jackie Robinson and the Integration of Baseball*, 79.

113. Hillstrom, 80–81. Robinson would ultimately regret this endorsement, not only because of Nixon's criminal activity but because Robinson became increasingly disillusioned with politicians in general after both Eisenhower and Kennedy refused to fully back the civil rights movement.

114. Jackie Robinson, *First Class Citizenship: The Civil Rights Letters of Jackie Robinson*, ed. Michael G. Long (Henry Holt, 2008), 225.

115. Robinson, *First Class Citizenship*, 207.

116. Robinson and Duckett, *I Never Had It Made*, 76.

117. Jackie Robinson, *Beyond Home Plate: Jackie Robinson on Life After Baseball*, ed. Michael G. Long (Syracuse University Press, 2013), 239.

118. Robinson, *Beyond Home Plate*, 67.

119. Malcolm X, "Open Letter to Jackie Robinson," *Amsterdam News*, November 30, 1963.

120. Robinson, *I Never Had It Made*, 85.

121. Robinson, *I Never Had It Made*, 166.

122. Brad Snyder, *A Well-Paid Slave: Curt Flood's Fight for Free Agency in Professional Sports* (Viking, 2006), 158–59.

123. Snyder, *Well-Paid Slave*, 159.

124. *Jet* 37, no. 19 (1970): 52.

125. Snyder, *Well-Paid Slave*, 164–65.

126. Leonard Koppett, "Ex-Stars Back Reserve Clause Change," *New York Times*, May 22, 1970, 22.

127. Hearings Before the Senate Subcommittee on Antitrust and Monopoly of the Committee on the Judiciary, 85th Cong., 2d Sess. 295 (1958).

128. Yohuru Williams, "'I've Got to Be Me: Robinson and the Long Black Freedom Struggle," in *42 Today: Jackie Robinson and His Legacy*, ed. Michael G. Long (New York University Press, 2021), 122.

129. Robinson, *I Never Had It Made*, 2.

130. Lanctot, *Negro League Baseball*, 394.

131. Rhiannon Walker, "The State of the Black Manager in Major League Baseball Would Disgust Jackie Robinson," *Undefeated*, April 20, 2018, https://andscape

.com/features/the-state-of-the-black-manager-in-major-league-baseball-would-disgust-jackie-robinson/.

132. Rob Ruck, "Reflections on African Americans in Baseball: No Longer the Vanguard of Change," *Race and Social Problems* 13 (2021): 172–81.

133. Cal Fussman, *After Jackie: Pride, Prejudice, and Baseball's Forgotten Heroes* (ESPN Books, 2007).

134. Rocco Constantino, *Beyond Baseball's Color Barrier: The Story of African Americans in Major League Baseball, Past, Present, and Future* (Rowman & Littlefield, 2021), 181–82.

135. David C. Ogden and Michael L. Hilt, "Collective Identity and Basketball: An Explanation for the Decreasing Number of African-Americans on America's Baseball Diamonds," *Journal of Leisure Research* 35, no. 2 (2003): 213–27.

136. Ruck, "Reflections on African Americans in Baseball," 178.

137. Gerald Early, "Performance and Reality: Race, Sports, and the Modern World," *Nation*, August 10–17, 1998, 11.

138. Tygiel, *Extra Bases*, 276–77.

139. Tygiel, *Extra Bases*, 276–77.

CHAPTER 4

AAGPBL Player Maybelle Blair in an interview with *Advocate*, January 19, 2024, https://www.advocate.com/sports/maybelle-blair-heaven-aloto-cubs.

1. John Montgomery Ward, *Base-Ball: How to Become a Playe*r (Outlook Verlag, 2018), 10.

2. *Morning Chronicle and London Advertiser*, January 16, 1775.

3. Carol Berkin, *Revolutionary Mothers: Women in the Struggle for America's Independence* (Knopf Doubleday, 2007), 16.

4. Rosemarie Zagarri, *Revolutionary Backlash: Women and Politics in the Early American Republic* (University of Pennsylvania Press, 2007), 26.

5. Linda Kerber, "The Republican Mother: Women and the Enlightenment—An American Perspective," *American Quarterly* 28, no. 2 (1976): 187–205.

6. Kerber, *Women of the Republic: Intellect and Ideology in Revolutionary America* (University of North Carolina Press, 1980), 200.

7. Mary Beth Norton, *Liberty's Daughters: The Revolutionary Experience of American Women, 1750–1800* (Little, Brown, 1980); Sara M. Evans, *Born for Liberty: A History of Women in America* (Free Press Paperbacks, 1997).

8. Thomas Jefferson, "From Thomas Jefferson to Anne Willing Bingham, 11 May 1788," *The Papers of Thomas Jefferson*, vol. 13, *March–7 October 1788*, ed. Julian P. Boyd (Princeton University Press, 1956), 151–52.

9. Brian Steele, "Thomas Jefferson's Gender Frontier," *Journal of American History* 95, no. 1 (2008): 17–42.

10. Benjamin Rush, *Thoughts upon Female Education Accomodated to the Present State of Society, Manners, and Government in the United States of America: Addressed to the Visitors of the Young Ladies' Academy in Philadelphia, 28 July, 1787, at the Close of the Quarterly Examination* (Prichard & Hall, 1787), 6–7.

11. John Adams and Abigail Adams, *My Dearest Friend: Letters of Abigail and John Adams*, ed. C. James Taylor and Margaret A. Hogan (Harvard University Press, 2010), 109–11.

12. Judith Sargent Murray, *Selected Writings of Judith Sargent Murray* (Oxford University Press, 1995), 8.

13. Zagarri, *Revolutionary Backlash*, 41.

14. Philip Pettit, "Republican Elements in the Thought of Mary Wollstonecraft," in *The Social and Political Philosophy of Mary Wollstonecraft*, ed. Sandrine Bergès and Alan M. S. J. Coffee, 135–47 (Oxford University Press, 2016); Susan James, "Mary Wollstonecraft's Conception of Rights," in *The Social and Political Philosophy of Mary Wollstonecraft*, ed. Sandrine Bergès and Alan M. S. J. Coffee, 148–65 (Oxford University Press, 2016).

15. Mary Wollstonecraft, *A Vindication of the Rights of Woman* (Dover, 1996), 2.

16. Wollstonecraft, *Vindication of the Rights of Woman*, 150.

17. Wollstonecraft, 3.

18. Wollstonecraft, 145.

19. Wollstonecraft, 146. For more on Wollstonecraft's understanding of property, see Lena Halldenius, "Mary Wollstonecraft's Feminist Critique of Property: On Becoming a Thief from Principle," *Hypatia* 29, no. 4 (2014): 942–57.

20. Zagarri, *Revolutionary Backlash*, 38.

21. Zagarri, 31.

22. Zagarri, 33.

23. Judith Apter Klinnghoffer and Lois Elkis, "'The Petticoat Electors': Women's Suffrage in New Jersey, 1776--1807," *Journal of the Early Republic* 12, no. 2 (1992): 159–93.

24. Robert C. Plumb and Elizabeth Griffith, "Women in Post–Civil War America," in *The Better Angels: Five Women Who Changed Civil War America* (University of Nebraska Press, 2020), 150–69.

25. Carolyn M. Moehling and Melissa A. Thomasson, "Votes for Women: An Economic Perspective on Women's Enfranchisement," *Journal of Economic Perspectives* 34, no. 2 (2020): 3–23.

26. Daniel Carpenter and Colin D. Moore, "When Canvassers Became Activists: Antislavery Petitioning and the Political Mobilization of American Women," *American Political Science Review* 108, no. 3 (2014): 479–98.

27. *New Berne Times*, December 7, 1865, 4.

28. Catherine A. Jones, "Women, Gender, and the Boundaries of Reconstruction," *Journal of the Civil War Era* 8, no. 1 (2018): 111–31.

29. Debra A. Shattuck, "Bats, Balls and Books: Baseball and Higher Education for Women at Three Eastern Women's Colleges, 1866–1891," *Journal of Sport History* 19, no. 2 (1992): 91–109.

30. Annie Glidden to John Glidden, April 20, 1866, in Glidden Papers, Vassar College Special Collection.

31. Shattuck, "Bats, Balls and Books," 94–35.

32. Debra Shattuck, "Women's Baseball in the 1860s: Reestablishing a Historical Memory," *Journal of Baseball History and Culture* 19, no. 2 (2011): 1–26.

33. *Utica Daily Gazette*, October 27, 1867, 2.

34. *Weekly Register*, September 5, 1867, 1.

35. Shattuck, "Women's Baseball in the 1860s," 15.

36. *Louisiana Daily Courier*, July 6, 1868, 2.

37. *Ashtabula Daily Telegraph*, November 23, 1867, 2.

38. Edward H. Clarke, *Sex in Education; or a Fair Chance for the Girls* (James R. Osgood, 1873), 118–62.

39. *Reading Times*, February 15, 1876, 2.

40. *Wichita Eagle*, September 23, 1875, 2.

41. Shattuck, "Bats, Balls and Books," 99–101.

42. Shattuck, "Bats, Balls and Books," 100.

43. Shattuck, "Bats, Balls and Books," 100.

44. In Philadelphia in 1883, John Lang, an enterprising white barber who had founded several Black male teams and a Chinese male team throughout the 1870s, decided to form three all-Black women teams to capitalize on baseball's popularity and the rise of novelty teams. One of the three teams, the Captain Jinks, only played one game before being disbanded, but the two Dolly Vardens hung on for a season. Not much is known about the teams, as newspapers largely ignored their existence or found them too amateur to bother reporting, and the accounts that do exist focus on their appearance and are largely racist. Reporting on one of the games, *The Detroit Free Press* remarks about the women's gaudy attire: "One wore a calico scarlet dress trimmed with blue, another pink trimmed with white, another cardinal red trimmed with yellow, another blue trimmed with white, and all wore red and white peaked caps." Similar accounts begrudgingly applaud Ella Harris, captain of one of the teams, for her leadership skills, and feign surprise over the players' toughness, asserting that "none of the women flinched" on injuries that would have "doubled up men." One other existing newspaper report called the first game between the two teams "a failure," despite the gathering of a large, enthusiastic crowd. These crowds were not enough for Lang to continue organizing the teams, as a group of Black women in the 1880s was not a profitable as he assumed it would be—the novelty of the act could not overcome the deep racism and sexism of the time.

45. Shattuck, *Bloomer Girls*, 138.

46. Shattuck, *Bloomer Girls*, 138.

47. *Atchison Daily Globe*, August 23, 1892, 4.

48. *Topeka Plaindealer*, July 28, 1911, 3.

49. Debra A. Shattuck, "Women's Baseball in Nineteenth-Century New York and the Man Who Set Back Women's Professional Baseball for Decades," in *The National Pastime: Baseball in the Big Apple*, ed. Cecelia M. Tan, (McFarland, 2017), 34–47.

50. *Weekly Sun*, November 20, 1897, 1.

51. *Valley Daily Times-News*, May 24, 1922, 1.

52. Barbara Gregorich, *Women at Play: The Story of Women in Baseball* (Harcourt Brace, 1993), 10–11.

53. *Reading Eagle*, July 6, 1898, 2.

54. Shattuck, *Bloomer Girls*, 146.

55. *Ogden Standard*, June 14, 1909, 2.

56. This endeavor was greatly aided by A. G. Spalding's insistence that women did not belong in baseball, as well as his efforts to tie baseball to American myth and American political institutions.

57. Michael S. Kimmel, "Baseball and the Reconstitution of American Masculinity, 1880–1920," in *Sport, Men, and the Gender Order: Critical Feminist Perspectives*, ed. Michael A. Messner and Don Sabo (Human Kinetics, 1992), 61.

58. Cohen, *No Girls in the Clubhouse*, 41.

59. Marilyn Cohen, *No Girls in the Clubhouse: The Exclusion of Women from Baseball* (McFarland, 2009), 131.

60. Jennifer Ring, *Stolen Bases: Why American Girls Don't Play Baseball* (University of Illinois Press: 2009), 72.

61. Ring, *Stolen Bases*, 43.

62. Cohen, *No Girls in the Clubhouse*, 32–34.

63. Barbara Gregorich, "Blues, Bloomers, and Bobbies," *Pennsylvania Heritage* (1993): 32–40.

64. Sarah K. Fields, "Baseball," in *Female Gladiators: Gender, Law, and Contact Sport in America* (University of Illinois Press, 2005), 19.

65. Merrie A. Fidler, "The Establishment of Softball as a Sport for American Women, 1900–1940," in *Her Story in Sport: A Historical Anthology of Women in Sports*, ed. Reet Howell (Leisure Press, 1982), 527–40.

66. Cohen, *No Girls in the Clubhouse*, 134–35.

67. Shattuck, *Bloomer Girls*, 180. Little League Baseball did not make the ban official until 1951, but the unofficial ban functioned in the same way as MLB's unofficial ban.

68. *Washington Sunday Herald*, July 7, 1891, 4.

69. *Boston Globe*, August 18, 1895, 27.

70. For instance, *The Brooklyn Citizen* noted in 1900 that many men began to complain about women who constantly "flocked to the grounds early and corralled all the best seats" (April 9, 1899, 4). *The Atlanta Constitution* declared that "there appeared to be a great interest in the game" on the part of women fans (March 30, 1895, 5).

71. Robert Thompson, Tim Wiles, and Andy Strasberg, *Baseball's Greatest Hit: The Story of "Take Me Out to the Ballgame"* (Hal Leonard, 2008), 59.

72. Jaime Schultz and Andrew D. Linden, "From Ladies' Days to Women's Initiatives: American Pastimes and Distaff Consumption," in *American National Pastimes—A History* (Routledge, 2016), 156–80.

73. *St. Louis Post-Dispatch*, April 14, 1912, 15.

74. *York Dispatch*, January 9, 1912, 8.

75. William Borst, "Helene Britton: The Matron Magnate," *Baseball Research Journal* 6, no. 1 (1977): 75–84.

76. Joan M. Thomas, *Baseball's First Lady: Helene Hathaway Robison Britton and the St. Louis Cardinals* (Reedy Press, 2010).

77. "Oregon Slogan Says Victory in November," *Women's Journal* (1912), 139.

78. Lindsay Parks Pieper, "'Make a Home Run for Suffrage': Promoting Women's Emancipation Through Baseball," *Women in Sport and Physical Activity Journal* 20, no. 1 (2020): 101–10.

79. For instance, earlier that season, anti-suffragist pamphlets had been distributed during several Boston Braves-Boston Red Sox games.

80. *New York Times*, May 19, 1915, 5.

81. *New York Sun*, April 29, 1916, 6.

82. Elizabeth York Enstam, "The Dallas Equal Suffrage Association, Political Style, and Popular Culture: Grassroots Strategies of the Woman Suffrage Movement, 1913–1919," *Journal of Southern History* 69, no. 4 (2002): 817–48.

83. *Nashville Tennessean*, July 20, 1915, 5.

84. *Daily Arkansas Gazette*, August 31, 1917, 3.

85. *Nashville Banner*, August 22, 1916, 3.

86. Roberts Ehrgott, *Mr. Wrigley's Ball Club: Chicago and the Cubs During the Jazz Age* (University of Nebraska Press, 2013), 55.

87. *Piqua Daily Call*, April 16, 1942, 12.

88. Jean Hastings Ardell, *Breaking into Baseball: Women and the National Pastime* (Southern Illinois University Press, 2005), 56.

89. Kimberly Young, "'TAKE ME OUT TO THE BELLEGAME': How the AAGPBL Gained and Maintained Its Highly Respected Reputation" in *A Locker Room of Her Own: Celebrity, Sexuality, and Female Athletes*, ed. David C. Ogden and Joel Nathan Rosen (University of Mississippi Press, 2013), 23–42.

90. Lois Browne, *Girls of Summer: In Their Own League* (HarperCollins, 1992), preface.

91. Young, "TAKE ME OUT TO THE BELLEGAM," 25.

92. Sue Macy, *A Whole New Ball Game: The Story of the All-American Girls Professional Baseball League* (Henry Holt, 1993), 52–53.

93. Kat D. Williams, *The All-American Girls After the AAGPBL: How Playing Pro Ball Shaped Their Lives* (McFarland, 2017), 12.

94. Martha Ackmann, *Curveball: The Remarkable Story of Toni Stone, the First Woman to Play Professional Baseball in the Negro League* (Lawrence Hill Books, 2010).

95. Amira Rose Davis, "No League of Their Own: Baseball, Black Women, and the Politics of Representation," *Radical History Review* 125 (2016): 81.

96. Davis, "No League of Their Own," 85–86. Although Stone enjoyed her career, immediately after her retirement, she remarked to her husband, "my years in negro baseball has not meant anything. The owner has capitalized on me . . . that's all." (88).

97. David Pietrusza, *Judge and Jury: The Life and Times of Judge Kenesaw Mountain Landis* (Diamond Communications, 1998), 433.

98. Wrigley told each city that owning an AAGPBL team would demonstrate the city's patriotism and provide entertainment for entire families. Each city contributed twenty thousand dollars to the teams, with Wrigley's nonprofit matching the sums.

99. Browne, *Girls of Summer*.
100. Browne, 98–102.
101. Browne, 116.
102. "Doc' Wagner," *Abilene (TX) Reporter-News*, July 30, 1948; "Doc' Wagner," *Alton (IL) Evening Telegraph*, July 28, 1948; "Doc' Wagner," *Arizona Republic*, July 30, 1948; "Doc' Wagner," *Bakersfield Californian*, August 3, 1948; "Doc' Wagner," *Bismarck (ND) Tribune*, July 30, 1948; "Best Girl," *Arizona Republic*, January 4, 1949; "Best Girl," *Bakersfield Californian*, November 27, 1948; "Best Girl," *Daily Times* (New Philadelphia, OH), December 22, 1948; "Best Girl," Evening News (Harrisburg, PA), November 24, 1948; "Best Girl," *Independent Record* (Helena, MT), December 20, 1948; "Best Girl," *Miami (OK) Daily News-Record*, December 5, 1948; "Best Girl," *News-Herald* (Franklin, PA), November 26, 1948; "Best Girl," *Rhinelander (WI) Daily News*, November 27, 1948; "Best Girl," *Sedalia (MO) Democrat*, December 1, 1948.
103. Sharon Roepke, "Diamond Gals: The Story of the All American Girls Professional Baseball League," *UW-L Journal of Undergraduate Research* 7 (2004): 6.
104. Gregorich, *Women at Play*, 92.
105. Gregorich, *Women at Play*, 95.
106. Kat D. Williams, *All-American Girls After the AAGPBL*, 8.
107. Williams, *All-American Girls*, 9–11.
108. Carol J. Pierman, "Baseball, Conduct, and True Womanhood," *Women's Studies Quarterly* 3, no. 1 (2005): 79–80.
109. Williams, *All-American Girls After the AAGPBL*, 156.
110. Ackmann, *Curveball*, 110.
111. Williams, *All-American Girls After the AAGPBL*, 161.
112. The debate over girls' participation in Little League continues to this day, and many girls choose softball over baseball because there is more of a community for them in softball than in the male-dominated sport of baseball.
113. Jennifer Ring, *A Game of Their Own: Voices of Contemporary Women in Baseball* (University of Nebraska Press, 2015), xxxi.
114. Fields, "Baseball,", 20–28.
115. As an example of such violence, in 2018, two coaches with the Oyster River Youth Association in New Hampshire were accused of instructing their players to throw at a girl's head in order to intimidate her out of the league. John Doyle, "Parent: Baseball Coaches Talked of 'Beaning' Daughter," *Foster's Daily Democrat*, April 10, 2018, https://www.fosters.com/news/20180410/parent-baseball-coaches-talked-of-beaning-daughter.
116. Marilyn Cohen, *No Girls in the Clubhouse*, 94.
117. Cohen, *No Girls in the Clubhouse*, 94.
118. "Words of the Week," *Jet* 57, no. 19 (1977), 40.
119. Gregorich, *Women at Play*, 181.
120. Cohen, *No Girls in the Clubhouse*, 96.
121. Cohen, 96.
122. Cohen, 100.

123. Cohen, 107–8.

124. Cohen, 113. After she lost a 1988 sex discrimination lawsuit against her varsity high school team, she emerged from the courtroom to see the players "celebrating like they'd won the World Series," an experience that "really will break a person." Pat Graham, "'A League of Their Own' Inspired Baseball Pioneer Croteau," *San Diego Union-Tribune*, April 17, 2020.

125. Andrew Bryce, "From Fitting in to Standing Out: Baseball's Couteau Recounts Journey as Pioneer for Women," *Daily Hampshire Gazette*, February 1, 1996.

126. Ila Jane Borders and Jean Hastings Ardell, *Making My Pitch: A Woman's Baseball Odyssey* (University of Nebraska Press, 2017), 179.

CONCLUSION

Philip Roth, "My Baseball Years," *The New York Times*, April 12, 1973

1. "Cooperstown Comes to California," *BART News*, November 17, 2005.

2. National Constitution Center, "'Baseball as America' Exhibition Overview," press release, 2008.

3. Michael L. Butterworth, *Baseball and Rhetorics of Purity: The National Pastime and American Identity During the War on Terror* (University of Alabama Press, 2010), 62.

4. Jules Tygiel, "Introduction," in *Baseball as America: Seeing Ourselves Through Our National Game* (National Geographic Society, 2002), 25.

5. Tom Brokaw, "The Front Lines to the Backyard," in *Baseball as America: Seeing Ourselves Through Our National Game* (National Geographic Society, 2002), 63.

6. Jules Tygiel, "Introduction to 'Ideals and Injustices,'" in *Baseball as America: Seeing Ourselves Through Our National Game* (National Geographic Society), 75.

7. Jules Tygiel, "Enterprise & Opportunity," in *Baseball as America*, 175.

8. David Rockwell, "Beyond the Bleachers: Enhancing the Fan Experience," in *Baseball as America: Seeing Ourselves Through Our National Game* (Washington, DC: National Geographic Society, 2002), 208.

9. Elliott J. Gorn, "Baseball as America: Seeing Ourselves Through Our National Game," *Journal of Sport History* 30, no. 2 (2003): 274–76.

10. Sharon Bohn Gmelch, *American Anthropologist* 104, no. 4 (2002): 1208–11.

11. For the exhibition as an excess of capitalism, see Butterworth, 59. For a critique of the triumphant tone of the exhibition, see Gorn, "Baseball as America," 275.

12. Butterworth, *Baseball and Rhetorics of Purity*, 60.

13. The phrase "sense of normalcy" has been used by many to describe the return to baseball post-9/11, including sports historian John Smith. See: Larry Olmstead, *Fans: How Watching Sports Makes Us Happier, Healthier, and More Understanding* (Algonquin Books, 2021), 63.

14. Butterworth, *Baseball and Rhetorics of Purity*, 40.

15. Hilary Giorgi, "Yankees Magazine: The Ultimate Comeback," September 11, 2018, MLB.com, https://www.mlb.com/news/baseball-helped-heal-the-nation-after-9-11-c294183722.

16. Allan H. (Bud) Selig, "Baseball in a Time of Crisis," in *Baseball as America*, 66.

17. Gorn, "Baseball as America," 275.

18. Sally Jenkins, "Is the District Being Sold a Bill of Goods?" *Washington Post*, September 30, 2004.

19. David Nakamura, "D.C. Seizes 16 Owners' Property for Stadium," *Washington Post*, October 26, 2005,.

20. Derek Hyra and Sabiyha Prince, "Beyond Gentrification: Investment and Abandonment on the Waterfront" in *Capital Dilemma* (Routledge, 2015), 245–56; Arthur Jones II, "How the Nationals Ballpark Helped Change Washington, D.C., from 'Chocolate City,'" *Andscape*, June 28, 2017; Marissa J. Lang, "In the Shadow of Nationals Park, Longtime Residents Face Threats Beyond Gunfire," *Washington Post*, July 21, 2021.

21. Hal Bodley, "President Loves, Follows Baseball," *USA Today*, April 15, 2005.

22. George Bush, "Islam Is Peace," September 17, 2001, https://georgewbush-whitehouse.archives.gov/news/releases/2001/09/20010917-11.html; "A NATION CHALLENGED; Excerpts from Bush Speech on Travel," *New York Times*, September 28, 2001.

23. Marc Sandalow, "A Brand-New Ballgame: The New Stadium of the Nationals," *Washingtonian*, March 1, 2008.

24. Sandalow, "A Brand-New Ballgame."

25. Tim Lemke, "Park Deemed Success: Mayor Praises Nationals' Completed Stadium," *Washington Times*, March 29, 2008.

26. Thomas Boswell, "House of Representativeness," *Washington Post*, March 28, 2008.

27. Jacques Barzun, *God's Country and Mine: A Declaration of Love Spiced with a Few Harsh Words* (Little, Brown, 1954), 160.

28. Roger Angell, *Five Seasons: A Baseball Companion* (Open Road Media, 2013), 237.

Bibliography

Ackmann, Martha. *Curveball: The Remarkable Story of Toni Stone, the First Woman to Play Professional Baseball in the Negro League*. Chicago Review Press, 2010.

Adams, John. "John Adams to James Sullivan, 26 May 1776." In *The Adams Papers*, vol. 4, *February–August 1776*, edited by Robert J. Taylor. Harvard University Press, 1979.

Adams, John. *The Political Writings of John Adams*. Edited by George W. Carey. Regnery, 2000.

Adams, John, and Abigail Adams. *My Dearest Friend: Letters of Abigail and John Adams*. Edited by C. James Taylor and Margaret A. Hogan. Harvard University Press, 2010.

Aiello, Thomas. "A Case for the Negro Southern League." *Black Ball* 3, no. 2 (2010): 37–45.

Alexander, Charles C. *Our Game: An American Baseball Story*. Macmillan, 1991.

Alexander, Charles C. *Turbulent Seasons: Baseball in 1890–1891*. Southern Methodist University Press, 2011.

Alexander, Gregory S. *Commodity and Propriety: Competing Visions of Property in American Legal Thought, 1776–1970*. University of Chicago Press, 2008.

Angell, Roger. *Five Seasons: A Baseball Companion*. Open Road Media, 2013.

Ardell, Jean Hastings. *Breaking into Baseball: Women and the National Pastime*. Southern Illinois University Press, 2005.

Aristotle. *Aristotle's Politics*. Translated by Carnes Lord. University of Chicago Press, 2013.

Bailyn, Bernard. *Faces of Revolution: Personalities and Themes in the Struggle for American Independence*. Knopf, 1990.

Baker, Kevin. "At the Park." *Creative Nonfiction*, no. 34 (2008): 8–20.

Banner, Stuart. *The Baseball Trust: A History of Baseball's Antitrust Exemption*. Oxford University Press, 2013.

Barth, Gunthar. *City People: The Rise of Modern City Culture in Nineteenth-Century America*. Oxford University Press, 1980.

Barzun, Jacques. *God's Country and Mine: A Declaration of Love Spiced with a Few Harsh Words*. Little, Brown, 1954.

Beisel, Nicola. "Class, Culture, and Campaigns Against Vice in Three American Cities, 1872–1892." *American Sociological Review* 55, no. 1 (1990): 44–62.

Benezet, Anthony. *The Complete Antislavery Writings of Anthony Benezet, 1754–1783: An Annotated Critical Edition*. Edited by David L. Crosby. Louisiana State University Press, 2014.

Bergès, Sandrine, and Alan M. S. J. Coffee, eds. *The Social and Political Philosophy of Mary Wollstonecraft*. Oxford University Press, 2016.

Bergh, Rio. "Blackness in the 'Grey Area': Representations of Virtuous Labor in Venture Smith's Narrative." *Early American Literature* 56, no. 2 (2021): 415–40.

Berkin, Carol. *Revolutionary Mothers: Women in the Struggle for America's Independence*. Knopf Doubleday, 2007.

Berman, David, and Thomas R. Cole. *The Strange Demise of Jim Crow: How Houston Desegregated Its Public Accommodations, 1959–1963*. California Newsreel, 1998.

Borders, Ila Jane, and Jean Hastings Ardell. *Making My Pitch: A Woman's Baseball Odyssey*. University of Nebraska Press, 2017.

Borst, William. "Helene Britton: The Matron Magnate." *Baseball Research Journal* 6, no. 1 (1977): 75–84.

Boswell, Thomas. "House of Representativeness." *Washington Post*, March 28, 2008.

Bradbury, John Charles, Dennis Coates, and Brad R. Humphreys. "Public Policy Toward Professional Sports Stadiums: A Review," *Journal of Policy Analysis and Management* 43 (2024): 899–937

Breslin, Jimmy. *Branch Rickey*. Viking, 2011.

Briley, Ron. "Danny Gardella and Baseball's Reserve Clause: A Working-Class Stiff Blacklisted in Cold War America." In *Sport and the Law: Historical and Cultural Intersections*, edited by Samuel O. Regalado and Sarah K. Fields.

Brokaw, Tom. "The Front Lines to the Backyard." In National Baseball Hall of Fame, *Baseball as America*.

Brown, Maury. "1985–1988—Collusions I, II . . . and III (A Hard Lesson Learned)." In *The Big Book of Baseball Blunders*, edited by Rob Neyer. Simon and Schuster, 2006.

Browne, Lois. *Girls of Summer: In Their Own League*. HarperCollins, 1992.

Brunson, James E. *Black Baseball, 1858–1900: A Comprehensive Record of the Teams, Players, Managers, Owners and Umpires*. McFarland, 2019.

Bryce, Andrew. "From Fitting in to Standing Out: Baseball's Couteau Recounts Journey as Pioneer for Women." *Daily Hampshire Gazette*, February 1, 1996.

Buell, Lawrence. "American Pastoral Ideology Reappraised." *American Literary History* 1, no. 1 (1989): 1–29.

Bunting, Thomas David. *Democracy at the Ballpark: Sport, Spectatorship, and Politics*. State University of New York Press, 2021.

Burk, Robert F. *Marvin Miller, Baseball Revolutionary*. University of Illinois Press, 2015.

Burk, Robert F. *Much More Than a Game: Players, Owners, and American Baseball Since 1921*. University of North Carolina Press, 2001.

Burk, Robert F. *Never Just a Game: Players, Owners, and American Baseball to 1920*. University of North Carolina Press, 2001.

Bush, George. "Islam Is Peace." September 17, 2001. https://georgewbushwhitehouse.archives.gov/news/releases/2001/09/20010917-11.html

Bush, George. "A NATION CHALLENGED; Excerpts from Bush Speech on Travel." *New York Times*, September 28, 2001.

Butterworth, Michael L. *Baseball and Rhetorics of Purity: The National Pastime and American Identity During the War on Terror*. University of Alabama Press, 2010.

Caivano, Dean. "The Question of Sharing: Thomas Jefferson and the Idea of Communal Property." *Histories* 1, no. 3 (2021): 85–99.

Calcaterra, Craig. "Shocker: Bud Selig Believes That Which Has Been Thoroughly Debunked." *NBC Sports*, November 8, 2010.

Carlino, P. J. "Bleacher Bugs and Fifty-Centers: The Social Stratification of Baseball Fans Through Stadium Design, 1880–1920." *Buildings and Landscapes: Journal of the Vernacular Architecture Forum* 28, no. 1 (2021): 5–29.

Carpenter, Daniel, and Colin D. Moore. "When Canvassers Became Activists: Antislavery Petitioning and the Political Mobilization of American Women." *American Political Science Review* 108, no. 3 (2014): 479–98.

Casway, Jerrold. "Octavius Catto and the Pythians of Philadelphia." *Pennsylvania Legacies* 7, no. 1 (2007): 5–9.

Catto, Octavius. "Our Alma Mater: An Address." May 10, 1864. C. Sherman, Son, 1864.

Chadwick, Henry. "Baseball in the South." *Outing: An Illustrated Monthly Magazine of Recreation* 12, no. 6 (September 1888).

Clarke, Edward H. *Sex in Education; or a Fair Chance for the Girls*. James R. Osgood, 1873.

Cline, Scott. "'To Foster Honorable Pastimes': Baseball as a Civic Endeavor in 1880s Seattle." *Pacific Northwest Quarterly* 87, no. 4 (1996): 171–79.

Cohen, Kenneth. *They Will Have Their Game: Sporting Culture and the Making of the Early American Republic*. Cornell University Press, 2017.

Cohen, Marilyn. *No Girls in the Clubhouse: The Exclusion of Women from Baseball*. McFarland, 2009.

Colclough, William G., Lawrence A. Daellenbach, and Keith R. Sherony. "Estimating the Economic Impact of a Minor League Baseball Stadium." *Managerial and Decision Economics* 15, no. 5 (1994): 497–502.

Conklin, Carli N. *The Pursuit of Happiness in the Founding Era: An Intellectual History*. University of Missouri Press, 2019.

Constantino, Rocco. *Beyond Baseball's Color Barrier: The Story of African Americans in Major League Baseball, Past, Present, and Future*. Rowman & Littlefield, 2021.

Curtis, Christopher Michael. *Jefferson's Freeholders and the Politics of Ownership in the Old Dominion*. Cambridge University Press, 2012.

Danielson, Michael N. *Home Team: Professional Sports and the American Metropolis*. Princeton University Press, 2021.

Davis, Amira Rose. "No League of Their Own: Baseball, Black Women, and the Politics of Representation." *Radical History Review* 125 (2016): 74–96.

de Crèvecœur, Michel-Guillaume Jean. *Letters from an American Farmer; and Sketches of Eighteenth-Century America.* Edited by Albert E. Stone. Penguin Books, 1981.

Desrochers, Robert E. "'Not Fade Away': The Narrative of Venture Smith, an African American in the Early Republic." *Journal of American History* 84, no. 1 (1997): 40–66.

Devine, James R. "Baseball's Labor Wars in Historical Context: The 1919 Chicago White Sox as a Case-Study in Owner-Player Relations." *Marquette Sports Law Review* 5, no. 1 (1994): 18–25.

Di Salvatore, Bryan. *A Clever Base-Ballist: The Life and Times of John Montgomery Ward.* Pantheon Books, 1999.

Duquette, Jerold J. *Regulating the National Pastime: Baseball and Antitrust.* Praeger, 1999.

Ehrgott, Robert. *Mr. Wrigley's Ball Club: Chicago and the Cubs during the Jazz Age.* University of Nebraska Press, 2013.

Elias, Robert. "The National Pastime Trade-Off: How Baseball Sells US Foreign Policy and the American Way." In *Mapping an Empire of American Sport: Expansion, Assimilation, Adaptation and Resistance*, edited by Mark Dyreson, J. A. Mangen, and Roberta Park. Routledge, 2013.

Enstam, Elizabeth York. "The Dallas Equal Suffrage Association, Political Style, and Popular Culture: Grassroots Strategies of The Woman Suffrage Movement, 1913–1919." *Journal of Southern History* 69, no. 4 (2002): 817–48.

Evans, Christopher H. "The Kingdom of Baseball in America: The Chronicle of an American Theology." In *Faith of 50 Million: Baseball, Religion and American Culture*, edited by Christopher H. Evans and William R. Herzog II. Westminster John Knox, 2002.

Evans, Sara M. *Born for Liberty: A History of Women in America.* Free Press Paperbacks, 1997.

Fatovic, Clement. *America's Founding and the Struggle over Economic Inequality.* University Press of Kansas, 2015.

Ferling, John. *Jefferson and Hamilton: The Rivalry That Forged a Nation.* Bloomsbury, 2014.

Fidler, Merrie A. "The Establishment of Softball as a Sport for American Women, 1900–1940." In *Her Story in Sport: A Historical Anthology of Women in Sports*, edited by Reet Howell. Leisure Press, 1982.

Fields, Sarah K. *Female Gladiators: Gender, Law, and Contact Sport in America.* University of Illinois Press, 2005.

Finkelman, Paul. "Baseball and the Rule of Law." *Cleveland State Law Review* 46, no. 2 (1998): 239–60.

Finkelman, Paul. "Baseball Is a Civics Education." *Atlantic*, October 24, 2019.

Finkelman, Paul. *Slavery and the Founders: Race and Liberty in the Age of Jefferson.* M. E. Sharpe, 2014.

Flood, Curt, and Carter Richard. *The Way It Is*. Trident Press, 1971.

Florio, John, and Ouisie Shapiro. *One Nation Under Baseball: How the 1960s Collided with the National Pastime*. University of Nebraska Press, 2017.

Ford, Lacy K. *Deliver Us from Evil: The Slavery Question in the Old South*. Oxford University Press, 2009.

Freehling, William W. "The Founding Fathers and Slavery." *American Historical Review* 77 (1972): 81–93

Freneau, Philip, and Hugh Henry Brackenridge. "A Poem on the Rising Glory of America." In *The Poems of Philip Freneau*, edited by Fred Lewis Pattee. The University Library, C. S. Robinson & Co. University Press, 1902.

Furst, R. Terry. *Early Professional Baseball and the Sporting Press: Shaping the Image of the Game*. McFarland, 2014.

Furstenberg, François. "Beyond Freedom and Slavery: Autonomy, Virtue, and Resistance in Early American Political Discourse." *Journal of American History* 89, no. 4 (2003): 1295–330.

Fussman, Cal. *After Jackie: Pride, Prejudice, and Baseball's Forgotten Heroes*. ESPN Books, 2007.

Gelber, Steven M. "Working at Playing: The Culture of the Workplace and the Rise of Baseball." *Journal of Social History* 16, no. 4 (1983): 3–22.

Gelzheiser, Robert P. *Labor and Capital in 19th Century Baseball*. McFarland, 2006.

Giamatti, A. Bartlett. *Take Time for Paradise: Americans and Their Games*. Bloomsbury, 2011.

Gibson, Alan. *Understanding the Founding: The Crucial Questions*. 2nd ed. University of Kansas Press, 2010.

Gift, Thomas, and Andrew Miner. "DROPPING THE BALL: The Understudied Nexus of Sports and Politics." *World Affairs* 180, no. 1 (2017): 127–61.

Glasser, Ira. "Branch Rickey and Jackie Robinson: Precursors to the Civil Rights Movement." *World and I*, 18, no. 3 (2003).

Goldstein, Warren Jay. *Playing for Keeps: A History of Early Baseball*. Cornell University Press, 2014.

Gorn, Elliot J. "Baseball As America: Seeing Ourselves Through Our National Game." *Journal of Sport History* 30, no. 2 (2003): 274–76.

Gourevitch, Alex. "William Manning and the Political Theory of the Dependent Classes." *Modern Intellectual History* 9, no. 2 (2012): 331–60.

Graham, Pat. "'A League of Their Own' Inspired Baseball Pioneer Croteau." *San Diego Union-Tribune*, April 17, 2020.

Gregorich, Barbara. "Blues, Bloomers, and Bobbies." *Pennsylvania Heritage* (1993): 32–40.

Gregorich, Barbara. *Women at Play: The Story of Women in Baseball*. Harcourt Brace, 1993.

Grella, George. "Baseball and the American Dream." *Massachusetts Review* 16, no. 3 (1975): 550–67.

Grossman, James R. *Land of Hope: Chicago, Black Southerners, and the Great Migration*. University of Chicago Press, 1989.

Grow, Nathaniel. *Baseball on Trial: The Origin of MLB's Antitrust Exemption*. University of Illinois Press, 2014.

Grundy, Pamela, and Benjamin G. Rader. *American Sports: From the Age of Folk Games to the Age of Televised Sports*. Taylor and Francis, 2016.

Guttman, Allen. *Essays on Sport History and Sport Mythology*. University of Texas at Arlington Press, 1990.

Halchin, Elaine, Justin Murray, Kathleen Ruane, and Jon Shimabukuro. "Congressional Responses to Selected Work Stoppages in Professional Sports." U.S. Library of Congress, Congressional Research Service, R40160 (2013).

Hall, Jacquelyn Dowd. *Like a Family: The Making of a Southern Cotton Mill World*. University of North Carolina Press, 1987.

Halldenius, Lena. "Mary Wollstonecraft's Feminist Critique of Property: On Becoming a Thief from Principle." *Hypatia* 29, no. 4 (2014): 942–57.

Hamilton, Alexander. *The Papers of Alexander Hamilton*. Vol. 4, *January 1787–May 1788*. Edited by Harold C. Syrett. Columbia University Press, 1962.

Hamilton, Alexander. "Alexander Hamilton's Final Version of the Report on the Subject of Manufactures, [5 December 1791]." In *The Papers of Alexander Hamilton*, vol. 10, *December 1791–January 1792*, edited by Harold C. Syrett. Columbia University Press, 1966.

Handlin, Oscar, and Mary Handlin, eds. *The Popular Sources of Political Authority: Documents on the Massachusetts Constitution of 1780*. Harvard University Press, 1966.

Harrigan, Patrick Joseph. *The Detroit Tigers: Club and Community, 1945–1995*. University of Toronto Press, 1997.

Hartz, Louis. *The Liberal Tradition in America: An Interpretation of American Political Thought Since the Revolution*. Harcourt, Brace, 1955.

Haupert, Michael. "Major League Baseball's Salary Leaders, 1874–2012." *Business of Baseball Research Committee Newsletter*, Fall 2012.

———. "William Hulbert and the Birth of the National League." *Baseball Research Journal* 44, no. 1 (2015): 83–92.

Haynes, Lemuel. *Preacher to White America: The Collected Writings of Lemuel Haynes, 1774–1833*. Carlson, 1990.

Heike, Paul. *The Myths That Made America: An Introduction to American Studies*. Transcript Verlag, 2014.

Helfand, Zach. "Invasion of the Robot Umpires." *New Yorker*, August 23, 2021.

Hillstrom, Laurie Collier. *Jackie Robinson and the Integration of Baseball*. Omnigraphics, 2001.

Hines, Thomas S. "Housing, Baseball, and Creeping Socialism: 'The Battle of Chavez Ravine, Los Angeles, 1949–1959.'" *Journal of Urban History* 8, no. 2 (1982): 123–44.

Hoang, Gia Phan. *Bonds of Citizenship: Law and the Labors of Emancipation*. New York University Press, 2013.

Hofstadter, Richard. *The American Political Tradition and the Men Who Made It*. Knopf, 1951.

Hofstadter, Richard. *The Age of Reform: From Bryan to F.D.R.* Knopf Doubleday, 1955.

Hogan, Lawrence D. *The Forgotten History of African American Baseball.* Praeger, 2014.

Hughes, Richard T. *Myths America Lives By: White Supremacy and the Stories That Give Us Meaning.* University of Illinois Press, 2018.

Hyra, Derek, and Sabiyha Prince. "Beyond Gentrification: Investment and Abandonment on the Waterfront." In *Capital Dilemma*, edited by Derek Hyra and Sabiyha Prince. Routledge, 2015.

James, Cyril Lionel Robert. *Beyond a Boundary.* Duke University Press, 2013.

James, Susan. "Mary Wollstonecraft's Conception of Rights." In Bergès and Coffee, *Social and Political Philosophy of Mary Wollstonecraft.*

Jefferson, Thomas. "Autobiography." In *The Writings of Thomas Jefferson*, edited by Paul Leicester Ford. G. P. Putnam's Sons, 1892.

Jefferson, Thomas. "From Thomas Jefferson to Anne Willing Bingham, 11 May 1788." In *The Papers of Thomas Jefferson*, vol. 13, *March–7 October 1788*, edited by Julian P. Boyd. Princeton University Press, 1956.

Jefferson, Thomas. "From Thomas Jefferson to James Madison, 20 December 1787." In *The Papers of Thomas Jefferson*, vol. 12, *7 August 1787–31 March 1788*, edited by Julian P. Boyd. Princeton University Press, 1955.

Jefferson, Thomas. *Notes on the State of Virginia.* Wells and Lilly, 1966.

Jefferson, Thomas. "Thomas Jefferson to John Jay, August 23, 1785." In *The Papers of Thomas Jefferson*, vol. 8, edited by James P. McLure. Princeton University Press, 2019.

Jenkins, Sally. "Is the District Being Sold a Bill of Goods?" *Washington Post*, September 30, 2004.

Johnson, Arthur T. "Professional Baseball at the Minor League Level: Considerations for Cities Large and Small." *State and Local Government Review* 22, no. 2 (1990): 90–96.

Johnston, Isaac. "Baseball in the Masculine Age: Sport and Popular Media as a Means of Revolution." *Ezra's Archives* 8, no. 1 (2018): 63–78.

Jones, Arthur, II. "How the Nationals Ballpark Helped Change Washington, D.C., from 'Chocolate City.'" *Andscape*, June 28, 2017.

Jones, Catherine A. "Women, Gender, and the Boundaries of Reconstruction." *Journal of the Civil War Era* 8, no. 1 (2018): 111–31.

Jordan, Alley M. *Virgil in Virginia: Eighteenth-Century Pastoralism and the Novus Ordo Seculorum.* University of San Diego, 2016.

Kaplan, Sidney, and Emma Nogrady Kaplan. *The Black Presence in the Era of the American Revolution.* University of Massachusetts Press, 1989.

Kerber, Linda. "The Republican Mother: Women and the Enlightenment—An American Perspective." *American Quarterly* 28, no. 2 (1976): 187–205.

Kerber, Linda. *Women of the Republic: Intellect and Ideology in Revolutionary America.* University of North Carolina Press, 1980.

Khan, Abraham Iqbal. *Curt Flood in the Media: Baseball, Race, and the Demise of the Activist Athlete.* University Press of Mississippi, 2012.

Kimball, Richard Ian. "Beyond the 'Great Experiment': Integrated Baseball Comes to Indianapolis." *Journal of Sport History* 26, no. 1 (1999): 142–62.

Kimmel, Michael. "Baseball and the Reconstitution of American Masculinity, 1880–1920." In *Sport, Men, and the Gender Order: Critical Feminist Perspectives*, edited by Michael A. Messner and Don Sabo. Human Kinetics, 1992.

Kimmel, Michael. *The History of Men: Essays on the History of American and British Masculinities*. State University of New York Press, 2005.

Kirsch, George B. *The Creation of American Team Sport: Baseball and Cricket, 1838–1872*. University of Illinois Press, 1989.

Kirsch, George B. "The War's Legacy." In *Baseball in Blue and Gray: The National Pastime During the Civil War*. Princeton University Press, 2003.

Klinnghoffer, Judith Apter, and Lois Elkis. "'The Petticoat Electors': Women's Suffrage in New Jersey, 1776–1807." *Journal of the Early Republic* 12, no. 2 (1992): 159–93.

Knight, Athelia. "The Fans Go to Bat vs. Strike." *Washington Post*, August 18, 1994.

Koppett, Leonard. "Ex-Stars Back Reserve Clause Change." *New York Times*, May 22, 1970.

Kraus, Rebecca S. *Minor League Baseball: Community Building Through Hometown Sports*. Haworth Press, 2003.

Kruse, Kevin M., and Julian E. Zeiler. *Myth America: Historians Take on the Biggest Legends and Lies About Our Past*. Basic Books, 2023.

Lamb, Chris. "Baseball's Whitewash: Sportswriter Wendell Smith Exposes Major League Baseball's Big Lie." *Nine* 18, no. 1 (2009): 1–20.

Lamb, Chris. *Conspiracy of Silence: Sportswriters and the Long Campaign to Desegregate Baseball*. University of Nebraska Press, 2012.

Lanctot, Neil. *Negro League Baseball: The Rise and Ruin of a Black Institution*. University of Pennsylvania Press, 2008.

Land, Kenneth C., and Walter R. Davis, and Judith R. Blau. "Organizing the Boys of Summer: The Evolution of U.S. Minor-League Baseball, 1883–1990." *American Journal of Sociology* 100, no. 3 (1994): 781–813.

Lang, Marissa J. "In the Shadow of Nationals Park, Longtime Residents Face Threats Beyond Gunfire." *Washington Post*, July 21, 2021.

Larson, Edward J., James Madison, and Michael P. Winship. *The Constitutional Convention: A Narrative History from the Notes of James Madison*. Random House, 2011.

Lauck, W. Jett, and Edgar Sydenstricker. *Conditions of Labor in American Industries*. Funk & Wagnall, 1917.

Lemke, Tim. "Park Deemed Success: Mayor Praises Nationals' Completed Stadium," *Washington Times*, March 29, 2008.

Letwin, William L. "Congress and the Sherman Antitrust Law: 1887–1890." *University of Chicago Law Review* 23, no. 2 (1956): 221–58.

Levine, Peter. *A. G. Spalding and the Rise of Baseball: The Promise of American Sport*. Oxford University Press, 1985.

Lewis, Robert F. *Smart Ball: Marketing the Myth and Managing the Reality of Major League Baseball*. University Press of Mississippi, 2010.

Light, Jonathan Fraser. *The Cultural Encyclopedia of Baseball*. 2nd ed. McFarland, 2005.

Locke, John. *Some Thoughts Concerning Education*. Edited by Ruth W. Grant and Nathan Tarcov. Hackett, 1996.

Locke, John. *Two Treatises of Government*. Edited by Lee Ward. Hackett, 2016.

Lomax, Michael. "'Curt Flood Stood up for Us': The Quest to Break down Racial Barriers and Structural Inequality in Major League Baseball." *Culture, Sport, Society* 6, nos. 2–3 (2003): 44–70.

Lord, John B. *Bill Giles and Baseball*. Temple University Press, 2014.

Lussana, Sergio. "To See Who Was Best on the Plantation: Enslaved Fighting Contests and Masculinity in the Antebellum Plantation South." *Journal of Southern History* 76, no. 4 (2010): 901–22.

Machor, James L. "The Garden City in America: Crevecoeur's Letters and the Urban Pastoral Context." *American Studies* 23, no. 1 (1982): 69–83.

MacLeod, Duncan J. *Slavery, Race, and the American Revolution*. Cambridge University Press, 1974.

Macpherson, C. B. "Locke on Capitalist Appropriation." *Western Political Quarterly* 4, no. 4 (1951): 550–66.

Macy, Sue. *A Whole New Ball Game: The Story of the All-American Girls Professional Baseball League*. Henry Holt, 1993.

Madison, James. "No. 54." In *The Federalist*, edited by George W. Carey and James McClellan. Liberty Fund, 2001.

Madison, James. *Notes on the Debates in the Federal Convention of 1787*. W. W. Norton, 1987.

Mann, Arthur William. *Branch Rickey: American in Action*. Houghton Mifflin, 1957.

Manning, William. *The Key of Liberty*. Manning Association, 1922.

Martin, Brian. *Baseball's Creation Myth: Adam Ford, Abner Graves and the Cooperstown Story*. McFarland, 2013.

Martin, Christopher R. *Framed!: Labor and the Corporate Media*. Cornell University Press, 2004.

Mason, Matthew. *Slavery and Politics in the Early American Republic*. University of North Carolina Press, 2006.

McCoy, Drew. *The Elusive Republic: Political Economy in Jeffersonian America*. University of North Carolina Press, 2012.

McGimpsey, David. *Imagining Baseball: America's Pastime and Popular Culture*. Indiana University Press, 2000.

McGowan, John. *American Liberalism: An Interpretation for Our Time*. University of North Carolina Press, 2007.

McGregor, Robert Kuhn. *A Calculus of Color: The Integration of Baseball's American League*. McFarland, 2015.

McKee, Theodore A. "Judges as Umpires." *Hofstra Law Review* 35, no. 4 (2007): 1709–24.

McNeese, Tim. *The Labor Movement: Unionizing America*. Facts on File, 2007.

Miller, James Edward. *The Baseball Business: Pursuing Pennants and Profits in Baltimore*. University of North Carolina Press, 1990.

Moehling, Carolyn M., and Melissa A. Thomasson. "'Votes for Women': An Economic Perspective on Women's Enfranchisement." *Journal of Economic Perspectives* 34, no. 2 (2020): 3–23.

Moore, Glenn. "Ideology on the Sportspage: Newspapers, Baseball, and Ideological Conflict in the Gilded Age." *Journal of Sport History* 23, no. 3 (1996): 228–55.

Morse, Jacob. *Sphere and Ash: History of Base Ball.* Camden House, 1984.

Murray, Judith Sargent. *Selected Writings of Judith Sargent Murray.* Oxford University Press, 1995.

Nakamura, David. "D.C. Seizes 16 Owners' Property for Stadium." *Washington Post,* October 26, 2005.

Nathanson, Mitchell. *A People's History of Baseball.* University of Illinois Press, 2012.

Nathanson, Mitchell. "Who Exempted Baseball, Anyway? The Curious Development of the Antitrust Exemption That Never Was." *Harvard Journal of Sports and Entertainment Law* 4, no. 1 (2013): 1–50.

National Baseball Hall of Fame, ed. *Baseball as America: Seeing Ourselves Through Our National Game.* National Geographic Society, 2002.

Nell, William Cooper. *The Colored Patriots of the American Revolution: With Sketches of Several Distinguished Colored Persons: To Which Is Added a Brief Survey of the Condition and Prospects of Colored Americans.* R. F. Wallcut, 1855.

Nelson, John R. *Liberty and Property: Political Economy and Policymaking in the New Nation, 1789–1812.* Johns Hopkins University Press, 1987.

Newman, Roberta J., Joel Nathan Rosen, Monte Irvin, and Earl Smith. *Black Baseball, Black Business: Race Enterprise and the Fate of the Segregated Dollar.* University Press of Mississippi, 2014.

Norton, Mary Beth. *Liberty's Daughters: The Revolutionary Experience of American Women, 1750–1800.* Little, Brown, 1980.

Obojski, Robert. *Bush League: A History of Minor League Baseball.* Macmillan, 1975.

O'Donnell, Edward T. *Henry George and the Crisis of Inequality: Progress and Poverty in the Gilded Age.* Columbia University Press, 2015.

Ogden, David C., and Michael L. Hilt. "Collective Identity and Basketball: An Explanation for the Decreasing Number of African-Americans on America's Baseball Diamonds," *Journal of Leisure Research* 35, no. 2 (2003): 213–27.

Olmstead, Larry. *Fans: How Watching Sports Makes Us Happier, Healthier, and More Understanding.* Algonquin Books, 2021.

Orens, Jeffrey. *Selling Baseball: How Superstars George Wright and Albert Spalding Impacted Sports in America.* Rowman & Littlefield, 2025.

Overman, Steven J. *The Protestant Ethic and the Spirit of Sport: How Calvinism and Capitalism Shaped America's Games.* Mercer University Press, 2011.

Pessah, Jon. *The Game: Inside the Secret World of Major League Baseball's Power Brokers.* Little, Brown, 2016.

Pettit, Philip. "Republican Elements in the Thought of Mary Wollstonecraft." In Bergès and Coffee, *Social and Political Philosophy of Mary Wollstonecraft.*

Pieper, Lindsay Parks. "'Make a Home Run for Suffrage': Promoting Women's Emancipation Through Baseball." *Women in Sport and Physical Activity Journal* 20, no. 1 (2020): 101–10.

Pierman, Carol J. "Baseball, Conduct, and True Womanhood." *Women's Studies Quarterly* 3, no. 1 (2005): 68–85.

Pietrusza, David. *Judge and Jury: The Life and Times of Judge Kenesaw Mountain Landis*. Diamond Communications, 1998.

Plumb, Robert C., and Elizabeth Griffith. *The Better Angels: Five Women Who Changed Civil War America*. University of Nebraska Press, 2020.

Pocock, J.G.A. *The Machiavellian Moment: Florentine Thought and the Atlantic Republican Tradition*. Princeton University Press, 2016.

Polgar, Paul J. "'To Raise Them to an Equal Participation': Early National Abolitionism, Gradual Emancipation, and the Promise of African American Citizenship." *Journal of the Early Republic* 31, no. 2 (2011): 229–58.

Postell, Joseph. "Regulation During the American Founding: Achieving Liberalism and Republicanism." *American Political Thought* 5, no. 1 (2016): 80–108.

Priest, Claire. "The End of Entail: Information, Institutions, and Slavery in the American Revolutionary Period." *Law and History Review* 33, no. 2 (2015): 277–319.

Rader, Benjamin G. *Baseball: A History of America's Game*. University of Illinois Press, 2018.

Rahe, Paul A. *Republics Ancient and Modern: Classical Republicanism and the American Revolution*. Vol. 1. University of North Carolina Press, 1992.

Reed, Christopher Robert. *The Rise of Chicago's Black Metropolis, 1920–1929*. University of Illinois Press, 2011.

Riess, Steven. "Baseball Myths, Baseball Reality, and the Social Function of Baseball in the Progressive America." *Stadion* 3, no. 2 (1977): 273–311.

Riess, Stephen. *City Games: The Evolution of American Urban Society and the Rise of Sports*. University of Illinois Press, 1991.

Ring, Jennifer. *A Game of Their Own: Voices of Contemporary Women in Baseball*. University of Nebraska Press, 2015.

Ring, Jennifer. *Stolen Bases: Why American Girls Don't Play Baseball*. University of Illinois Press, 2009.

Roberts, Carey. "Alexander Hamilton and the 1790s Economy: A Reappraisal." In *The Many Faces of Alexander Hamilton: The Life and Legacy of America's Most Elusive Founding Father*, edited by Douglas Ambrose and Robert W. T. Martin. NYU Press, 2006.

Robinson, Jackie. Acceptance Address at Special Luncheon Honoring Him on Presentation of 41st Spingarn Medal. New York, December 8, 1956.

Robinson, Jackie. *Beyond Home Plate: Jackie Robinson on Life After Baseball*. Edited by Michael G. Long. Syracuse University Press, 2013.

Robinson, Jackie. *First Class Citizenship: The Civil Rights Letters of Jackie Robinson*. Edited by Michael G. Long. Henry Holt, 2008.

Robinson, Jackie, and Alfred Duckett. *I Never Had It Made: An Autobiography of Jackie Robinson*. Harper Collins, 2013.

Rockwell, David. "Beyond the Bleachers: Enhancing the Fan Experience." In National Baseball Hall of Fame, *Baseball as America*.

Roepke, Sharon. "Diamond Gals: The Story of the All American Girls Professional Baseball League." *UW-L Journal of Undergraduate Research* 7 (2004): 1–7.

Romans, Bernard. *A Concise Natural History of the East and West of Florida*. R. Aitken, 1776.

Rosenblatt, Helena. *The Lost History of Liberalism: From Ancient Rome to the Twenty-First Century*. Princeton University Press, 2020.

Ross, Robert B. *The Great Baseball Revolt: The Rise and Fall of the 1890 Players League*. University of Nebraska Press, 2016.

Ruck, Rob. "Reflections on African Americans in Baseball: No Longer the Vanguard of Change," *Race and Social Problems* 13 (2021): 172–81

Rush, Benjamin. *Thoughts upon Female Education Accomodated to the Present State of Society, Manners, and Government in the United States of America: Addressed to the Visitors of the Young Ladies' Academy in Philadelphia, 28 July, 1787, at the Close of the Quarterly Examination*. Prichard and Hall, 1787.

Sacks, Marcy. "'To Be a Man and Not a Lackey': Black Men, Work, and the Construction of Manhood in Gilded Age New York City." *American Studies* 45, no. 1 (2004): 39–63.

Sandalow, Marc. "A Brand-New Ballgame: The New Stadium of the Nationals." *Washingtonian*, March 1, 2008.

Schiff, Andrew J. *"The Father of Baseball": A Biography of Henry Chadwick*. McFarland, 2008.

Schultz, Jaime, and Andrew D. Linden. "From Ladies' Days to Women's Initiatives: American Pastimes and Distaff Consumption." In *American National Pastimes—A History* Routledge, 2016.

Scully, Gerald W. "Player Salary Share and the Distribution of Player Earnings." *Managerial and Decision Economics* 25, no. 1 (2004): 77–86.

Searls, David T. "Trade or Commerce Among the Several States or with Foreign Nations" *Section of Antitrust Law* (1953): 58–59.

Selig, Allan H., Thomas J. Ostertag, and Matthew J. Mitten. "Baseball's Antitrust Exemption for Franchise Decisions: Its Justifications and Antitrust Law Implications for Other Professional Leagues." *Wisconsin Law Review*, no. 3 (2019): 421–50.

Selig, Allan H., Thomas J. Ostertag, and Matthew J. Mitten. "Baseball in a Time of Crisis." In National Baseball Hall of Fame, *Baseball as America*.

Sentance, David P. *Cricket in America, 1710–2000*. McFarland, 2006.

Seymour, Harold. *Baseball: The Early Years*. Oxford University Press, 1960.

Seymour Mills, Dorothy, and Harold Seymour. *Baseball: The Early Years*. Oxford University Press, 1989.

Shattuck, Debra. A. *Bloomer Girls: Women Baseball Pioneers*. University of Illinois Press, 2017.

Shattuck, Debra. "Bats, Balls and Books: Baseball and Higher Education for Women at Three Eastern Women's Colleges, 1866–1891." *Journal of Sport History* 19, no. 2 (1992): 91–109.

Shattuck, Debra. "Women's Baseball in Nineteenth-Century New York and the Man Who Set Back Women's Professional Baseball for Decades." In *The National Pastime: Baseball in the Big Apple*, edited by Ceclia M. Tan, 2017.

Shattuck, Debra. "Women's Baseball in the 1860s: Reestablishing a Historical Memory." *Journal of Baseball History and Culture* 19, no. 2 (2011): 1–26.

Slotkin, Richard. *A Great Disorder: National Myth and the Battle for America*. Belknap Press of Harvard University Press, 2024.

Slotkin, Richard. "Nostalgia and Progress: Theodore Roosevelt's Myth of the Frontier." *American Quarterly* 33, no. 5 (1981): 608–37.

Smith, Henry Nash. *Virgin Land: The American West as Symbol and Myth*. Harvard University Press, 2007.

Smith, Rogers M. *Civic Ideals: Conflicting Visions of Citizenship in U.S. History*. Yale University Press, 1999.

Smith, Venture. *A Narrative of the Life and Adventures of Venture, a Native of Africa: But Resident Above Sixty Years in the United States of America. Related by Himself*. Printed by C. Holt, at The Bee-office, 1798.

Smith-Rosenburg, Carroll. *"Fusions and Confusions" in This Violent Empire: The Birth of an American National Identity*. University of North Carolina Press, 2010.

Snyder, Brad. *A Well-Paid Slave: Curt Flood's Fight for Free Agency in Professional Sports*. Viking, 2006.

Snyder, David L. "Anatomy of an Aberration: An Examination of the Attempts to Apply Antitrust Law to Major League Baseball Through *Flood v. Kuhn* (1972)." *DePaul Journal of Sports Law* 4, no. 2 (2008): 177–200.

Sokolow, Michael. *Bush League, Big City: The Brooklyn Cyclones, Staten Island Yankees, and the New York-Penn League*. State University of New York Press, 2023.

Sovereign, J. R. *Preamble and Declaration of Principles of the Knights of Labor*. Knights of Labor, 1890.

Spalding, A. G. *America's National Game: Historic Facts Concerning the Beginning, Evolution, Development and Popularity of Base Ball*. American Sports Publishing Company, 1911.

Spalding, A. G. *Spalding's Official Base Ball Guide*. A. G. Spalding & Bros., 1889.

Starr, Paul. *Entrenchment: Wealth, Power, and the Constitution of Democratic Societies*. Yale University Press, 2019.

Staudohar, Paul D. "The Baseball Strike of 1994–95." *Monthly Labor Review* 120, no. 3 (1997): 21–27.

Steele, Brian. "Thomas Jefferson's Gender Frontier." *Journal of American History* 95, no. 1 (2008): 17–42.

Stewart, J. B. *Venture Smith and the Business of Slavery and Freedom*. University of Massachusetts Press, 2010.

Storing, Herbert J. "Slavery and the Moral Foundations of the American Republic." In *The Moral Foundations of the American Republic*, 3rd ed., edited by Robert H. Horwitz. University Press of Virginia, 1986.

Struges, Mark. "Enclosing the Commons: Thomas Jefferson, Agrarian Independence, and Early American Land Policy, 1774–1789." *Virginia Magazine of History and Biography* 119, no. 1 (2011): 42–74.

Sullivan, Dean A. "Faces in the Crowd: A Statistical Portrait of Baseball Spectators in Cincinnati, 1886–1888." *Journal of Sport History* 17, no. 3 (1990): 354–65.

Swanson, Krister. *Baseball's Power Shift: How the Players Union, the Fans, and the Media Changed American Sports Culture*. University of Nebraska Press, 2016.

Swanson, Ryan A. *When Baseball Went White: Reconstruction, Reconciliation, and Dreams of a National Pastime*. University of Nebraska Press, 2014.

Taylor, Shakeia. "Effa Manley's Hidden Life." *SB Nation*, April 20, 2020.

Thomas, Joan M. *Baseball's First Lady: Helene Hathaway Robison Britton and the St. Louis Cardinals*. Reedy Press, 2010.

Thompson, Robert, Tim Wiles, and Andy Strasberg. "Baseball's Greatest Hit: The Story of 'Take Me Out to the Ballgame.'" Hal Leonard, 2008.

Thorn, John. *Baseball in the Garden of Eden: The Secret History of the Early Game*. Simon & Schuster, 2012.

Thorn, John. "Why Baseball: An American Eden of the Mind." *Our Game* (blog), October 19, 2018, https://ourgame.mlblogs.com/why-baseball-8849e118519c.

Tone, Andrea. *The Business of Benevolence: Industrial Paternalism in Progressive America*. Cornell University Press, 1997.

Traubel, Horace. *With Walt Whitman in Camden*. Vol. 1. Small, Maynard, 1906.

Turner, Frederick Jackson. *The Significance of the Frontier in American History*. Penguin Books, 2008.

Twombly, Robert. "Cuds and Snipes: Labor at Chicago's Auditorium Building, 1887–1889." *Journal of American Studies* 31, no. 1 (1997): 79–101.

Tygiel, Jules. *Baseball's Great Experiment: Jackie Robinson and His Legacy*. Oxford University Press, 1997.

Tygiel, Jules. "Enterprise & Opportunity." In National Baseball Hall of Fame, *Baseball as America*.

Tygiel, Jules. *Extra Bases: Reflections on Jackie Robinson, Race, and Baseball History*. University of Nebraska Press, 2002.

Tygiel, Jules. "Introduction to 'Ideals and Injustices.'" In National Baseball Hall of Fame, *Baseball as America* (National Geographic Society, 2002).

Vaught, David. "Abner Doubleday, Marc Bloch, and the Cultural Significance of Baseball in Rural America." *Agricultural History* 85, no. 1 (2011): 1–20.

Voigt, David Q. *American Baseball*. Pennsylvania State University Press, 1983.

Walker, James R., and Robert V. Bellamy. *Center Field Shot: A History of Baseball on Television*. Bison Original, 2008.

Walker, Rhiannon. "The State of the Black Manager in Major League Baseball Would Disgust Jackie Robinson." *Undefeated*, April 20, 2018. https://andscape.com/features/the-state-of-the-black-manager-in-major-league-baseball-would-disgust-jackie-robinson/.

Ward, John Montgomery. *Base-Ball: How to Become a Player*. Outlook Verlag, 2018.

Ward, John Montgomery. "Is the Base Ball Player a Chattel?" *Lippincott's Monthly Magazine: A Popular Journal of General Literature* 40 (1887): 310–19.

Ward, John Montgomery. "Notes of a Base-Ballist." *Lippincott's Monthly Magazine: A Popular Journal of General Literature, Science, and Politics* 34 (1886): 215–23.

Washington, George. *The Writings of George Washington from the Original Manuscript Sources, 1745–1799*. Edited by John C. Fitzpatrick. Government Printing Office, 1931.

Webb, Clive, and David Brown. *Race in the American South: From Slavery to Civil Rights*. Edinburgh University Press, 2007.

West, Thomas G. *Political Theory of the American Founding: Natural Rights, Public Policy, and the Moral Conditions of Freedom*. Cambridge University Press, 2017.

White, G. Edward. *Creating the National Pastime: Baseball Transforms Itself, 1900–1953*. Princeton University Press, 1996.

White, Richard. "Baseball's John Fowler: The 1887 Season in Binghamton, New York." *Afro Americans in New York Life and History* 16, no. 1 (1992): 7–17.

Wilentz, Sean. *No Property in Man: Slavery and Antislavery at the Nation's Founding*. Harvard University Press, 2018.

Williams, Yohuru, "'I've Got to Be Me: Robinson and the Long Black Freedom Struggle." In *42 Today: Jackie Robinson and His Legacy*, edited by Michael G. Long. New York University Press, 2021.

Williams, Kat D. *The All-American Girls After the AAGPBL: How Playing Pro Ball Shaped Their Lives*. McFarland, 2017.

Williams, Loretta J. *Freemasonry and Middle-Class Realities*. University of Missouri Press, 1980.

Wolfe, Edgar F. "The Benevolent Brotherhood of Baseball Bugs." *Literary Digest*, 1923.

Wollstonecraft, Mary. *A Vindication of the Rights of Woman*. Dover Publications, 1996.

Wood, Gordon S. *The Radicalism of the American Revolution*. Alfred A. Knopf, 1992.

WPA Federal Writers Project. *Slave Narratives: A Folk History of Slavery in the United States from Interviews with Former Slaves*, Vol. 1, *Alabama, Aarons-Young*. Library of Congress, 1941.

WPA Federal Writers Project. *Slave Narratives: A Folk History of Slavery in the United States from Interviews with Former Slaves*. Vol. 16, *Texas, Part 2, Easter-King*. Library of Congress, 1941.

WPA Federal Writers Project. *Slave Narratives: A Folk History of Slavery in the United States from Interviews with Former Slaves*. Vol. 3, *Florida, Anderson-Wilson*. Library of Congress, 1941.

WPA Federal Writers Project. *Slave Narratives: A Folk History of Slavery in the United States from Interviews with Former Slaves*. Vol. 2, *Arkansas, Part 1, Abbott-Byrd*. Library of Congress, 1941.

Wright, Robert E., and David J. Cowen. *Financial Founding Fathers: The Men Who Made America Rich*. University of Chicago Press, 2006.

Young, Kimberley. "'TAKE ME OUT TO THE BELLEGAME' How the AAGPBL Gained and Maintained Its Highly Respected Reputation." In *A Locker Room of Her Own: Celebrity, Sexuality, and Female Athletes*, edited by David C. Ogden and Joel Nathan Rosen. University Press of Mississippi, 2013.

Young, Whitney. "To Be Equal." *Michigan Chronicle*, November 21, 1964.

Zagarri, Rosemarie. *Revolutionary Backlash: Women and Politics in the Early American Republic*. University of Pennsylvania Press, 2007.

Zeiler, Thomas W. *Ambassadors in Pinstripes: The Spalding World Baseball Tour and the Birth of American Empire*. Rowman & Littlefield, 2006.

Zimbalist, Andrew. *Baseball and Billions: A Probing Look Inside the Big Business of Our National Pastime*. HarperCollins, 1992.

Zimbalist, Andrew. *In the Best Interests of Baseball?: The Revolutionary Reign of Bud Selig*. Wiley, 2006.

Index